GUNS, LIES AND SPIES

Chris Cowley was born and educated in Britain. After training as a metallurgist, he travelled to the Alps and worked there as a mountain guide. His love of the outdoor life and his profession have enabled Chris to travel and live in places as far-flung and remote as East Africa, South America and Tibet. From 1984 to 1989 he worked for the Brussels-based Space research Corporation. He now lives in Bristol with his wife and family.

GW00685915

GUNS, LIES AND SPIES

HOW WE ARMED IRAQ

Chris Cowley

Introduction by Paul Foot

HAMISH HAMILTON · LONDON

HAMISH HAMILTON LTD

Published by the Penguin Group
Penguin Books Ltd, 27 Wrights Lane, London W8 5TZ, England
Penguin Books USA Inc., 375 Hudson Street, New York, New York 10014, USA
Penguin Books Australia Ltd, Ringwood, Victoria, Australia
Penguin Books Canada Ltd, 10 Alcorn Avenue, Toronto, Ontario, Canada M4V 3B2
Penguin Books (NZ) Ltd, 182–190 Wairau Road, Auckland 10, New Zealand

Penguin Books Ltd, Registered Offices: Harmondsworth, Middlesex, England

First published 1992
10 9 8 7 6 5 4 3 2 1

Filmset in Bembo by Intype, London
Printed in Great Britain by Clays Ltd, St Ives plc, Bungay, Suffolk

A CIP catalogue record for this book is available from the British Library

ISBN 0–241–13447–1

For Balbir Dhillon

The subject now before us is the construction of the gun – its length, its composition, and its weight. We may end up giving it gigantic dimensions; but, however great may be the difficulties, our mechanical genius will readily overcome them.

Jules Verne: *From the Earth to the Moon* (1864)

In the popular mind, guns are associated only with war and destruction. Minds of limited vision . . . prefer sensationalised stories of the combination strife between nations.

Gerald Bull: *The Paris Guns and H.A.R.P.* (1988)

ACKNOWLEDGEMENTS

This story would not have been told without the willing assistance of many people. They gave time, borrowed and loaned documents and photographs, and provided constant support. These people deserve only credit. Any shortcomings in the book are entirely my responsibility.

Many miles were travelled and numerous people were interviewed before slowly the jigsaw came together. Along the way I was to learn the true meaning of friendship. On occasions it came in the form of letters of support and encouragement from near and distant lands, or even of a brief word of greeting by neighbours or shop-keepers who knew of my situation – not to mention an ever-friendly NatWest bank manager.

At other times I have been inspired by the continual and sustained efforts of certain individuals on my behalf. A number of these have requested that I do not mention either their names or the assistance given. In respecting their wishes I acknowledge the personal risk to which they have exposed themselves. Significant pieces of information have come from individuals whose identities I do not even know, nor do I know why they have helped. I can only extend my heart-felt appreciation.

Those who are not being allowed to escape acknowledgement are Robin Blake, whose generosity of time, clarity of thought and writing skills have earned my unbounded thanks; Jonathan Foster of the *Independent*, who provided much background information and who sustained us with his humour; Bernard de Witt, with his deep knowledge of the Belgian dimension of this story; Jane Corbin of the BBC, who quite unknowingly upset the government the most; Tom Archer of CST Productions Ltd, who pointed me towards Paul Foot; and Paul Foot of the *Mirror*, who said 'You have to tell this story.'

I must also offer my profound thanks to Kevin Robinson for his calming influence; Monique Jamine, who possesses more backbone than most; Liep Sie, who is a real friend in a storm; Mohinder

Dhillon for his kind words; Pat and Harold Morris, who are such good people; Vanessa Stevens for typing continuously when others were apprehensive; Cliff and Ginny Granger for their great Thai food; the entire Dunn family (what a bunch!); Dianne Eley, who is a tough act to follow; and my son Ian, who produced so many fine drawings and sketches and who pedalled so many miles.

Professional help was provided by Gill Coleridge, of Rogers, Coleridge and White, who worked so hard to find the right publisher.

Finally I acknowledge the emotional support provided by my family and especially Glenys, whom I am privileged to have as a wife, and who in the early days turned into an answering machine.

How could I ever doubt we would win?

WHERE ARE THEY IN 1992?

THE COMPANIES

Astra Holdings This has been the subject of an enquiry by K.M.P.G. Peat Marwick on behalf of the D.T.I., which is now in its third year and has cost well over a million pounds. The company still exists, but as no more than a shell. Its absence has left the field of defence supplies largely to the B.Ae. subsidiary Royal Ordnance.

Matrix Churchill It was sold by the Official Receiver in 1991 to B.S.A. machine tools company. In November the former Matrix Churchill directors were acquitted at the Old Bailey of all charges brought by H.M. Customs over Iraqi exports.

The Midland Bank After a run of lean years, it has been bought by the Hong Kong and Shanghai Bank.

Poudreries Réunies de Belgique It is still making powders, propellants and artillery shells. But P.R.B. has changed ownership again, being now part of GIAT, the major French government arms-manufacturer.

Sheffield Forgemasters It was substantially intact after the Super-gun affair, and continues to manufacture large, high-quality forgings. Indeed, the company appears to have gained a certain kudos from the Babylon contracts.

Société Générale de Belgique This continues as the largest and most influential company in Belgium, although the majority of its shares are owned by Générale de Banque. S.G.B. engaged London solicitors to attend and report on the D.T.I. Select Committee hearings, although it did not give evidence.

Walter Somers A very long-established company, it has gone through difficult times but continues to trade under the ownership of Eagle Trust plc.

Space Research Corporation It was placed in voluntary receivership by Michel Bull following his father's death and within a few weeks was wound up. Company files seized by police after the murder have never been returned.

THE BRITISH

Paul Ashwell Following losses sustained through the Supergun affair, the haulage company for which Ashwell worked, owned by his father-in-law, became bankrupt.

Sir John Cuckney He has been appointed to track down millions of pounds missing from the pension funds of the late Robert Maxwell's companies. He retired from the chairmanship of the 3i Group in July 1992.

Chris Gumbley Following his alleged harassment by the Ministry of Defence police, he was charged with corrupting a government official and served a prison sentence. Gumbley told the Select Committee that, since meeting Bull hours before he was murdered, he 'had maintained the lowest possible profile'.

Gerald James He resigned from the board of Astra in March 1990, without compensation. He has since worked as a consultant. Although the Select Committee report gave scant credence to James's view of the Astra/P.R.B. affair, much of it has been confirmed by documents unearthed by Chris Cowley and by evidence given at the Matrix Churchill trial.

Stephan Kock Following the failure of Astra, he is still a consultant in military sales. In a remarkably unrevealing session, he gave evidence to the Select Committee on 19 February 1992.

Sir Hal Miller, Nicholas Ridley and Alan Clark They did not contest their parliamentary seats in the 1992 general election. Alan Clark's evidence at the Old Bailey contributed to the dismissal of charges against the Matrix Churchill defendants.

Peter Mitchell He is still managing director of Walter Somers, and was never charged with any offence. He gave evidence at the Select Committee in which he maintained that he never knew the S.R.C./Iraqi contracts were for guns.

Barry Penrose He no longer works for the *Sunday Times*.

Barry Riley He has recently taken early retirement from H.M. Customs. Riley appeared at the Select Committee, making few interventions. He still runs, and occasionally he and Chris Cowley train together.

Kevin Robinson He successfully represented Paul Henderson at the Matrix Churchill trial.

George Wong He has shed his directorship of Rothchilds Bank and no longer answers his telephone or replies to mail from his Berkeley Square address. He is now believed to be living in Hong Kong.

THE BELGIAN CONNECTION

Mike Bayne, Tony Slack and John Heath They did not give evidence at the Select Committee and have not returned to live in the U.K.

Monique Jamine She runs a business helping expatriates in Brussels to deal with Belgian bureaucracy.

Patrick Renoir He has been redeployed away from the Bull murder investigation.

Liep Sie He now works in partnership with Chris Cowley in an engineering consultancy based in Thailand.

Bernard de Witt He is a judge in the Belgian High Court.

Shabib Azzawi He survived Desert Storm and was seen on television showing a group of U.N. officials around the elevated 350-mm gun site.

Chris Drogoul At a time of writing, he is awaiting trial on several hundred counts of fraud and related charges in Atlanta, Georgia. Following his indictment in 1991, Drogoul was at liberty. His bail was then suddenly withdrawn after he gave an interview in which he stated that cash and credits from B.N.L. had been transferred to Iraq with U.S. Government knowledge. In May 1992 Drogoul suddenly changed his plea to guilty, which meant U.S. Government officials would be released from giving testimony at his trial. He has since changed his plea back to not guilty.

Kemal Hussein Previously Minister for Industries, he still holds a senior position in his father-in-law's government.

Saddam Hussein He remains President of Iraq, despite Desert Storm. He has recently been reported as supplying arms to the Serbian government.

Amir Saadi He is presumed to be still a senior minister in Saddam's government.

INTRODUCTION

A common illusion about a 'free enterprise' society is that it encourages the free flow of information. On the contrary, the freer the enterprise, the more ruthlessly information about that enterprise is suppressed. Great corporations release only the information which shows how wonderful they are – and punish with the utmost severity any employee who talks to the media about anything else. I remember my surprise, as an investigative journalist employed by Mr Robert Maxwell, to be asked in my contract of employment to agree that if I released a single piece of information about any company in the Maxwell empire, I would be instantly dismissed (I refused, but many journalists were forced to comply).

Another illusion is that information about the world we live in gets 'dug out' by assiduous journalists. My experience is that you can 'dig' all your life long and come up with next to nothing. The only important published information comes from the inside, passed over by so-called 'whistle-blowers' who make available the information which they've been pledged to keep secret.

Sometimes, rarely, such moles emerge because they suddenly realise that the social consequences of what they are doing are intolerable. They might have some religious or moral objection to consistent lying, cheating and stealing. Usually, however, the 'whistle-blowers' decide to speak out because something in their scheme of things has gone wrong – something which shakes to the foundations the central aims and purposes in their lives. Such a person, for instance, was Ron Smith, the former Leeds policeman who was asked to accept that his daughter had fallen from the top of a high block of flats in Saudi Arabia with hardly any injuries, save those of an obvious rape, which were deliberately hushed up; or Ann Whelan, who refused to believe that her son had murdered the newspaper boy Carl Bridgewater; or Colin Wallace, who told his intelligence minders in Northern Ireland that his job as information officer for the British army did not include smearing Labour Ministers. All these people were happily living their lives in tune with accepted values. Their experiences shocked them into the belief that the world was not what it is made out to be.

Chris Cowley is an engineer who was employed in the arms industry by the eccentric Canadian-born Gerald Bull, whose ambition was to shoot satellites into space with a gun. Cowley was put in charge of Bull's Babylon Project – to build such 'Superguns' for Iraq and its dictator Saddam Hussein. Cowley left the project in the spring of 1989. A year later he was suddenly swept up in the political scandal known as 'Supergun'. The British people were rather surprised to discover, as they were being prepared for a war against Tyrant Hussein, that British engineering companies had been manufacturing guns for the same tyrant to use with equal vigour against his enemies and against his own people.

The government were embarrassed. They sought to cover up their embarrassment by blaming anyone else who came to hand. Chris Cowley was arrested, cast into prison, released, leaned on by Customs and Excise. His phones were tapped, his mail interfered with and he seemed to be followed wherever he went.

Fortunately for all of us, he is not the kind of man to be broken by this nonsense. He is persistent, sometimes stubborn. The victimisation infuriated him and stiffened his resolve. When he came to see me, he was anxious to disclose information about the whole Supergun scandal.

When I visited his home in Bristol, Chris showed me a document prepared for his defence but which also told his story. I could see (and hear) at once that he had a remarkable story to tell, but not in its then existing form. Events and times were jumbled together without structure. Worse, it assumed scandalous interpretations to events, without proving them. For instance, it alleged (as Chris Cowley did later to the House of Commons Select Committee on Trade and Industry) that the criminal case against him was being masterminded from 10 Downing Street. The only 'proof' of this was, apparently, the statement of one Customs Officer one night that 'she' (whom he had rung to find out if Cowley could be released) had 'gone to bed'. The assumption without proof that this 'she' was the Prime Minister sounds ridiculous. And this willingness to leap to dramatic conclusions without anything but the vaguest proof did Chris Cowley great disservice, when, in January 1992, he gave oral evidence for a whole day to the Select Committee. Barry Porter, a portly solicitor, who sits as Tory MP for Wirral South, concluded with portentous solemnity that

Cowley was a mischievous fantasist, and his story a lot of bunkum.

When I saw the document again, it had developed into the story of what happened to Chris Cowley. Chris's narrative is dramatically and tightly told, and expertly interwoven with the Supergun scandal. It is a thriller and an exposé at the same time.

For two years after he first told his story, Chris Cowley's seemed a lonely voice, echoed only by a small group of independent journalists and other 'whistle-blowers' like Gerald James, the former chairman of the ill-fated arms company Astra. The theme of all these stories is that a gang of important people across the world were determined to export arms to Iraq, and in so doing to defy the arms embargos of their own governments and those of the United Nations. At the centre of the British part of this operation were the intelligence services, a small group of high-placed Tories, including at least one Minister, civil servants in the D.T.I. and the Ministry of Defence, big businessmen 'with intelligence connections' and their bankers. This group was entirely unaccountable. They made up the laws they honoured, and dishonoured ones they didn't make. They were strong enough to defy an embargo which had been expressly announced in the House of Commons. It all seemed a little fanciful, almost incredible. Then, in October 1992, three directors of a Midlands engineering firm, Matrix Churchill, were acquitted of illegal arms sales to Iraq. Their defence had been that they had been encouraged to break the arms embargo by the Government which had imposed it. Suddenly, everybody was interested in 'Iraqgate'. Suddenly, Chris Cowley's story wasn't so fanciful. Its publication now, with its new information from the hitherto unpublished tapes of Bull's conversations shortly before his bizarre murder in 1990 (a murder closely followed by, and undoubtedly associated with, the assassination of the Deputy Prime Minister of Belgium), could not be more appropriate.

Until Anthony Sampson wrote his famous book *The Arms Bazaar* (1987), most people thought the international arms trade was run by sleazy businessmen, working behind the scenes. Sampson showed how the main players are the biggest businessmen in the world, helped again and again by senior government figures. The big businessmen in Britain – and the head of state – are all here in this book.

Like so many people forced to expose the world in which they once flourished, Chris Cowley has changed his mind. He used to revere Gerald Bull, for instance. Now he sees the fanatical and almost maniacal side to Bull's character. He used to work and prosper in the international arms industry. Now he finds the whole business a 'force for evil', a cesspool of corruption. The closing pages, in which Cowley contemplates with horror the filth in which he once revelled, is a remarkable conclusion to a most remarkable story.

Paul Foot
December 1992

1

Some days and dates have more significance than others. The date in 1938 on which I was born in Liverpool, England. My marriage to Glenys and the births of my three sons. Celebrations, birthdays, happy times.

But there are dates in 1990 which I do not celebrate, though I'll never have difficulty calling them to mind. On one I was threatened. On another my friend was killed. And on a third I went to jail.

My house is in a quiet, respectable suburb of Bristol, England. On 23 February 1990 I had been working all afternoon in my makeshift home-office, a bedroom at the top of the house. It was nearing dusk and, as the surrounding room sank into half-light, I sat in a pool of bright grey radiance cast by the screen of my computer terminal. The only sound was the clack of my fingers on the keyboard, and the occasional whirr of a passing car.

Absorbed in my work, I was startled by the telephone ringing on the table to my left. I only had to stretch into the shadow and pick up the receiver.

'Yes?'

'*Is that Dr Christopher Cowley?*'

It was good, clear English, but not Queen's English. I wasn't sure if it was a British voice at all.

'Yes, speaking.'

'*This is a warning.*'

There was a hint of a guttural, vaguely Germanic accent there. A foreigner, then, but one who was easy with the language, who spoke English every day.

'I'm sorry. I didn't—'

'*Never return to Iraq.*'

I hesitated, not knowing how to respond. Then I said,

'Actually I haven't worked there since last May.'

'*We know. Don't return.*'

The line went dead, but it was a moment before I replaced the receiver. I was thinking hard, my heart thumping. *Never return to Iraq*. That was fairly unequivocal. I had been warned off, that was as transparent as the window through which I saw the cold, dusky, West of England sky. The unspoken words *or face the consequences* had lingered like smoke around the curt message.

But who had threatened me? And why? Was it Chris Cowley they were targetting? Or did someone at last want to stop Project Babylon, to which I'd donated twelve months of my life?

I had been in Baghdad a lot in that period. It was during the last phase of the Iran-Iraq war, and I had witnessed at first hand the summary cruelties, the authoritarianism of officials and police, the spying and the paranoia of Saddam Hussein's regime. Yet I had never considered Iraq a dangerous place for me personally. Iraqis we had known and worked with had been as genuinely friendly, and as professionally motivated, as anyone I have ever done business with. They had shown every indication of liking us, every appreciation of what we were doing for them.

Even when one of our team had fallen under the suspicion of the secret police, I had been allowed to deal with the matter quietly and in my own way. After all I was British, along with a significant number of my team. Britain was a crucial supplier of technology to Iraq, and Iraq was a very important customer of Britain, one of the few countries in which the balance of trade was tilted in our favour. Moreover, most educated Iraqis were graduates of British universities. Religion and culture apart, the two countries saw themselves as virtually hand-in-glove.

After the decade-long Iran-Iraq war had come to an end, this basically chummy situation flourished briefly as never before, and then began to sour. In September 1989 a young *Observer* journalist called Farzad Bazoft made an unauthorised visit to the Al-Qaqa explosives plant near Al-Iskandariya, 60 kilometres south of Baghdad. Bazoft was chasing rumours of massive damage and loss of life from an explosion, although officially he was part of a delegation of journalists invited to witness Iraq's efforts at post-war reconstruction. In the hope of confirming the rumours of nuclear or chemical fall-out from the blast, Bazoft had brought back soil samples from around the base for later analysis.

Had Bazoft found a moderately subtle way to export his soil samples the whole escapade would probably have gone unnoticed. Unfortunately, Iraq is one of those countries whose Customs are concerned less about goods coming in than with the contents of your bags as you leave. So, when the samples from Al-Qaqa were found in his luggage at the airport, Bazoft was arrested. Daphne Parrish, the British nurse who'd given him a lift to the site, was also arrested. Although it hardly boded well that Bazoft was of Iranian descent, in happier times his British residency would probably have got him a summary expulsion and an end to the matter. As it was, both he and Parrish were now to be tried as spies.

I considered my own situation, here, in respectable Bristol. If I were in danger from the Iraqis, I would have to be a danger *to* them. How much did I know about Saddam's secrets?

A fair amount, I had to admit. I had, for instance, been in Al-Qaqa, though only in the part of the plant where explosives and propellants were made. It was here that the Iraqis had planned to make propellant charges for Project Babylon; Gerald Bull would be furious if the supplies were cut off because of the explosion.

Al-Qaqa had a more secret section, a section where, it was reasonable to suppose, Saddam was creating his arsenal of chemical weapons. I had been in other secret locations, such as Saad-16, the advanced missile research station in the north of the country and the Nassr weapons research establishment.

Most of all, though, I knew about Project Babylon. This had certainly been confidential, and at times clandestine. Yet a lot of people – all the people who really mattered – knew about it. I had sat in the Al-Rasheed hotel in Baghdad and discussed it with agents of western banks, even of governments. And even if, in negotiating manufacturing contracts with some of the biggest steel companies in Europe, I had preferred not to speak openly of the project's real purpose, I became perfectly aware that these companies knew what this purpose was. We had even put a table-top model of it openly on display at the 1989 Baghdad International Arms Fair. Yes, a lot of individuals and agencies knew about Babylon, and the Iraqis knew they knew. It wouldn't make any kind of sense for them to target me on that score. Whoever had made that phone call was not trying to *protect* Project Babylon. They were trying to ensure that I never returned to it. They were trying to *hurt* it, and I could tell from the man's tone of voice that they would not bother if, along the way, they also hurt me.

After a few minutes of thought I gathered together some kit, my tracksuit and trainers, and got changed. I would go for a run.

2

Whenever I need to think, or shed stress, I run. At 50-odd I may not quite be in the Olympic class, though I can still do a three-hour marathon. But running isn't only fitness with me, it's a combination of stimulant and stress-relief.

My house stands near the bottom of a hill. Below us a trunk road conducts traffic out of Bristol and into an entanglement of flyovers and slip roads around the head of Plimsoll Bridge. Here a driver can either cross and go away south towards the Mendips, or continue along the north bank of the river which sweeps almost immediately between the precipitous limestone walls of Clifton Gorge, under the 75-metre high suspension bridge, and then away to Avonmouth and the Severn Estuary.

The runner has different possibilities. Still trying to loosen up, I jogged across Plimsoll Bridge and, reaching the south bank of the river, then struck uphill along a mud path into Leigh Woods, the nature reserve which covers the land to the west of the Gorge. The tracks here are steep, passing through a thick ancient woodland which stands in direct line of descent from Britain's primeval forest. Rare broadleaf trees such as whitebeam and wych elm grow here alongside the more familiar oak and beech. Roe deer roam wild.

The runner on these trails is working hard with no time for continuous reflection. But after three or four kilometres I paused, breathing hard and looked through the trees towards Brunel's great suspension bridge, which leaps the Gorge from clifftop to clifftop. In its day the bridge had been at the leading edge of engineering technology, the work of a man whose thought was never less than large and bold, and who loved nothing better than to hear others telling him 'It can't be done'.

It was a cast of mind overwhelmingly evident in the man I had worked for on Babylon. Isambard Kingdom Brunel and Gerald Vincent Bull were two of a kind.

It wasn't hard to see why certain individuals in certain countries

4

might want to put the skids under Project Babylon. It was an epoch-making venture – an exploit in engineering and ballistics that had no precedent. That meant, like any great enterprise such as that bridge over there, that Babylon's success would carry enormous prestige and would also arouse corresponding jealousies, suspicions, enmities. Iraq, moreover, was a country with powerful enemies – Iran, Syria and, most potent of all, Israel. None of these would relish Project Babylon and to scare away scientists and technicians would be one possible way of pulling the plug on it.

A mere 12 months ago I had been project manager as well as metallurgist, an obvious target for such tactics. But why would they be warning me off now? I had ended my association with the enterprise nine months earlier, in May 1988, and had not been near Iraq since.

'*We know*', the voice on the phone had said. '*Don't return.*'

Did they want to preempt my return? Did they know something I didn't? After all, what reason could there possibly be for me to return, unless . . .

Christ! An unwelcome thought dropped with a thud into my mind.

Immediately I started down the precipitous track which would take me to the River Avon's tow-path. If something should happen to Bull, then it *might* be supposed I could be rehired by the company in his place. The idea was preposterous, of course, but there is no accounting for the mistaken assumptions of outsiders. I pounded the tow-path hard until I reached Plimsoll Bridge once more. I recrossed the river and completed the short distance to my home in a sprint finish.

In my office I seized the telephone and keyed the well-remembered number of the company, Space Research Corporation of Brussels. This was where Project Babylon had been conceived, and where design and development work were still, as far as I knew, continuing. I waited impatiently for the connection.

Anyone who thought Bull replaceable on Project Babylon was, of course, in a state of gross error. Bull *was* Project Babylon. He was the presiding genius, he had given 30 years of thought, study and experiment to its concepts. It was impossible to imagine the thing without him, but those who had telephoned me – whoever they were – would not necessarily know that. They might not know much about Gerald Bull at all.

Bull's prime quality was persistent, infectious enthusiasm. Ever

5

since he had conceived the broad outline of the scheme as a Canadian research scientist in the late 1950s, he had run up against antagonists and sceptics. Engineers said his designs could not be built. Rocket scientists insisted he was a walking anachronism. Bureaucrats and politicians told him he was slipshod and bumptious. But Bull took no notice. When politicians started talking about science and technology, Bull used to give a hollow laugh and quote Tony Benn, who as Minister of Technology in Britain in the 1960s, once said, 'I see no value in application satellites.'

'Why should politicians be trusted in business or science?' he would ask. 'They've got no training in either.'

And yet, because of the nature of his work, Bull was required to spend much of his time dealing with governments. His strategy was to ride roughshod over all their cautions and objections. Nothing, so far as he was concerned, was insuperable.

And, on top form, the man could *convince* you. He always carried along with him a corps of devoted disciples of whom, at that time, I was one. It was the force of Bull's spirit that swept us forward to do ever more extraordinary things.

Bull's personality and scientific reputation must have been the factor which convinced Kamil Hussein, the powerful son-in-law of the Iraqi dictator, to buy Project Babylon in the first place. In retrospect it was rather a strange progression. Bull had failed once to sell it to his own Canadian Government. He had failed, ultimately, to sell it to the U.S. Army. But he had sold it at last – and sold it (you might say) lock, stock and barrel – to the biggest bully in the Middle-Eastern arena.

But somehow, those who worked for him didn't think too hard about the worthiness of our client. It was Bull we cared about, doing a good job for him. He inspired people, he mesmerised them. *He* wasn't concerned with who was going to use his invention, he wasn't concerned with power games. If he had something to prove, *that* was his objective. Everything else was just a means to that overriding end – the establishment, as he saw it, of truth, his truth.

Yes, I thought, the best way to injure Project Babylon would be to injure its begetter.

'Hello Chris. It's been a long time. How are you?'

Bull's secretary in Brussels, Pascale, was friendly as ever, but she couldn't put me in touch with her boss.

'Sorry, Chris, he's not here. He's on his travels as usual.'

'Do you know when he'll be back?'

Her laugh was full of affection for her wayward, unpredictable boss.

'Do I ever?'

'Okay, I'll call again. But tell him I phoned, will you?'

'I'll tell him. Bye, Chris.'

I hung up.

The weekend passed and everything was normal. There were no more threatening phone calls and the immediate fright had already begun to recede. I called Pascale on Monday to be told Bull was now due to return to his office two days later.

'Right,' I said. 'I'll call him then.'

Bull may have been unpredictable, but he had certain habits. One was to turn up around mid-morning at the office, coming in straight from the airport. He would then begin a gruelling session of work on his backlog, which might last until midnight. I decided to delay my call until after lunch, when I reckoned he would have got his phonecalls out of the way and be well stuck into his paperwork.

It was the wrong choice.

'I'm sorry, Chris. Dr Bull did return this morning but he's already left again. Hasn't he phoned you? I gave him your message.'

'Look, Pascale, I urgently want to talk to him. Get him to phone me back as soon as you can.'

She promised she would. I wasn't altogether surprised that Bull had touched base only to wing off again. He was a restless, driven man, always on the move and utterly uninterested in recreation. Well, maybe he would contact me, eventually. And maybe I was unnecessarily paranoid, imagining the danger. After all, Pascale had seen Bull this morning and she hadn't said there was anything the matter with him. I went back to my work on the design for the chiropractor's couch, a new venture I had become involved in.

Bull never did contact me, and meanwhile I made no further effort to reach him. If I had, it might have saved his life.

In a world preoccupied by the disintegration of the Soviet empire in Eastern Europe, the Middle East had been less in the news than usual. However, on 15 March 1990, Farzad Bazoft was executed by hanging in Baghdad's central prison. I considered him a victim of the Thatcher Government's uncompromising, get-tough approach to the situation, which involved public demands for Bazoft's immediate release and repatriation. My own experience with Arabs is that most things are negotiable in private, so long as you don't publicly push the guy into a corner. As things stood, Saddam Hussein believed he had to show his own strength or lose face.

On the same day Yitzak Shamir became the first Israeli Prime Minister ever to lose a vote of no confidence in the Knesset. He was the victim of a revolt by the more extreme Zionist parties in his coalition, who wanted Israel to get even tougher with the Arabs.

I am not saying these happenings are connected to the events of the following week. Nor would I rule out a connection.

It was on 23 March that I heard. This time the voice on the phone was friendly, though downbeat, a voice carrying the weight of bad news. It was Tony Perez and he was calling from somewhere in France.

'I was in the car, Chris. I just caught the tail end of the news. Have you heard?'

'Heard what, Tony?'

'Bull's dead.'

I shut my eyes and opened them again. I couldn't have heard right.

'I'm sorry, Tony. What was that you said?'

'Gerald Bull – he's dead.'

I had known Tony in the days when I worked for S.R.C. He lived in Switzerland, but drove all over Europe listening obsessively – I knew – to the B.B.C., in an endless quest to improve his English. But surely he hadn't interpreted this news item right.

'Are you sure?'

'Yes, absolutely. He's been killed.'

'What do you mean, *killed?* Was it a heart attack, a road accident?'

'No heart attack, no accident, Chris. Bull was murdered.'

At this point I almost dropped the phone.

'*What* did you say?'

'He was shot at his flat in Brussels last night. That's all I got from the radio.'

'I don't believe this. Who killed him and why? Haven't you got any details?'

'Sorry Chris, nothing. Nothing at all. I only caught the end of the bulletin.'

8

There was nothing more to say. I thanked Tony for the call and hung up.

It was numbing. Bull dead? There was something incredible about it. He'd been my boss but I also considered him my friend. He was such a powerful, inescapable presence. It was hard – no, it was impossible to take in.

I stared for a few moments vacantly out of the window. Then I remembered my radio. I switched it on, trying to tune to the next news bulletin, my hand suddenly shaking with shock and anxiety. Finally I found one: it supplied only the bald facts.

The Canadian artillery designer Dr Gerald Bull had been shot dead by an unknown assailant at the front door of his Brussels flat the previous evening. He had been hit in the head and body by a number of gunshots. Police had no suspects and knew of no motive. In a 30-year career Dr Bull had developed a reputation as a maverick in the world's arms industries. In 1980 a U.S. court sentenced him to six months imprisonment after he was found guilty of breaking the arms embargo against South Africa. Since then he had moved his operations to Europe.

Murder. It was hard to take in. Murder happened, of course. In the newspapers, in feature films, in novels. It happened to strangers. Friends were never murdered, ex-employers were not assassinated, people you had travelled with for weeks, joked with, confided in – these people were not *murdered*!

I was thinking about Bull. Why had he died? There had to be a reason, because murder always had a reason.

Then that thin menacing voice came back to me. *Never return to Iraq.* It was the voice of someone who was not about to listen to arguments, justifications. Had Bull been warned and ignored that warning? Had he been told not to go back to Iraq, and done so?

Again I went running. I turned right out of my house this time, up the hill towards the high open green space known (oddly enough) as Clifton Downs. It was lunchtime, and people were out to take the midday air. Office workers occupied park benches in the pale sunlight, bending to their sandwiches. It seemed too cold to sit long, but there were hardy souls amongst them who, having crushed their sandwich papers to a ball of waste, sat tensely over paperback books, wrapped in scarves and mittens. I jogged past wine bars and pubs, hearing the controlled roar of the conversation and the busy ringing of the tills. So normal, so English, so far from the desert west of Mosul, where perhaps Gerald Bull had been only two or three days ago, at the Babylon test-bed.

9

It was very likely. Project Babylon would still be a year or more from completion, but it had come a long way and with each new stage of progress there would be test-firings to attend, results to analyse. And apart from this, there were the other areas of Iraq's military development programme in which Bull had become involved. I was very hazy about details, but I knew certain requests from Baghdad had arrived, and hints had been dropped that technical advice would be appreciated. I knew, too, that Bull could never resist an appeal like that. If Saddam's generals asked him to attend to some problem on their behalf, he would see it as a challenge to his skill and expertise and he would do it.

Yes, he must have shuttled back and forth many times since I'd seen him last, eight or nine months ago. What had Pascale said? *He's on his travels, as usual.* Well, he wouldn't be going on them any more.

3

I would later try to imagine the scene.

It is of the dockside, Teesport, in the North East of England. The quays are quiet and sparsely occupied, but two or three freighters are loading. Beside one of these, with the cranes hovering overhead, is a consignment of eight packing cases in the shape of gigantic cotton reels, 1.5 metres in diameter by 6 metres long. Loading of these huge crates seems likely to begin any time.

Suddenly a car engine is heard in the middle-distance, revving high as the vehicle buckets along the uneven surface of the quayside. It stops beside the cotton reels and two men in suits get out, one of them unfolding a piece of paper. He checks the name of the ship. GUR MARINER Port of registration: Basra.

They walk among the yet-to-be-loaded cargo, speaking to the dockers, identifying themselves.

'H.M. Customs,' they say. 'Anyone know what this lot is?'

'Main-drains,' someone chips in. 'In sections. Bloody big sewer pipes.'

'Oh yeah?'

The senior of the Customs men smiles grimly, counting the huge boxes. He makes some notes and then walks towards the ship, scanning the superstructure for any member of the crew. He sees a head and shoulders bobbing up over the rail like a glove puppet.

'Captain on board?' he calls up. The puppet dips out of sight.

When at last he finds the ship's master, he adopts an official voice. It is his duty to inform Captain X that, acting on information received by H.M. Customs regarding the nature of his intended cargo of eight steel tubes for the Republic of Iraq, H.M. Customs was hereby detaining the said shipment, pursuant to their powers under such-and-such a section of such-and-such an Act, and that therefore loading operations must cease forthwith. The Captain's jaw goes slack, he begins to stutter and then to protest.

11

All the paperwork is in order, isn't it? He *must* get the shipment to his country. Perhaps he could lose more than his job if he doesn't.

This ship is a private vessel, but it is on charter to the Iraqi Maritime Organisation. This, like all Iraqi state concerns, is quasi-military and the Captain is therefore technically under the military code of a state whose discipline would undoubtedly rank as among the harshest in the world. So the Captain is sweating.

The Customs officer remains impassive. He writes something out on a form pad, rips the top copy and hands it to the Captain. He tells him crisply to remain in port and stand by for a squad of officers who will be arriving shortly to carry out a comprehensive search of the vessel.

This was to be the first action undertaken by H.M. Customs in what was to be a seven-month operation: codename Bertha.

That was on Wednesday, 11 April 1990. Next day the front page of every paper in the land screamed the same story.

SEIZED: THE TUBES OF DEATH!
DOOMSDAY GUN FOUND!

While Bull's murder, a fortnight earlier, had occasioned precious little comment in the press, this was a cat of a different colour. The discovery at Teesport quayside let loose the Fourth Estate on a frantic and greedy ruck as they ferreted for angles on the story.

I suppose I should have known. With Bull's company in disarray after his death in Brussels, and the Sheffield steel companies who had made the tubes denying the whole thing, I was obviously the only reliable source available. Companies have the safety of numbers, they have lawyers and press officers. I was on my own.

In mosquito country, if you sleep without nets, it's only a matter of time before the pests find you. And when they've done so, they like to suck your blood. So it is with most journalists. By the weekend our house was under siege.

My initial decision was to say and do nothing. Watching events unfold in print and on television, I knew, of course, exactly what the tubes were for and was obtaining some quiet amusement at the expense of the media speculators, many of whose guesses were miles off target. In fact the journalists were feverish with wild speculation. Their notion of a great big phallic gun in the hands of some trigger-happy Arab dictator provided a perfect vehicle to

12

promulgate their vivid, endlessly simplified and melodramatic view of the world. This was an instrument of chemical warfare or a cannon designed to fire shells filled with 'death-bugs' across continents. Others claimed it was not a gun but a rocket launcher. Or else they said it *was* a gun, but designed specifically for nuclear shells. It was a Doomsday Gun.

Iraq's nuclear ambitions had been particularly highlighted in the press on 28 March, when Heathrow Customs officials had grabbed a cargo of nuclear-bomb triggering devices, illegally ordered for Iraq from a high-tech Californian firm. The operation was in fact a complex sting. The triggers were dummies, despatched in order to expose the London end of Iraq's chain of supply for nuclear high-technology. This was accomplished very effectively.

Now, only two weeks later, there was something even more sensational. It did not take long for the link between the seized tubes and Gerald Bull to be established. Then the papers, remembering that he had been murdered in Brussels only weeks before, started to give the impression that Bull was a Dr Strangelove figure, or a megalomaniac, Ian Fleming-type villain dreaming of world domination. In this scenario, Bull's murder was easy to explain: he had quite simply been taken out by some agent with a licence to kill.

Goaded by the more puerile fantasies of the press, other experts came along and scoffed openly. Supergun, they brayed, was a myth. It was a wonderful bogey perhaps, but an idea so frivolous and anachronistic as to be laughable in the real world. You couldn't *have* a gun this size. What are we doing in the late twentieth century, in the age of 'Star Wars', talking seriously about a gun with a bore of one metre? A *gun!* This was an ana-chronistic thriller plot, a Bulldog Drummond fantasy. Pull the other one.

They were all agreed, however, on one thing. The tubes discovered at Teesport were designated on the paperwork as 'petro-chemical equipment'. But no one could say how they were intended to be used as such.

Day after day Glenys and I sat tight. If we went out we were pestered all the way to the shops. We stopped going to the shops. Men lounged constantly by the wall across the street, making no attempt to conceal their ready cameras. Reporters came in a seemingly endless relay. At regular intervals they would be there, thumbing our doorbell. Some became increasingly frustrated and took to pressing the bell more angrily, in sharp staccato bursts or

13

in agonisingly long ones. Others – most – lacked persistence and were got rid of fairly easily.

'Mr Cowley?'

Two men in padded Alpine jackets, holding miniature dictaphones. I hear the tapes whirring.

'We're from *The Sun* newspaper. Could he possibly give us a few words regarding this Supergun business?'

'I'm sorry, he's not here. He's in Brussels.'

'But it'll only take a minute, if we can just ask—'

'I'm very sorry, but there's no comment. Good-bye.'

Others required a degree of sarcasm.

'Mr Cowley, did you personally design—?'

'Still out there, are you? Well, not today thanks.'

Or a curt answer.

'Mr Cowley, about the Supergun—'

'Just go away and leave us alone, will you?'

When the time came to speak, I wanted to be able to pick my own ground. Then I would tell my story, and it would be asserted simply, for I was sure of my facts: the Sheffield contracts had not been what the papers were claiming, they were *not for a weapon* and I had done nothing wrong or illegal. End of message. But I didn't want to speak in the middle of this clamour and confusion, this talk of arms smuggling and other skulduggery. Although I didn't know this until later, the Customs had already raided the offices of Sheffield Forgemasters and Walter Somers Ltd, co-signatories with the Iraqis of Project Babylon contracts. Now there was speculation about imminent arrests and prosecutions. Hysteria was mounting and I was trying to stay cool.

And then something happened which rattled my confidence badly.

A lorry en route to Iraq, driven by a young self-employed British haulier, Paul Ashwell, had been intercepted in Greece, where the police were clearly acting on information supplied by British Customs. Ashwell's truck, which was filmed by television news, was carrying a giant forging which could clearly be identified on the screen. As the canvas was pulled from the load, anyone familiar with artillery could see precisely what it was – a conventional breech-slide mechanism or 'cradle' for a very large gun. But there was something wrong. *We* had not designed such an item. There was no such breech-slide mechanism in the Babylon specification.

What could it mean? Was it some kind of a set-up? The load on

Ashwell's lorry seemed to confirm the existence of the gun and it certainly (as far as the public was concerned) put the lid on the petro-chemical cover-story. Yet I knew that the gun cradle found in Greece and the Teesport tubes had nothing to do with each other. Furthermore, I could explain the tubes, but I had no way of accounting for Ashwell's load.

Meanwhile the broadsheet press had established that political pressure was mounting on the Customs to stay its hand. Rumours were rife that the British Government was impaled on the horns of a sharp dilemma, that officials had been well warned from the start about this order for steel pipes to go to Iraq, and that these might indeed be sections of a gun barrel. If this were true, and they then prosecuted the manufacturers, they stood accused of allowing the company to go ahead with a possibly illegal contract, only to turn around and throw the book at the company just as the order was completed.

The Conservative M.P. for Bromsgrove, Sir Hal Miller heard on 18 April that the Department of Trade and Industry was denying all prior knowledge of the Iraqi order. On the same day he stood up in the House of Commons and accused these officials of lying. Miller knew that Trade and Industry civil servants had been told of the contracts, he said, because *he*, on behalf of the company, had told them. He had passed on the company's disquiet about the order, and indicated that Walter Somers, although they were desperate for the work, would withdraw from the deal if the Government advised them to do so.

Miller informed Nicholas Ridley, Secretary of State for Trade and Industry, that he put the same offer to people at the Ministry of Defence. Miller had good contacts there, having previously been Parliamentary Private Secretary to the Defence Minister himself. In addition, he said, he had contacted a 'third agency' and briefed them.

Miller declined to name this agency, but the whole world assumed he meant M.I.6, and he did not contradict the assumption.

With all this going on it seemed more important than ever that I should not entrust my story to the press. Then the reporters began to melt away, finally discouraged, and we began to believe we'd won. We hadn't. Suddenly, hell bent on getting a story for the 'Insight' section, a man named Barrie Penrose arrived from *The Sunday Times*.

I suppose it was half past four in the afternoon when he knocked loudly on our door. I opened it. Penrose stood there with a smirk on his face, as if he had news for us.

'Dr Cowley?'

He didn't know it but he'd got off to a very poor start. I hate to be called *Doctor* – apart from anything else, I find people are always asking my opinion on some medical condition or other. However Penrose, having got my address and details through the Institute of Metallurgists, thought he was being correct. I said,

'Who wants him?'

'Well I'm from *The Sunday Times* – it's er, Barrie Penrose.'

This, he seemed to say, was a name I couldn't possibly fail to have heard of. I just said,

'Yes?'

'Well look, I need a quick word, okay?'

I looked the man up and down. Mid-40s, brown trousers, greenish sports jacket and a startling, canary-yellow cardigan.

'I'm sorry, he's not here. He's in Brussels.'

Penrose was regarding me now with a cunning look. What were his expectations of his quarry? He was asking himself: this guy in running gear with a noticeable Scouse accent, could it be Cowley? He must have decided it couldn't. He said,

'Well you see, I don't wish to contradict you, but I've been talking to the neighbours and they all say they've seen Dr Cowley around.'

'Sorry. Like all the other newspaper men have been told, he's in Brussels right now.'

'But as I said I—'

'Good-bye.'

I shut the door. A few minutes later he knocked again. This time Glenys went to the door.

The conversation lasted as long as five minutes, but Penrose's foot-in-the-door technique cut no ice with her. Telling Penrose she was cooking and had no time to talk, she firmly closed the door on him. So next, he put a note through the letter-slot, written in an untidy hand on a piece of ruled paper. It asked 'Dr Cowley for an interview'.

Another five minutes passed and the phone rang.

'*Dr Cowley, please.*'

'Who wants him?'

'*It's Barrie Penrose of The Sunday Times.*'

'He's not here.'

'*Well I happen to be able to confirm that he is, and I'd like an interview*

16

and I may say I'm not going to go away. So would you tell him I'm staying at the Avon Gorge Hotel?'

'I'm afraid I can't help you,' I said, and hung up.

The telephone rang again, and this time my son Bryn answered, just for a change. Penrose was shifting his ground too.

'*I've got a deadline,*' Penrose said. '*I don't want to leave the area without a statement from Dr Cowley. But if I have to I'll run the story anyway. Do you understand what that might mean?*'

Penrose sounded like he was saying he would make the story up. I felt furious and very tense at the powerlessness of my position. I just said,

'Well let him make it up then.'

4

I had been doing my Clifton Downs run, and was now coming downhill, in the dark, towards home. If I had been thinking about hit-men waiting in dark doorways, if I had been thinking about what it is like to be shot, it would not have been surprising.

The civilised streets of the Clifton district rise sharply for a kilometre before levelling off at the Downs. The run calls for a hard climb up these precipitous streets, a few circuits of open common, a drop back towards the house and then, perhaps, a kilometre or two more along the tow-path. The Downs are popular, in daytime at least, with strollers, dog walkers, joggers, pram-pushers and students from the University's nearby Halls of Residence. But now the area was deserted. It was half an hour before midnight.

Tonight I was in dire need of this. Glenys and I had already decided we would go to rural Wales for the weekend to get away from the unremitting media attention, but we hadn't planned to leave until the morning. Meanwhile the stress of this last week had left my system pumped up with adrenalin. Much of it came from being cooped up. I could hardly bear being a prisoner at home. But there was something in this beyond frustration and incipient claustrophobia. There was a more sinister worry lurking in the pit of my mind.

Bull had been dead a month. At the time, what little press comment there was had focussed mainly on the work of the Space Research Corporation, and Bull's sanctions-busting reputation. These had all pointed to the obvious political dimension of his murder. But there was a certain amount of more salacious speculation. Bull's wife, the papers said, was living in Canada and, on the night he was killed, Bull had been due to meet a woman who was not his wife. Furthermore, the same woman – her name was Hélène Grégoire – had arrived at his door to keep the appointment, only to discover his body lying at the threshold. The uninformed press allowed itself to build small, ill-defined castles of conjecture

18

upon these bare facts. Was this perhaps a grudge murder? Was it the act of a husband or lover insane with jealousy, a classic *crime passionel*?

I never believed a word of it. While Bull's wife Mimi certainly *was* living in Montreal, I knew of no marital estrangement between them. Having shared his nomadic existence for three decades, Mimi wanted to build a home in which she could visualise herself and Bull settling down in retirement. The fact that Bull would never, of his own will, have contemplated retirement was neither here nor there. Mimi had her own strength, and it was enough to retain Bull's devotion so that, during their long periods apart, he phoned and consulted her constantly.

Apart from anything else, Hélène Grégoire was one of Mimi Bull's closest friends.

No, the killing was no crime of passion. To me, the facts as I had them had always suggested a professional hit, carried out by the secret service goons of one country or another. A wet job. If Bull was not liquidated by the agents of an unknown government, then the murder must have been done by contractors hired by a government. From this hypothesis flowed two numbing questions. If there was a hit, was there a hit *list?* And, even more to the point, was the name of Chris Cowley on it?

With this thought perhaps no more than a wisp in my mind, and with the enforced idleness of the media siege, I had started to become very jumpy. Running was the best way to ease the build-up of tension, but I would do so only, as now, at night, reasoning that the assorted hacks would be drifting off to their hotel bars shortly after sunset, to compare notes and hatch their plans for the morning. Tonight, however, it had taken a while for the sovereign remedy to start working.

I was near the top of Clifton Village, trying to achieve that fast but relaxed lope that the marathon runner strives for. Still, looking out for trouble, I couldn't give myself up to it. I tried to penetrate each dark shop door. I flinched past roadside trees, the mouths of alleys, parked cars. For greater safety I stepped into the road and ran there until a car brushed me and I saw that I was more vulnerable on the road than on the pavement.

With my running shoes slapping the pavement, I at last began to relax as gravity took me downhill again. Now I was closing on my home. I could see virtually the whole street and it was deserted. The few parked cars, as far as I could make out, were unoccupied.

I was only 20 metres past my door when someone stepped out of shadow and into my path. He was three metres in front of me and had been lurking behind the bonnet of a car. It was a man, but I only saw his silhouette against streetlighting. Something glinted in his hand, as he raised it up between us.

Quite deliberately, with no conscious thoughts except self-preservation, I careered on down and cannoned into the figure. He was a big man, at least 80 kilogrammes, but I heaved him sideways so that he seemed almost to fly away from me before falling into the road. Whatever he had been holding flew from his hands and I heard it clatter to the ground.

All my normally well-controlled reflexes of anger were activated as I advanced on the guy, ready to attack him again.

He was half on his feet now, trying to escape. He looked around him as if to locate his fallen equipment. I saw his fear. Scrabbling on his hands and knees in the road to get away from me, he called out, his voice quavering.

'Look, I'm a photographer. I only wanted a picture.'

For the first time I realised this was the truth: the metal object which he'd held in his hands was a camera. He'd wanted to shoot me with nothing but that. All the frustration of the last seven days came to the surface and suddenly I was shaking as I felt the anger and the self-protective reflex dissipate. I felt suddenly drained. I walked towards my front door, vaguely aware of the man across the street, picking up his camera. I fumbled with my key and at last, despite my trembling, got it into the lock. Letting myself in I shut the door firmly.

5

I was breathing heavily, leaning back against the front door, looking at the two suitcases which stood, fully packed for tomorrow's
trip, in the hall. I called to Glenys. She came and stood on the stairs
looking down at me. I said,
'Let's not go in the morning.'
Our weekend away was planned, but not rigidly. We thought
we might find some remote rural guest house, it didn't matter
where, just going wherever the fancy took us. Now she looked at
me, puzzled.
'But I thought you wanted to get away.'
'I do. But not in the morning. Those vultures are still there, and
they're not about to leave us alone. Let's get out of here right now.
They won't be able to follow in the dark.'
The car was parked beside the door, and it took no more than a
few minutes for me to shower and change. Then I threw the cases
into the boot and we were gone, away into the night. I saw no sign
of the men from *The Sunday Times*. It was just after midnight.
As we surged over the Severn Bridge and into Wales my pulse
began reverting to its normal rhythm. I kept checking the mirror.
It was hard to distinguish the headlights of one car from another,
but I was pretty sure no one was following us. I drove as fast as I
dared, and all the time I could feel the tension seeping out of me. It
felt fantastic. It felt like freedom.
Then Glenys said,
'Okay, where are we going to stay the night?'
I hadn't given it any thought. Wales, as a country, is not known
for keeping late hours, and it was a fair assumption that most hotel
landlords would be tucked up in bed by this time. However we
saw an illuminated sign for a hotel that was a kilometre ahead and I
turned into its driveway full of hope. But all was dark and the door
was locked. I drove on.
After successive roadside hotel signs produced no happier result
and we were beginning to resign ourselves to a night spent in the

car, we saw a police station ahead. I pulled in and asked the desk sergeant if he knew of any hotels that would still be open.

'At this hour, no sir, can't say I do. But there's a working men's club just up ahead that'll still be open. You could ask in there.'

These clubs are the Welshman's way of circumventing the licensing hours, which forbid alcohol to be publicly sold over the counter after 10.30 pm. When we got there we entered a still-lively scene, talkers and live cabaret competing with each other to fill the place with noise. Heads turned as we came in and conversation ceased. At least a dozen club members heard my request to the bar man for information about hotels, and one of them came up with the answer.

'There's a place in Usk, down the road here, that's sure to be still open. Want to give them a ring from this phone here?'

My telephone call secured a room at this establishment and, although it was well after two am by the time we arrived, the bar was almost as lively as it had been at the club. We had a drink with the regulars, chatted for half an hour, then went upstairs and fell gratefully into bed.

In the morning we drove north, through the Usk valley which separates the Black Mountains from the Brecon Beacons. It was more than thirty years since I had last visited the area, and I'd nearly forgotten that it contains some of the finest scenery in Europe. We passed the day like any tourists, looking at antiques in country towns and villages, stopping at the Dolaucothi gold mine, last worked by slave labour in the Roman period. Finally we checked into a guest house, which had once been a farm, on a hill between the Cambrian Mountains and the sea.

It was a pleasant room looking out towards the vast blue mountain range in the east. I was enjoying the view as I sat on the bed and picked up the phone.

At that time we shared our Bristol home with our son Bryn. If I wanted to know what had been going on at home, the easiest thing was to dial his number.

'Dad, the police have been here. They want to know where you are.'

I said, 'Are you sure it was police? Did you see their I.D.?'

'One was in uniform. The other did all the talking. There's been a complaint from that news photographer you had that fracas with in the street last night. Claims he was assaulted or something. Now they want a statement from you.'

'What did you tell them?'

'That I don't know where you are, which I don't. Where *are* you?'

'Guest house near Aberystwyth. Want the phone number?'

I read him the number off the telephone dialling unit. Then I said,

'Look, I'll call this policeman. What's his name, what station?'

'Detective Sergeant Evans, Redlands Police Station.'

He gave me the Bristol number and I dialled again. After a minute I was put through to D.S. Evans. I asked what the trouble was.

'Well, I'm afraid I have an official complaint against you, sir. Gentleman, a Mr Justin Sutcliffe, alleges you assaulted him at 23.33 on Friday last, 20 April, outside your house. I'd like you to come in tonight, sir, and make a statement, if you don't mind.'

I told him I didn't mind making a statement, but that I was away for the weekend.

'Mind telling me where exactly, sir?'

'That's irrelevant at the moment, Sergeant. I can't get to you tonight in any case. Also I think I'd better talk to my solicitor first.'

'That might be wise, sir.'

With a promise to call him back, I hung up and sat for a while on the bed, staring out of the window. Dusk was beginning to fall by now and the country beyond the guest house garden had darkened.

Ever since the seizure of the tubes at Teesport ten days ago I had known that some sort of prosecution might ensue. The Customs would never have been let loose in the first place, otherwise. But it hadn't been until the previous Wednesday, whilst talking to Jonathan Foster, one of the few journalists with whom I had a sensible relationship, that I realised in full what this might mean for me. I had asked Jonathan then if he knew any solicitor experienced in cases with a political complexion.

Jonathan had covered the Stalker affair for the paper he was then working for, *The Guardian*. He said,

'You could try Stalker's lawyers.'

In the mid-1980s John Stalker, the Deputy Chief Constable of Manchester, had been called in to investigate allegations of a 'shoot-to-kill' policy against terrorists by the Northern Ireland police, but he had been taken off the enquiry a few days before he was due to present his report. Later, in spite of his outstanding and blameless record of service, Stalker was driven out of the police altogether, when his own force made accusations of corruption against him. It was a case with enough elements of cover-up

23

and vindictiveness to leave the suspicion of political interference hanging around it like a foul smell.

I had already smelled a hint of the same aroma from statements made by officials about H.M. Customs' Operation Bertha. Yes, I thought, Stalker's solicitors might be the very people for me. I therefore garnered from Jonathan the telephone number of Messrs Irwin Mitchell, a firm of solicitors established in Sheffield, South Yorkshire. He also gave me the private number of Mike Napier, one of the firms senior partners.

I used the number immediately.

'I'm sorry, Mr Cowley. Mike's out at the moment. I'm expecting him back in about half an hour, though.'

'Please could you tell him I called, and that it's to do with the so-called Iraqi Supergun affair.'

'Can he call you back?'

'No, I'll call back myself at half past eleven. Thanks.'

Standing up I moved to the window. I could see the skyline of the enormous mountain range cut out against the lighter intensity of the night sky. Glenys was tired and said she would go to bed. I wanted to go out and breathe the cool night air, and be surrounded by silence and peace. I put on a coat, and went for a walk.

To reach the guest house we had turned off a A-road and driven for half a kilometre up a narrow lane. I now walked back down the lane, meaning to reach the road and stroll a little way along it. The night was cool, with a light breeze. I could hear the occasional vehicle changing gear in the distance, but there were no other sounds bar the wind. Before I reached the junction with the road, however, I saw something new: a car parked, facing away from me. It was occupied by two men.

When I came abreast of the car – it was a fairly new Vauxhall Cavalier – a couple of things struck me. One was that instead of the usual single car radio aerial, this vehicle was equipped with two antennae, one on the roof and another on the rear wing. The second point of interest was that, instead of turning to look at me as I passed, the men ducked away as if to hide their faces in the interior of the car. These men, it seemed, were anxious not to be recognised.

I walked for a mile along the A-road, and then retraced my steps, thinking about this car. By the time I reached the lane once more I had convinced myself there was nothing sinister in it. The car was probably just a mini-cab and, for all I knew, the men were a couple of homosexuals who didn't want to be identified.

However, when I reached the junction of the lane leading to the guest house, my suspicions returned. The car had been moved. Now it faced away from the road and was on the other side of the lane. I could see, as I walked past, that its occupants were still inside. I glanced back into the rear window, catching sight of a heap of rugs and a thermos flask. Then I moved crisply up the lane, returning directly to my room where the telephone was waiting.

I did not tell Mike Napier about the men in the car, not wanting him to think he was dealing with a paranoiac. I did explain, though, that I had been Gerald Bull's Project Manager for the so-called Supergun, and that I thought I might be the subject of some kind of Customs action in the fairly near future. I also told him about the incident with the photographer outside my home, and of the man's subsequent complaint to the police.

Napier immediately grasped the situation and took charge.

'Tomorrow's Sunday. I suggest you come at once to Sheffield. Don't, whatever you do, go back to Bristol. Come early because tomorrow afternoon I've got to go to London and I'd like to see you in the morning before I leave.'

I thought about Glenys. Should I drag her all the way to Sheffield? And what about the men in the Cavalier?

I told Mike Napier it might be difficult to do as he suggested, but I would try. He gave me the directions I needed to find him and wished me luck. Then I hung up and telephoned D.S. Evans at Redlands Police Station.

I told Evans I intended to see my solicitor before making any statement to the police.

'Is your solicitor in Bristol?'

'No.'

'I really must insist, sir, that you return to Bristol right away.'

'Well, I'm sorry Sergeant Evans, but that won't be possible. I will return as soon as I can.'

There was a pause, as if Evans was trying to think what to say next. On the other hand he might have been conferring with another officer. When his voice came back down the line its earlier, rather friendly tone had hardened.

'Dr Cowley, I must warn you. If you won't tell me where you are speaking from, and if you won't undertake to return at once to make your statement, then it shall be necessary for me to put out an instruction to police forces nationwide, asking that you be apprehended.'

25

'But Sergeant Evans, surely this is a very minor matter—'
'I can only repeat what I have just said, sir.'
I told him goodbye and hung up.

It was midnight now as I slipped downstairs and out of the house. This time, instead of going down the lane I climbed a fence and crossed the field which stood between the guest house and the road. This way I could approach the Cavalier from behind, and without being seen.

Looking through the rear window I could see the silhouette of only one head, a man sitting in the front passenger seat. I crept nearer, trying not to disturb any loose stones or chippings underfoot. At last I came near enough to see that the mound of rugs in the back of the car looked bulked out, and protruding from them was a stockinged foot which was propped beside the headrest on top of the driver's seat. The second man was clearly taking his turn to kip.

I returned the way I had come without attracting attention. Now I was sure of it. The car was not a mini-cab, and the men were not here on a gay date. They could have only one reason to be hanging around in this remote country lane at midnight.

By the time I had recrossed the field, the decision was made. I would go to Sheffield. Glenys would telephone our youngest son Ross after my departure and he would come and pick her up and take her back to Bristol. If the men in the Cavalier tried to follow me, I would lose them.

As I climbed into bed, suddenly dog-tired, a thought struck me. How in God's name had those men known how to find us?

6

The Welsh countryside was bright and alive with the movements of birds and animals. Only human beings were scarce in this early morning scene as my car rolled cautiously out of the guest house gate and into the lane. I craned round and caught a glimpse of Glenys watching from an upstairs window. I gave as cheery a wave as I could manage.

The watchers were still at their station. I drove cautiously towards them, ready to plunge down on the accelerator if they tried to block the road. I need not have worried: the man in front was asleep. Then, as I drew up alongside, his head rolled sideways and his eyelids came open. For an instant our eyes met. Then I had passed, turned left into the main road, and driven on. My intended direction was the other way but I wanted to test the men in the Cavalier first.

They were not press. I was confident no reporters could have followed me all the way from Bristol to this remote spot. But I didn't know who they *were*.

I was pretty sure of one thing. If they hadn't tailed us from Bristol, there was only one way they could have known where to look. They must have intercepted my telephone conversation with Bryn, in which I'd relayed the phone number of the guest house.

Few motor cars would be able to keep up with the Peugeot Mi 16 I was driving, but I kept the speed down to 50 kilometres per hour at first, looking repeatedly in the rear-view mirror and seeing no Cavalier. I began to think that, after all, I must have been mistaken. They weren't going to follow me, the whole thing was a paranoid fantasy spun by a brain plagued by worry and hassle.

I had gone about two kilometres now, and there was still no sign of them. I passed over the brow of a hill, went on for 200 metres, and looked in the mirror again. I saw the Cavalier appearing over the bump, gliding into view at the same leisurely speed as myself.

So this was it. I increased the pressure of my foot on the accelerator, picking up speed and moving a little ahead of the pursuers until they, too, accelerated just enough to make up the deficit. We were travelling on a major road now, the A470 towards Rhayader. All the time I was putting on more speed, and they were responding. Soon we were hurtling south at more than 160 kilometres per hour.

I was thinking only that somewhere soon I would have to turn around, for we were going in diametrically the opposite direction from Sheffield. But I wanted to lose those two in the Cavalier first. I guessed if they lost me going south they would gamble on London and probably look for me on the M4 motorway.

On straight stretches of road I could see them sticking to their work, a few hundred metres behind my tail. Only over twisting stretches did I lose sight of them, so it would have to be on one of these that I must try to shake them off. I screamed through a chicane. A roadsign showed ahead, a left turn, signed to Cross-gates. In front the road went into a right-hand bend.

Desperately I visualised the road map I had studied at breakfast. I thought I knew which road it must be. If I could take the corner before the Cavalier came round the bend behind me they would think I had already gone through the bend in front. By the time they'd shot past the turn, gone on ahead and realised I wasn't there, I might have put enough distance between us to reach the cross roads at Crossgates before they picked up my tail again. Once the men in the Cavalier got there they'd have only a one in three chance of picking my direction right – even if their thinking wasn't biased towards London.

I blasted the Peugeot into that corner, corrected the skid and jammed my foot down. I shot forward. In front of me was another bend, and I took the car through it, almost skidding into the ditch. But I was sure I got round it before the Cavalier flashed past behind me.

Then I settled down to do some serious driving along the twisty side road. Within minutes I passed through Crossgates and turned north. By the time I reached Welshpool I knew I had lost the Cavalier.

7

In Welshpool I saw a small general store and bought a bunch of Sunday newspapers. Then, in this border country somewhere near the path of Offa's Dyke, I found a lay-by beside the Shrewsbury road and sat reading all about the latest developments.

The Government had by now cautiously moved towards acceptance of the position of H.M. Customs, who were firmly convinced that the tubes seized at Teesport were for a great gun. At the same time the Department of Trade continued to stonewall any questions about their own advance knowledge of the deal. In answer to unwelcome questions they were saying that this was a matter for the Ministry of Defence.

The manufacturers of the seized tubes, Forgemasters plc, until recently a division of British Steel and now privatised, had initially denied that the tubes were for a cannon or gun. The tubes were of varying diameters, their press statements argued, and couldn't be made to fit together to make a gun barrel with a consistent bore. But within a day or two the company had been forced to shift their position. They now said that, when the contracts were signed, and throughout the manufacturing process, they had unquestioning believed these tubes to be high-specification petro-chemical equipment. They were beginning to fear they had been duped.

This didn't quite fit with what Sir Hal Miller, member for Bromsgrove, was saying. Miller continued to insist that he had been made aware by one of the other companies involved, Walter Somers, of their anxieties about the contracts.

The apparent inconsistency coming from the manufacturers gave Nicholas Ridley, Secretary for Trade and Industry, the opportunity he needed to wipe some of the egg from his own face. Hitherto he had been on the defensive, caught off balance. It had been his department's job to see that export licenses were sought by companies for sensitive contracts, and that no sector of British industry broke sanctions or otherwise jeopardised British foreign-policy objectives.

Now that the companies were seeming to protest too much, Ridley went on the attack. In answer to Opposition questions in the House of Commons he accused these companies of conspiring to export advanced gun technology to Iraq. It appeared to him that they had signed covert contracts for gun barrels at a time when that country was a belligerent in a war with Iran, and when arms-technology transfers to it were restricted. The nature of these contracts had been disguised in order to deflect the attentions of the authorities. He concluded, therefore, that these companies had been either 'negligent or dishonest' in the matter.

But Ridley's tactics were not working, and judging from my reading of that Sunday's papers, the Opposition believed that the steam had far from gone out of the issue. The Prime Minister, Margaret Thatcher, though she had tried to stay aloof, had already been forced to step in and, on the Friday 21 April, had promised an enquiry into the affair. That, if nothing else, would keep the boiler hot.

It was when I turned to *The Sunday Times* that I found out how busy Barrie Penrose had been on the Saturday, elaborating details of my encounter with his photographer in lurid terms.

> The British scientist alleged to be at the centre of the Iraqi 'supergun' project was being sought by Avon and Somerset police last night after he attacked a photographer working for *The Sunday Times* in Bristol.
>
> Detectives want to question Dr Christopher Cowley, said to be former project manager with a Brussels-based arms firm which ordered parts for what British companies believed to be a petrochemical project.
>
> The attack happened late on Friday night outside Cowley's house in the Clifton area of Bristol. Justin Sutcliffe, 22, a freelance photographer, said Cowley raced towards him, pushing him into the path of a passing car and then kicked him in the stomach.
>
> 'He told me, "You don't know who you're messing with. My wife and children's lives are at risk over this business. I've been in this game for 28 years",' Sutcliffe said. 'He asked me for the camera and when I said "No", he told me "Then I'm going to have to kill you." '
>
> Sutcliffe said Cowley then grabbed the camera and smashed it on the road after exposing the film. Sutcliffe, who has given a statement to the police, said Cowley threatened to 'fireball' his car.

Penrose's threat was not idly made.

Earlier in the same article, the 'Insight' team had secured a statement from a Customs source. The source dismissed 'the distinction between a gun and a more innocent-sounding satellite launcher' with the simple words 'a gun is a gun'. The tabloid view of what was essentially complex was beginning to prevail.

And my personal situation was beginning to look increasingly precarious.

8

Ordinary solicitors are not normally willing to open their offices at eleven o'clock on a Sunday morning to see clients whom they have never met before. Irwin Mitchell, though, is no ordinary firm.

Mike Napier listened to me for 45 minutes while I outlined some of the events of the past few days, including the incident with the photographer, the press speculation over charges relating to the export of Supergun, and the two men in the Cavalier. When I had finished he looked at his watch.

'Mr Cowley, I explained, didn't I, that I have to go to London this afternoon?'

I nodded.

'Then what I propose is this. You drive yourself to London and meet me there later this evening – let's say six o'clock at Euston Station. The firm has a place where we can talk in confidence and at length. We need to do that because this business is clearly very complicated and involves a number of heavyweight competing interests. We don't want you to be squashed between them. You will need to provide me with as much background as possible if we are to represent you.'

He wrote a London telephone number on the back of a business card and handed it to me.

'Contact me here if you have any trouble on the way.'

'Where *is* this?' I asked.

'Oh, it's a flat we own, a place where clients can meet us. It isn't known to many people.'

I felt like I was entering some John le Carré world of confidential addresses and secret meetings.

'You mean, a kind of safe house?'

He smiled.

'If you like. You can stay there without fear of discovery until we are ready to talk to the authorities – that is, if you are really sure that you are likely to be arrested.'

I was increasingly sure of this and said the safe house sounded like a good idea.

'But what do I do about Sergeant Evans at Redlands Police Station?'

'I think you shouldn't talk to the police at all just yet, not until you have filled *me* in on your involvement with these Iraqi contracts. If they know you've already given me your story they're less likely to play silly buggers when they do get hold of you.'

I didn't much like the sound of this.

'What do you mean, play silly buggers?'

Napier fixed me with a serious, searching look.

'Mr Cowley, from what you've told me it seems you have been under some sort of surveillance. It looks as if your phone is being tapped and as if some people are tailing you. This may be because they're worried – whoever they are – that you might be willing to share your knowledge of this affair, with the press, say, or whoever. They – I'm not saying this *is* the case, but it's a possibility – *they* might not wish this. I therefore advise, for your own safety, a kind of insurance policy if you like, that you don't talk to the police until I've taken down your full account of these events.'

I have to say I was now thoroughly shaken. I nodded and stood up. Right, I said, we would meet at Euston at six.

The flat was in a mansion block, almost palatial in size and furnished in a luxurious but impersonal style.

Napier fixed a meal and poured beers for us both. Then he sat down with a legal pad on his knee and began asking questions. We had to map out a statement, he said, a complete account of my involvement in Supergun, and of what I knew particularly about the British end of it – the contracts, the dates of meetings, the personnel involved.

'But first I'd like to know how you got involved in it. Where did it all start?'

It all started 54 years ago, when I was born in Liverpool. My father was an artist-craftsman, who worked all his life on what must be the last great building designed to medieval specifications – Giles Gilbert Scott's Anglican Cathedral. He spent his time either in the stonemason's shop or up the ecclesiastical scaffolding, hand-carving bosses and scrolls, gargoyles and capitals.

Son of a man who worked in stone, it might seem appropriate that I should concern myself with metals. However, my boyhood interests lay elsewhere. A passion for model aeroplanes led to an attempt to enlist in the Royal Air Force, but this was thwarted by my father, who flatly refused to sign the necessary paperwork.

No, my father had other ideas and so it was that higher education claimed me. I did eventually fulfill that old ambition to learn how to fly, but a part of me still regrets I never became a fighter pilot.

Over the past two years the press shorthand description of me has been as a scientist, but theoretical research doesn't appeal to me. I am above all interested in practical outcomes, and that, I consider, makes me an engineer.

After a spell at English Electric, another stint in South Africa with a mining company, and a third back in England with Henry Wigan, by then a subsidiary of International Nickel, I found myself returning to Africa, and a job supervising the railways engineering workshops of the newly-independent state of Kenya.

I found Jomo Kenyatta's young country an utterly captivating place to be. What you remember is the warmth, the light, the accessibility of wilderness, the sense of freedom. You had the freedom to learn to fly, and then pilot your own plane across the savannah to remote and inaccessible places; the freedom to go diving off the coral reefs which decorate the coastline; the freedom to drop down into South Africa and climb the Drakensberg Mountains, to wander in Uganda's Ruwenzorie Range – the Mountains of the Moon, or to scale the twin 5,500-metre peaks of Mount Kenya itself.

This makes my years in Kenya seem like a long holiday, but it was far from that. Independence had found the railway workshops, once the pride of British East African Railways, in a bad way. Investment in railways was in terminal decline and the country was so starved of hard currency that it could hardly afford to import the spares necessary to keep a minimal network running.

I realised, however, that the workshops themselves were an invaluable resource, and suggested my bosses should stop worrying about the absence of imported spares and start using the railway workshops to manufacture what was needed on site. I spent the next 12 years happily employed making this happen.

It ended more because of the internal politics of Kenya than for any other reason. Understandably, the Kenyan Government's goal was to Africanise as much of its management as it could, and so, inevitably for all of us European managers, the time arrived when we had trained the people who would supplant us. In 1983 it happened to me. At last, surplus to requirements, it was time to move on, but I left knowing it would not be easy adjusting once again to the grey weather, the chill wind, the cramped life of Britain.

'Okay,' said Mike, writing a note on his pad. 'What's next?'

'I went to work for Gerald Bull,' I said.

9

The advertisement from the Space Research Corporation in *The Daily Telegraph* was a trawl-net, highly generalised, as if they weren't quite sure what it was they wanted but thought they would see what they pulled in. Yet to me it looked enticing – foreign travel, good money and work with high-technology input.

I went to the hotel at Birmingham Airport where the interviews were being held. Alec Pappas, S.R.C.'s Vice-President of Engineering, and therefore one of Bull's deputies, met me.

'Do you object to working abroad?'

'No.'

'Any objection to China?'

I shrugged, thinking of Taiwan.

'Sounds okay.'

'This is Red China we're talking about. That still okay?'

I was surprised, but I said it would be no problem. I asked him about the company.

'Have you heard of Gerald Bull?'

'Yes. A gun scientist. Didn't he build a field gun for South Africa with an incredible range? That's about all I know.'

'Well if you come to work for us you'll soon know a hell of a lot more about him. This is Bull's company. What do you know about electro-slag remelting?'

Pappas was referring to a melting technique used to produce particularly clean and therefore very tough steels. The method is not generally available outside the developed world, but Bull believed it was an essential requirement for the manufacture of his guns. I said I was familiar with it.

'We used it at Henry Wigan in Hereford to manufacture jet-engine disc and blade materials.'

Pappas looked pleased and asked me about Kenya, wanting to know how I had adapted the engineering workshops in Nairobi to accommodate the railway's new requirements. I left Birmingham feeling very buoyant. The job sounded by far the most exciting of all those I had been looking at. I set about discovering as much as I could about the prodigious Canadian for whom I might soon be working.

Gerald Vincent Bull really had been a scientific prodigy. He qualified for entry to the University of Toronto at only 15 years old and, shortly after his twenty-third birthday, he became the youngest Ph.D. ever appointed by that University. His doctoral thesis was on shock-wave measurement at supersonic speeds and the aerodynamic characteristics of wind tunnels. It was highly precocious work and produced results which effectively replaced the old ballistic method of wind tunnel analysis. But, even before the thesis was finished, Bull was in full-time employment as the rising star of the Canadian defence industry.

Canada, in the 1950s, had decided it wanted to play in the big league of the cold war. Its Government, therefore, gave C.A.R.D.E., the Canadian Armament Research and Development Establishment, the task of developing an air-to-air missile capable of deterring a Soviet nuclear bomber strike. This programme was code-named Velvet Glove, and Bull went straight from graduate school to the leadership of the team designing the missile's body, wings and control fins. He had started his career at the very top.

But progress, apparently, was agonisingly slow. There were continual lapses in government concentration, interruptions in funding and breakdowns of will in the effort to perfect Velvet Glove. Thus, even before the missile was finished, it was found that the Russians had developed bombers fast enough to outpace it. By this time, too, the first intercontinental ballistic missiles were being tested, and it was clear that, against these, Velvet Glove would have been about as useful as firing a pea shooter to stop a swarm of bees. The missile was scrapped.

Still in his 20s, the experience taught Bull an important lesson. It was an axiom I would frequently hear him expound: you can't develop effective advanced technology systems in an atmosphere of caution and delay; bureaucracy impedes progress.

Certainly the Velvet Glove setback was none of his making and Bull stayed with C.A.R.D.E. for another ten years, becoming in his early 30s the highest-paid civil servant in Canadian history. His work continued to shine, and he was acquiring an international name in the field of ballistics, and, in particular, in the design of missile nose-cones able to withstand the complex problems of atmospheric re-entry. Yet, in spite of his official position as head of the Aerophysics Division, he never forgot the bureaucratic problems he had experienced over Velvet Glove, and always kept a number of pet projects under his personal control, projects which did not necessarily directly serve the defence needs of the Ottowa Government. One of these was soon to become his ruling passion: the design and use of big guns.

It was a spin-off from his Ph.D. subject. Wind tunnels are employed in aerophysical research to simulate the behaviour of large, solid objects moving through the atmosphere at speed. As he became increasingly involved in airframe and missile design, it occurred to Bull that firing prototypes through the air from a gun might be more informative than firing the air past *them*.

Such firing was done in the horizontal plane and into a distant earth mound. In this way, ballistic experiments could be observed, controlled and monitored more easily than with the gun barrel in an inclined position, and meant that you could readily recover the projectile. On the test-bed for Operation Babylon, at a desert location in north-western Iraq, the time would come when I myself would supervise such procedures.

But, back in the 1950s, Bull was already thinking beyond the use of a large gun as a mere simulator. If it could *simulate*, he reasoned, it could also do tasks in its own right. One of these, which seemed particularly promising at a time when Intercontinental Ballistic Missiles (I.C.B.M.) systems were an emerging threat, was to make a gun into a giant shotgun, firing pellets at high altitude into the path of incoming missiles and so destroying them.

Bull had to wait 30 years before he could demonstrate conclusively that this was a practical idea, and again it was in Iraq that he did it. But the details of that belong in a later section of my story.

In 1962, when he was 34, Bull left C.A.R.D.E. to accept the Chair of Aerophysics at McGill University in Montreal, and here he openly worked on the idea which years later would culminate in Project Babylon. He called it H.A.R.P. – the High Altitude Research Project – a programme to prove that big guns can be used to hurl instrument-carrying projectiles first into the upper atmosphere, and then into space itself. His partners were the U.S. Army and a slightly reluctant Canadian Government.

H.A.R.P. grew impressively, notching up a succession of technical achievements and records. In partnership with his father-in-law, Bull founded his own private artillery test-bed at Highwater, Quebec (straddling the U.S. border), where horizontal firings could be carried out using state-of-the-art equipment. But Bull's prize bit of hardware was Betsy, a scavenged, 'obsolete' 16-inch (400-mm) naval gun barrel, left over from the era of big battleships. Betsy gradually evolved into an enormous artillery piece. In fact, with her barrel specially extended to 36 metres and her bore increased to 424 millimetres, she was at that time the biggest gun in use anywhere in the world. At the Space Research Corporation test site on Barbados, in July 1965, inclined at an angle of 80 degrees, Betsy fired one of Bull's self-designed Martlet series of projectiles to a world record altitude of 150 kilometres.

Bull was showered with honours, including the McCurdy Award in 1968 for outstanding scientific achievements in space research, in part by a jealous missile lobby.

Then, in the late 1960s, the bottom dropped out of H.A.R.P. The Canadian Government, which at the best of times had found Bull difficult to work with, withdrew its funding and the Pentagon – now having its own big-gun facility at Yuma, Arizona – decided it would not carry Bull by itself. He and his company, Space Research Corporation, had been bounced out of space research, in part by a jealous missile lobby.

But Bull was a character of considerable resilience. As if leaving a marker down for the future, he refused to change the company name and S.R.C. carried on as a terrestrial artillery design consultancy. For governments as diverse as America, Iran, Taiwan and South Africa, Bull ironed out artillery problems and designed new systems. It was in working for South Africa that he scored one of his greatest triumphs. Yet it was, at the same time, a personal disaster.

As a lawyer, Mike Napier became really interested in Bull only at the point when the South African connection came up.

'I remember reading that South Africa got Bull in hot water.'

'It got him into gaol. He never completely forgave the Americans. I mean, in 1972 they made him an honorary U.S. citizen by special Act of Congress, just so he could participate in American military secrets. The only other person ever to receive that honour was Winston Churchill. But then, the Carter administration turned round and used the citizenship to nail him, just so they could prove they were tough on apartheid. They couldn't have touched Bull as a Canadian, of course.'

'So why did he break the law?'

'He said he didn't. The South Africans were losing the war against Angola, partly because their field guns couldn't shoot far enough. Bull told them his GC45 gun was the answer to their prayers. Used in combination with his specially designed extended-range shells, it's probably still the best field gun ever made.'

'He designed it specially for Pretoria?'

'No, he designed it for anybody. The ordinary 155-mm field gun is a standard piece of kit, but it never used to have a range of more than 20 kilometres. Russian missiles – the kind used by the Cuban army in Angola – could outdo that, so the South Africans needed something better. Bull was their man because he'd already designed the solution – a combination of a longer-barrelled field piece with his specially designed shells. The new system had a throw of 40 kilometres.'

'So why South Africa? Didn't everyone want this new gun?'

'No. The strange thing was, they didn't. The Americans rejected the new shells and other N.A.T.O. countries followed suit. It's the old story, Mike.'

'Meaning?'

'National defence industries are never economical, they tend to choose options at the highest possible cost. Bull was a designer of low-cost solutions, but he always found the large armaments people thinking, well, if it's cheaper it can't be so good, and there's also less profit.'

'And was it?'

'Of course it was. To put this in perspective, the combined national defence industries of Britain, Germany and Italy spent a decade and a billion pounds trying to develop an improved 155-mm self-propelled gun, the SP70. They couldn't do it. In the meantime the South African G6 self-propelled system – largely designed by S.R.C. – was developed all the way from initial design concepts into service at a fraction of the cost.'

'But N.A.T.O. countries weren't interested in Bull's products? Why not?'

'They patronise their own arms industries, don't they? And those industries don't make sufficient profits from low-cost systems. The Pentagon encouraged Bull's research, certainly, but they never bought the product. They'd found their own much more high-tech ways to spend money. South Africa looked like his only customer.'

'So he broke the law?'

'Technically, I don't know. He was arraigned for illegally exporting the empty long-range shells, but he had an export permit from the U.S. Munitions Control Office to do it. You see, when they left America the shells went either to Antigua in the West Indies, or to Spain – both friendly countries. In fact, of course, these countries were staging posts. The shells were filled with explosives and went off from there to South Africa where the fuses were fitted. Bull had even sent his two Vice-Presidents, Alec Pappas and Steve Adams, to Pretoria to oversee the design and development. He was also working in Brussels with the explosives company Poudreries Réunies de Belgique who supplied the South African propellant charges. P.R.B. later came into Project Babylon, you know.'

Napier nodded.

'So Bull went to gaol, did he?'

'In 1980. He was shattered. He believed he'd actually broken no federal laws and he'd come from being a scientific star to a convict. When he came out he moved the company to Brussels. He was very bitter. He fought for a pardon until the day he died.'

'But of course, you didn't know Bull in those days. You had nothing to do with South Africa.'

'No, I hadn't met Bull. I didn't do so until three years after his release. But what I think's so interesting is the way history repeats itself. Over South Africa it's obvious that the C.I.A., the Pentagon and the State Department all knew what S.R.C. was doing. They wanted South Africa to beat Angola, they wanted the Russian-supported Cubans thrashed, so they let Bull go ahead. Then, for whatever reason of internal politics, they let him go down. He was the fall-guy, the patsy.'

Mike leaned forward, with a smile.

'Well, we must try to prevent the same thing happening to you, Chris.'

10

In spite of exhaustion I woke early. I thought, for a moment, I was in some international hotel room – but where? Even before I went to the Middle East, I travelled on Bull's business constantly in all the continents of the world, as well as to virtually every country in Europe. So I was used to waking in those ubiquitous 'businessmen hotels', with bedrooms all similarly comfortable and bland. The decoration of this room, as you'd expect in a company flat, shared the same neutral, inoffensive, international good taste.

With S.R.C. the excitement of travel had in the end turned to boredom: too many bedrooms like this one, too many hours hanging around airports, sitting in aeroplane seats, listening to canned airline music. But Bull's original offer to me, on that first day in 1984 when I finally met him at the S.R.C. office in Brussels, had involved a type of business travel that fitted none of the stereotypes. It seemed an extraordinary and challenging prospect: he wanted me to go and work for him in the remote, northern provinces of China.

Since his gaol sentence and the move to Europe, Bull's old customers now felt unable to do business with him openly. They were willing enough to use his expertise but consultants' fees would not be enough to sustain the company. South Africa, in particular, pretended they had no further need of him: from the start which he had provided, they went on to develop Bull's 155-mm field gun system by themselves, first with their G5 towable gun, followed by the G6, a superb self-propelled weapon with a range of 40 kilometres. This gun was virtually mass-produced, first for the Angolan war, and then for sale all over the world, but it made no further contribution to S.R.C.'s bank balance. The South Africans felt no compulsion to volunteer any contributions, or to provide Bull with additional work.

Not only had Bull always believed in selling his ideas at bargain prices, he was chronically in need of cash liquidity to finance his on-going research – and this usually meant one-time cash fees. It had been the same in 1978, when he licensed manufacture of the GC45 design to an Austrian Government-owned company. Voest Alpine, for a one-off fee of only $2 million. It has been estimated that, if Bull had had a royalty of five per cent on the South African and Austrian guns, he would have earned $30 million from their sales alone in the following years. He didn't: he was a poor businessman.

So now he desperately needed a new client, and one promptly came along, but there was a small problem. The client was the People's Republic of China and Bull had always been a fervent anti-communist. What was he to do?

After some thought he realised that the Chinese, having experienced thousands of border incidents in its cold war period with Russia, and having studied the Angolan war with profit, required Bull's gun for exactly the same reason as the South Africans: to counter the threat of superior Soviet weaponry. This he could live with, even welcome. Most of his anti-communist beliefs had been targetted at the Soviets and, even though his notions of patriotism had been modified by the experience of prison, he knew that China was considered almost an ally of the anti-Soviet West during the latter days of the Cold War.

So, in 1984, Bull signed a three-year $25 million contract with the Chinese Government to supply drawings, prototypes and test-facilities for a 155-mm field artillery system, tailored to Chinese requirements. But this was not all. Even more than South Africa, the Chinese are committed to self-sufficiency in defence, and by the end of the three years they wanted to be able to make Bull's gun entirely from their own resources. Thus, along with the system's drawings and prototypes, S.R.C. was obliged to provide complete factory specifications and layouts, exhaustive operating instructions for the machinery and detailed training in assembly.

There was also the ammunition to consider. Bull had recently become the first ballistics engineer to develop a way of countering a problem in shell design which had always seemed intractable. When a shell moves through the air, it is affected by the creation of a vacuum immediately behind its flat base. This vacuum in turn creates drag at the base of the shell which impedes its forward momentum.

Bull's revolutionary 'base-bleed' ammunition had a mechanism which released (or 'bled') a gas from the base of the shell into this vacuum, filling it and thus cancelling the drag. The effect on the range of the ammunition was startling. Using Bull's older full-bore ammunition the 155-mm ordnance which Bull designed for China (they were to call the gun MF45) had a range of 30 kilometres. With base-bleed, the throw was increased by 33 per cent to 40 kilometres.

Naturally the Chinese wanted base-bleed technology as a part of the package.

My Kenyan experience of using and adapting local – and relatively primitive – manufacturing plant appealed to Bull. Using the Nairobi workshops I had made Kenyan railways largely self-sufficient in spares. If S.R.C. were going to help the Chinese adapt their own antiquated methods in order to manufacture the most advanced field-ordnance system in the world, this was just the kind of experience they would need.

I went home to my house in Devon. I had a talk with Glenys and a good night's sleep. In the morning I telephoned Bull and told him yes. China would be a fantastic idea.

The change of direction was not merely geographical. I had never had anything to do with weaponry, although I was aware that progress in my discipline of metallurgy has been linked throughout history with armaments. Its application to artillery is obvious. The stresses of firing are so enormous that the material intended for gun-barrel manufacture is required to have a high yield-strength. When you operate a 155-mm artillery piece, the whole thing jumps two metres in the air. The shockwave from the propellant – radiating outwards in a cone-shape from the breech end – is so great that anyone near the gun and within that cone could have every bone in their body broken, just by the shock alone.

This means that, if they are not going to self-destruct whilst firing at the expected frequency (in the GC45's case, a round every twelve seconds), these powerful weapons have to be made of steel with very special properties. Our problem in China was to find ways of producing high-quality steel from plant which the Russians had looted in post-war Austria and sold on to the Chinese shortly afterwards.

Within a few weeks I was trying to solve these, and a thousand other difficulties, with our team in the city of Qiqihar on the banks of the Heilong Jiang river in northern China. I travelled around, into some of the remotest provinces, most of them off-limits to foreigners since the Communist take-over. I looked at firing ranges, foundries, chemical plants, living all the while in some of the worst conditions I had thought it possible to imagine.

The diet was unspeakable, hygiene did not exist, and the climate was appalling, with temperatures falling as low as minus-45 degrees Celsius. Finally, the landscape was utterly bleak and unburdened by natural life of any kind. We were treated everywhere with incomprehension. They called us honoured guests but, in terms of the culture gap, we might have been from another planet.

The most soul-destroying aspect was the enforced conformity. In this part of China, to the outsider at any rate, the scope for individuality was down to anthill levels. Each morning at six-thirty the whole town was simultaneously blasted awake by martial music, broadcast at screeching-pitch from street corner loudspeakers. This eardrum-wrenching noise went on for an hour and could be heard 16 kilometres away. The tone was set for the rest of the day.

There was nothing at all to do except work, although bizarre attempts were sometimes made to entertain us. I remember an eight-hour drive to visit a zoo where, we were told, lived the only panda for nearly 2,000 kilometres. This poor wretch enjoyed a life entirely commensurate with what we were trying to get used to: it was kept in a box hardly bigger than a tea chest.

I remember a dance. We were told it was being organised for the benefit of the honoured guests and found the dining room of our sordid guest-house had been cleared for the occasion. Heavily-diluted orange squash was served and dance music, a sort of mangled military two-step, filled the room from a battered record player in the corner. As seven or eight of us waited, wondering who we were supposed to dance with, a detachment of male workers from a nearby factory trouped in wearing boilersuits. Our dancing partners were to be the night-shift from the neighbouring engineering works.

At the time it was not particularly easy to find this kind of thing hilarious. We could not get books. We were surrounded by rigidly-enforced conformity. The only places to go 'out' to were 'restaurants' – filthy roadside hovels with earth floors and unspeakable food. Here people found ways to cope with the conditions, or they went under. Two members of our team died from heart failure during my tour of duty, their own yield-stress ultimately proving too low.

A couple of years in China taught me a great deal about the capacity of the human spirit under stress.

11

Mike Napier was due to spend the whole day of Sunday 22 April representing the bereaved families at the judicial enquiry into a Thames pleasure boat disaster. I was to keep my head down, making notes about Project Babylon.

'I want you to note down the sequence of events from the moment you heard of the Supergun, okay?'

'What about the police in Bristol? I'm facing a charge of assault.'

'Leave that to me. Concentrate on those notes.'

I settled down to concentrate.

It was when I had been two years with S.R.C., my tour of duty in China coming to an end, that the first rumours began to circulate. Bull was thinking about big guns again. To me, still fairly inexperienced in the field, the 155-mm gun was big. I had no idea just how much bigger he was now thinking. Then one day he said to me,

'I'm writing a book, Chris. It'll be the standard textbook on big guns systems, the *only* textbook worth a damn, as a matter of fact.'

Bull had been ill, not seriously, but enough to provoke a transient sense of his own mortality. He convinced himself that his life's work could suddenly be lost, unless it was recorded for posterity. So he proceeded to write the book. His co-author was Charles Murphy, a U.S. army scientist who had been Bull's partner on H.A.R.P., and the second half of the book (with inputs by Murphy) told the whole story of Betsy, the Highwater test-bed and the McGill University work on big-gun systems. But the book was wider in scope, because Bull was anxious to establish the historical tradition in which he wished to be remembered. This tradition determined the book's title: *Paris Kanonen – the Paris Guns – and Project H.A.R.P.*

The historical survey with which the book was intended to start, quickly evolved into a piece of full-blown historical research, for which Bull himself did much of the work. The 'Paris Guns', precursors (as he saw them) of Bull's own work with large guns, were built by the Krupps company for the Kaiser's army during the First World War. They were, it seemed, the biggest practicable artillery pieces built prior to H.A.R.P.

The Paris Guns had come about because Germany's 1917 advance on the French capital had stalled at the River Marne, still a long way short of its objective. The distance was a great deal further than the range of any previous gun, but the German High Command now authorised the experimental construction of a new series of three enormous, long-barrelled howitzers which the German gunnery and ballistic engineers – clearly men after Bull's own heart – promised would be capable of lobbing high explosive shells from behind the line right into the heart of metropolitan Paris.

For a short time they even succeeded. But this was 1918 and the defeat of Germany was only a matter of time. Then, between the Armistice and the disarming of Germany at the Treaty of Versailles, the German military had the Paris Guns scrapped. Records were burned and personnel were strictly forbidden to speak of them. Gradually, the memory of the Paris Guns all but disappeared.

Such a story was meat and drink to a man like Bull. He relished the challenge of the detective work needed to provide a full account of the Paris Guns. He ferreted out scientific data from the Krupps archives and other German sources; he raised copies of suppressed scientific papers he tracked down nonagenarian former technicans and gunners in retirement homes all over the Federal Republic of Germany. Relatively few images of the guns were to hand – a scattering of technical drawings and photographs – but he used computer analysis to extrapolate from them, building up a complete specification for the guns, their shells, and the units' performance profile.

The book's chapters on H.A.R.P. were equally comprehensive and Bull used them in commercial presentations to show that, far from being anachronistic, big-gun systems were a practical low-cost way of investigating the upper atmosphere and space, as well as delivering payloads over long distances. In 1985 Bull had an opportunity to argue this case at a highly exclusive conference at the Pentagon. The subject was the place of guns in advanced weapons research, and the Americans, laying the South Africa misdemeanours to one side, accorded Bull the status of a world-class scientist. He responded by telling them that if they gave him a gun with a barrel 150 metres long and a bore of a metre, he could give them gun-fired orbiting satellites.

The Pentagon was sufficiently impressed to invite S.R.C. to prepare a formal proposal for such a gun. Bull asked me to prepare the proposal, and it was submitted in 1987. I remember him remarking sarcastically at the time, 'I gave the Americans this technology 30 years ago. They seem to have forgotten it.'

Nevertheless he was in a fever of excitement. He was again working on large-bore guns, the Americans were again paying court and he was once more in sight of completing his life's work.

The immediate outcome was great disappointment. On Bull's behalf I had sent a set of outline-design mechanical engineering drawings from Brussels to the Sandia Laboratory in Los Alamos – the secret research centre where much of the work on nuclear weapons had been carried out. Complete budget estimates for this 1,000-mm H.A.R.P. system were also submitted. Apart from an acknowledgement, the Pentagon never followed the proposal up.

However, in essence, work on Supergun had commenced with the Sandia proposal. All that Bull needed now was a hot client, a well-heeled paymaster.

Early in 1988 I had been in Rio de Janeiro on S.R.C. business. Bull had been asked to consult over a steelworks, to be built by Mannesmann De Mag of Germany, operated in Brazil but owned by the Islamic Republic of Iran. He had sent me out there to meet the Iranian Defence Minister and we had held talks surrounded, to the minister's slight bewilderment, by bare flesh on view as far as the eye could see along the beach Copa Cobana. I had just returned to Brussels and was sitting in my office, before climbing into the steelworks proposal, when the voice of the S.R.C.'s receptionist Martine came over the tannoy.

'Would Chris Cowley please go to Dr Bull's office immediately?'

I dropped what I was doing and went. Bull was sitting at his desk, which groaned under skyscrapers of papers, technical reports, manuals and books. He looked very pleased, almost triumphant, as he told me,

'Chris, we're going to build a one-metre gun.'

'One metre?'

At first I found myself at a loss. It was a year since we'd sent the proposal to Los Alamos and I'd forgotten all about it. I could now only relate the one-metre dimension to barrel-length. Surely we weren't going into rifles?

'Yes, we're going to do H.A.R.P., only bigger, more than twice as big. It'll be the biggest gun ever built, and we'll have $20 million to play with. So money's no problem. I want you to get involved.'

With Bull in this mood, you couldn't say no to him. I told him I'd be delighted, and within two days I was on my way to see our new client, the Government of Iraq.

12

By the time Mike returned at six o'clock on that Sunday evening, I had completed another ten pages of notes.

'We'll go through them in a minute. But first take a look at these.'

He dropped in my lap a bundle of the day's papers and went through to the kitchen to fix a drink.

GREECE HOLDS DRIVER IN IRAQ PIPE AFFAIR, said *The Daily Telegraph*. The British driver Paul Ashwell, whose lorry had been caught with the mysterious gun cradle, had been formally arrested in Greece and was facing what looked like quite serious charges of arms smuggling. Forgemasters, the company which had manufactured his load, were apparently doing nothing for Ashwell's firm, a small family outfit owned by his father-in-law. Ashwell meanwhile claimed not to have known what he was carrying, beyond some generalised description on his travelling papers. Whatever was going to happen to him now, the very least he could expect was the bankruptcy of his family's firm.

While most of the tabloids concentrated on the plight of Ashwell, *The Independent* had a different angle. Over the by-line of Jonathan Foster was the headline M.O.D. CANNOT TRACE SUPERGUN WARNINGS. Here we had the Government department, which Sir Hal Miller had told about the Iraq contracts two years ago, desperately trying to buy some time. It now no longer denied receiving Miller's warnings – it merely could find no paperwork on them.

The Times speculated about why neither the Department of Trade nor the Ministry of Defence, having been warned about the Babylon contracts, saw fit to advise Her Majesty's Customs. And if they didn't, who did tell Customs? 'The alert', said *The Times* 'may have been given by the Israeli secret service, Mossad.' The uses of the Supergun were also confidently described by the same paper: 'The gun was designed to enable Iraq to hit foes with nuclear or chemical weapons from the northern city of Mosul.' If that idea ever came to be generally accepted, I would really be in trouble.

'Still bubbling along nicely,' said Mike, coming back into the room and handing me a drink. 'It certainly looks as if the Customs are in full cry.'

'There's no mention of me anywhere.'

Mike settled in an armchair.

'That doesn't mean anything. Journalists rarely know more than officials want them to know. Now, let's look at your homework.'

I handed Mike the pages with my rough notes on the evolution of Project Babylon. He looked through them with intense concentration.

'Yes,' he said, laying the notes out on the coffee table in front of him. 'This gives me the bones I need – enough to prepare a preliminary defence statement on your behalf, in case you are picked up.'

He spread his hands wide.

'Though I don't say you will be. This whole thing's still up in the air. Nobody knows what's been going on, who's been told about what or who's approved what. The thing to remember is the politicians. When politicians are involved, no legal situation can be predicted.'

He picked up the notes and stacked them. Then he sat back and took out a pen.

'Now, I've just got a few supplementary questions.'

For the next hour he questioned me closely about the history of the Supergun contracts. He wanted to concentrate on Walter Somers and Forgemasters, asking me to recall the exact dates on which various meetings had taken place, and who had been present.

'A key question is who exactly placed the contracts with the steel manufacturers. Was it your lot, or the Iraqi Government?'

'You mean, who were the signatories?'

'Negotiators and signatories.'

'We certainly weren't the signatories. We were the design consultants, so of course we had to be in on discussions about manufacturing processes, specifications and so on. But only as advisers. All the financial arrangements, delivery times and suchlike, were negotiated and agreed directly.'

'By whom? Forgemasters are claiming Bull placed the contracts.'

'That's rubbish. It was the Iraqis. They're not idiots. They quite

51

rightly insisted on controlling all that side of things themselves. And they'd got a very tough negotiator Shabib Azzawi. He came over for the meetings and he signed the contracts himself.'

Mike seemed pleased. He slapped his knees and stood up.

'Good. Well I think that's quite enough work for today. These notes will need development eventually, and the time may come when we'll have to look for corroboration – some kind of hard evidence.'

'I've still got contacts in the company. I can't promise, but I might be able to get hold of documentation.'

'That sounds worth trying. But we've got enough to go on, for the time being anyway.'

Mike drained his glass.

'I don't know about you, but I've worked up quite an appetite. There's an Italian place round the corner where they do a very acceptable *saltimbocca romana*. You want to try it?'

We had got half way through a bottle of Chianti before he sprang his surprise.

'I spoke with your Detective Sergeant Evans today.'

I put down my knife and fork.

'And?'

'He still wants to see you. Since we're a Sheffield firm, I've suggested it should be somewhere in the South Yorkshire area. I've arranged for you to go and meet him tomorrow.'

I pondered this. I had a feeling of foreboding.

'Well at least I'll be going back to Bristol, see my wife,' I said.

Mike held up a hand, like a traffic cop.

'No, Chris. I don't think you should go to Bristol. For one thing I couldn't guarantee our presence there, and I do think that's essential. I also think, for psychological reasons, it's better to have the mountain come to Mohammed.'

'Here?'

'No, in Sheffield. I'm going to hand you over to a partner, Kevin Robinson, who'll take the case from here.'

I must have looked disappointed, because Mike hurriedly reassured me.

'Don't worry, he's good. I'll be in the background too, of course, but I've got a lot of very demanding work down here in London with this judicial enquiry. Kevin can give you more of his time. So what I've done, I've arranged for Detective Sergeant Evans to drive up from Bristol to interview you, with Kevin present, at Sheffield Police Station. That'll be late tomorrow after-noon. He will talk only about the so-called assault and won't touch on Supergun, so we shall have some more breathing space on that, anyway. Kevin will want a bit of time with you to get stuck into the case.'

I nodded my agreement.

'Okay, Mike. I take the point. I'll drive up to Sheffield tomorrow.'

Mike Napier smiled and raised his glass.

'Here's to success.'

On the way to bed back at the flat, I looked again at the newspapers. Paul Ashwell's picture was prominently featured, taken the day before in Athens. It showed a young man in trouble but trying to smile. The strain on his features was plain to see, as a grim-faced policeman escorted him to court.

As I lay in bed I thought of him tonight in his Athens police cell. An innocent. What had Mike Napier said?

'When politicians are involved no legal situation can be pre-dicted.'

It applied as much to him as to me. And, if my own future was a trifle shrouded, I wouldn't fancy swapping with Ashwell. I might wish I knew more, but at least I knew a little of what was going on.

And what's more, I wasn't in a cell.

13

I allowed plenty of time for the journey. Leaving the flat at ten o'clock in the morning, I walked to a nearby underground car park where the Peugeot was waiting in its bay.

The traffic was dense and unfamiliar. In my life I'd spent little enough time in London, and had driven through it even less. Now I drove warily, not only of the cars crowding impatiently around me, but of someone – some unknown operative, agent, policeman, whoever – who may be on my tail. I could not easily forget the Welsh experience and the two men in the Cavalier.

These suspicions left me as I drove up the motorway, going north. On a motorway it is relatively easy to tell if there's a car following you, and I was sure there wasn't. I found I was making good time. For once the M1 had few hold-ups, lane-closures or contra-flow systems and, in spite of a long lunch stop and a visit to a car-wash, I found myself in Sheffield city centre with two hours to spare. I left the Peugeot in the British Rail car park and mooched around, window shopping and killing time. But I am of little use with time on my hands and, half an hour ahead of time, I found myself in the offices of Irwin Mitchell. I was told Mr Robinson was in court, representing a client, and would I please wait. Leafing through the out-of-date magazines in the waiting room I felt anxious to get it over with. I wanted to go home.

Kevin came in, a dark, controlled, soft-spoken man, carrying a bulging briefcase. We shook hands.

'Hope you haven't been waiting long. I've been in court all afternoon, my usual place of work.'

Kevin had been briefed over the phone by Mike Napier but we again recapped the situation: I was to meet Detective Sergeant Evans at the Police Station, make a statement about the incident that happened the previous Friday night outside my home, and then leave. Kevin thought I would probably be back home by midnight.

Supergun was not on the agenda, and, at this stage, Kevin and I only touched on it tangentially. Then, at five minutes to five, we left Irwin Mitchell's offices and strolled round the corner to Sheffield Police Station. I had the sensation of butterflies in my stomach, but Kevin Robinson was a reassuring, competent presence by my side. We walked into the reception area together and approached the desk.

My first impression was that there seemed an inordinate number of uniformed officers milling around the hall. They fell silent as I strolled to the desk, where a sergeant was speaking on the phone, whilst writing some details on a report pad. He flicked a look at me and called a colleague over to take his call. I said,

'I am Chris Cowley. I'm due to meet Detective Sergeant Evans of the Bristol C.I.D. Can you tell me where I can find him?'

The desk sergeant didn't even answer. With a wave of his fingers at the knot of loitering officers, he picked up his phone and said,

'He's here.'

Suddenly there were police all around me, crowding me in towards the desk. I said,

'What's going on?'

'If you'll just wait there for a moment, sir. Be just a moment.'

I looked at Kevin, who motioned me to keep calm. A more senior officer then appeared on the scene. He asked,

'Are you Christopher Cowley of Clifton Vale, Hotwell, Bristol?'

'I am.'

'Then I must tell you I am arresting you, sir, on a charge of assaulting Justin Sutcliffe on the evening of the nineteenth of April last. You have a right to remain silent, and I must warn you that anything you do say may be used in evidence. All right sergeant.'

The senior officer handed me over to the desk sergeant. I was asked to remove my tie, trouser belt, shoe laces, and to place the contents of my pockets on the counter. I looked again at Kevin. He nodded. He looked completely taken by surprise. I did as I was asked, struck dumb with shock, laying the things on the counter: pen, wallet, keys, credit cards, watch, loose change. The sergeant wrote everything down on a pad, then looked up at me and stretched out his hand, palm up. I looked at the counter and checked my pockets again. Yes, I had completely emptied them. What did he want now?

'The ring. Take off the ring.'

I slid my wedding ring from my finger and dropped it into the middle of the small heap of coins. The sergeant wrote: *ring*. He swivelled the pad and handed me the pen.

'Sign.'

I wrote my name. The signature came out shaky, almost unrecognisable.

Kevin walked alongside as they took me to an adjacent room, bare and hardly furnished. Then he returned to the desk and I could just hear him talking to the sergeant. I sat on a wooden chair. Two policemen stayed with me. I said,

'What's going to happen next?'

'We just wait.'

'I want to see Mr Robinson, my lawyer. He came in with me.'

One of the officers went back into the hall, then returned.

'He'll be with you soon.'

We waited. Several minutes passed by, while I tried to hear what was going on in reception. There was nothing but muffled voices. Then Kevin strode into the room. He had recovered his composure and seemed master of the situation.

'You all right?'

'Well, it's not exactly what I'd imagined.'

'I know. I'm terribly sorry. They evidently had it all planned.'

'But they said they only wanted a statement.'

Kevin smiled grimly.

'Yes. So much for the word of a police officer.'

I could tell from his tone that he was well used to this type of situation. He was a criminal lawyer: he saw plenty of the insides of police stations. I said,

'So what happens now?'

'They want to fingerprint you. Then you'll see Detective Sergeant Evans.'

'Fingerprints. What for?'

'Just procedure.'

'And when I see Evans, will you be present?'

It was terrible. I had only the vaguest idea of my rights in this predicament. Kevin patted me on the shoulder.

'Don't worry. I won't be there for the fingerprinting, but they have to let me in when Evans questions you.'

Questions me! The language of police thrillers was being employed now. So how was I supposed to feel – like a criminal? But I *didn't* feel like a criminal.

Kevin told me that, when the time came, I must answer only questions relating to the specific charge of assault. Supergun had

56

nothing to do with Detective Sergeant Evans, and it was vital I say nothing on the subject.

'As yet we don't know what they're up to, and we mustn't let them see our hand, okay?'

'Okay.'

I was taken to a windowless locker room. There were narrow metal cupboards in rows around the walls. A man came in dressed in a suit. He was a large man in his mid-30s, with a courteous, deferential manner.

'I'm Detective Sergeant Evans from Bristol. I'd like to take your prints, if you don't mind.'

I looked around. The room must be the police officers' changing room, which they used as they came on and went off duty. Evans saw my expression and said,

'Yes, I know, but there seems to be no other room available.'

Evans conferred with one of the locals who had come in with him. After a whispered discussion he said,

'It appears we don't have fingerprint forms. Would you mind waiting while we locate them?'

I said, 'Do I have a choice?'

They both left the room and I heard the lock turning.

Twenty minutes passed before they came back. Evans and his uniformed Sheffield minder, who looked little more than a teenager. The minder had some forms in his hand. Evans turned to him and said,

'You got the ink?'

The constable seemed at a loss. He looked around, as if he might discover a tube of fingerprint ink lying on the floor. Then he leaned out of the door and called an older colleague to join them.

'It's usually kept in that cupboard,' said the newcomer, nodding towards a metal cabinet indistinguishable from all the others.

The youth opened the indicated locker and began fishing around inside. Evans, looking tense, turned to me and remarked in an attempt at ironic humour,

'Every station has its own system.'

The youth produced from the cupboard a flattened tube which had once contained lamp-black ink. He removed the screw-top and tried to milk something usable from it.

'It looks like it's been used up,' remarked the older man, helpfully.

'I'll go and fetch another,' said the youth. He passed the fingerprint forms to Evans and left us. Evans tapped his foot on the floor and looked around.

'Well now, let's see . . . '

He found the only suitable flat surface in the room, a shelf between two lockers. He was spreading out the fingerprint forms as another police officer, one I hadn't seen before, arrived with a fresh tube of ink and a brass plate. A blob of ink was dropped on the plate and spread around by the constable's broad forefinger.

'Normally we have a roller to spread the ink,' explained Evans, as if to imply that police work soared to heights of the most advanced technology.

One by one, the pads of my fingers and thumbs were pressed onto the brass plate and thence onto the fingerprint form. As he was completing the impression of my ringless ring-finger, Evans said, for no evident reason,

'Nobody's ever refused to let me take their fingerprints.'

He obviously meant the remark as a piece of light small-talk. 'If they did,' Evans went on with forced cheerfulness. 'I suppose we'd have to break their fingers.' I said nothing. I was in no mood to be amused.

With the prints taken, a second time-honoured police ritual ensued. From somewhere – perhaps from the cabinet which had held the spent ink-tube – a camera, a flashgun and a small blackboard painted with white lines was produced. Oh yes, I thought, of course. The mugshots.

'Just a couple, and then we're finished.'

Evans was chalking words and numbers on the board. Engrossed in his work, like a doctor writing up case notes, he didn't look at me.

'Stand by the wall, will you? Hold this.'

I stood at attention, holding the board propped against my chest. The back of my head and my shoulder blades touched the wall. An officer stood in front of me, examining the camera. He looked as if he'd never seen such a thing before.

'It's not our usual camera, this. I don't think it's got a film in it.'

Now another policeman had entered. He seemed to have some sort of authority.

'Somebody go and get a film,' he said.

Evans gestured towards me, a tired movement, and sighed.

'Look, you may as well put down the board.'

It took several minutes for two fresh policemen to return with a film. I caught them looking at me curiously as they came in, and for the first time I wondered if this whole drawn-out farce had a purpose. Surely not so that the entire shift could get a look at the famous Supergun man? I tried to look impassive, gazing up at the ceiling as they bickered over the correct procedure for loading the film. In the end I couldn't stand it. I joined the group of officers around the camera to offer my own suggestions.

By the time three portraits had been taken, a full-face and the two profiles, the paperwork attendant upon my arrest had been completed. I estimated that at least four man-hours had been expended on the process, but at last it was time for my interrogation.

14

Now that it had finally happened, the interview with Evans was perfunctory, a matter of form and no more. The man seemed to accept my version of events, and was now clearly in a hurry to get back home to the wife and kids. Had I gone through this whole absurd rigmarole just for the sake of procedure?

In my statement I simply told him what had happened: how it had been dark, close to 11.30 at night. I was running and this man had jumped out in front of me. I explained that, because of my previous employment, I had had well-founded reasons to be concerned for my and my family's safety, especially after threats had been issued and other events, which I didn't want to go into. I was therefore shocked and frightened, thinking I was being ambushed by someone intent on doing me harm. My reaction had been essentially a reflex of self-defence.

He asked a few supplementary questions and then wrapped up the session. He handed me a piece of paper, a form.

'It's just a notice explaining what will happen to the tape. I'll just put my details on it.'

He scribbled on the form, handed it to me and said,

'The time is now 6.30 pm, the interview is concluded and I am now switching off the recorder.'

Detective Sergeant Evans flipped the off button and ejected the cassette. He stood up, stretched.

'Well, Mr Cowley, I see no reason to detain you any further. As far as I'm concerned you will be free to go.'

'You mean you're releasing me?'

'Subject to the usual conditions, yes. All right, Mr Robinson?'

We both glanced across the room at Kevin, who looked serious. Carefully he gathered his papers together and tapped them into a neat stack.

'Come on,' he said to me, 'I suggest we leave.'

'Oh, Mr Cowley, there's one more thing,' said Evans. 'I felt it was my duty to inform the Customs and Excise that I was meeting you here.'

A minute later I was waiting at the desk to collect my effects when a short, fit-looking man who seemed much younger than his 50-plus years, approached. Behind him was another man. These were not police officers, though I was not absolutely sure why I knew this.

'Dr Cowley?' said the first man.

'Yes?'

'I am Mr Riley, an officer of her Majesty's Customs and Excise. I am re-arresting you.'

Kevin and I exchanged glances. What was this? This wasn't supposed to happen. Riley however had a piece of paper in his hand, from which he read, quite confident of his own powers.

'I am hereby arresting you for the illegal exportation of goods. Would you mind accompanying me please?'

I said, 'Only if he can come too. He's my lawyer.'

'No objection,' said Riley. 'This way.'

Feeling sick in my stomach, I thought, I see it all: the reason for the delays, the slow-motion, the apparent incompetence. I had run into a carefully-laid snare, but they'd needed to keep me in it just long enough to enable these Customs Officers to be on hand when the farce was over. Well, they'd got the timing right, and I was well and truly trapped.

We were led back into the same small interview room pre-viously used by Detective Sergeant Evans. Riley dropped a box file on the desk. Kevin and I sat where we had sat before. Riley took Evan's chair and the fourth seat was occupied by the other man. Riley now gestured towards him.

'This is my colleague, Raymond Gaubert.'

Gaubert was lean and drawn. His smile lacked warmth. I nodded. Riley produced a tape and loaded it into the machine.

'You've been informed of your rights, including the right to legal representation?'

His fingers were hovering over the record-button. I nodded, wondering if I could trust my tongue. He hit the button.

'Can I caution you now that you are not obliged to say anything unless you wish to but, if you do so that will be tape-recorded and may be given in evidence. Do you understand the caution?'

'Yes.'

The next few minutes were spent confirming my name, address, and other personal details. Then Riley settled into his chair, opened up his file and began.

'What is your occupation?'

'I'm retired.'

For some reason this disconcerted him. I was just about to elaborate on my newly developed engineering interest, but he interrupted.

'You're now retired?'

'Retired last May 1989.'

He flicked a look at Gaubert.

'What was your occupation prior to retirement?'

'I had the title Chief Metallurgist at A.T.I.'

'A.T.I.?'

'Yes, a company owned by S.R.C.'

'What do the initials A.T.I. stand for?'

'Advanced Technology Institute.'

'And what does S.R.C. stand for?'

'Space Research Corporation.'

'And where are these companies?'

'They are both based in Brussels.'

'How long did you work for A.T.I.?'

'A year.'

'And how many years did you work for S.R.C. before that?'

'Four.'

He referred to the file, finding a place with his index finger.

'Okay, now, were you in any way involved in P.C.2?'

I hesitated. P.C.2? I was not instantly familiar with the term. I replied cautiously.

'I am not sure what you mean by P.C.2.'

'It covered the purchase of certain pieces of manufactured steel – tubes for example – from U.K. suppliers, Sheffield Forgemasters and Walter Somers.'

'I know that as Project Babylon.'

Now it was Riley's turn to pause. He had obviously not heard this name before. He frowned.

'Babylon?'

'Yes, can we use that term? That's the term I was familiar with.'

Riley wrote on his notepad.

'Okay. Can you tell me, then, from your knowledge of, er, Project Babylon, what the exported items were for?'

I spent the next few minutes sketching Bull's earlier work on

H.A.R.P. and mentioning the testing facilities at Highwater, Quebec.

'That was the Walter Somers element of this contract, for research and development.'

'So what does it do, basically?'

'It's intended to research internal and external ballistics.'

Riley shifted a little uneasily in his chair.

'Yes, but when this system was used by Dr Bull in Canada and Barbados, do you know what it actually did? Was he able to release objects through this thing or what?'

I took in a deep breath and again described Bull's early work with Betsy and the part later played by the horizontal test-gun, mounted on rails, at Highwater.

'I could tell you a lot about this, but if you refer to Bull's book about H.A.R.P., you'll see all the facilities he had. There are hundreds of pictures in it.'

'And you said just now, there were two U.K. companies. Forgemasters and . . . ?'

'Walter Somers.'

'And they were contracted to supply the hardware for this sort of thing?'

'Correct.'

'Now you said earlier that there was also a model.'

'The model was produced by Walter Somers, the full-scale was produced by Forgemasters.'

'Let me see if I can get this quite clear. My interpretation of a model is something you put on a table-top. You're talking about a scaled-down working aspect of a larger object?'

'The model was intended to give us information. The problem was the enormous size of the full-scale thing. You can't just make a 1,000-mm gun the way you make a 155-mm artillery piece, only bigger. You have to go through a series of trials and iterations using larger and larger models to see how to do it.'

Riley made a note on his pad.

'So the item made by Somers was a model with a 350-mm bore?'

'Yes, and it closely resembled the pressure-chambers which Bull had in Canada.'

Riley turned over some pages in his file, laying them face down on the table beside it. He then started on a different tack asking me how the contract had been awarded.

I said,

'By tender. It was put out to V.E.W. in Austria, and to C3F in

France – that's the equivalent to the Royal Ordnance over there. I personally wanted to give it to the French, because they have no embargoes. But the Iraqis preferred the British companies.'

'Were you party to the negotiations of the contracts?'

'I was Project Manager when the contracts were initiated.'

'Were you present at a meeting in Frankfurt, when the contracts were signed?'

'I was present at all the significant meetings. The first meeting with Forgemasters was at Heathrow Airport and I remember Philip Wright, the Chief Executive of Forgemasters, getting on the phone to the Department of Trade and Industry to clear their approval.'

I looked from Riley to Gaubert and back. They remained impassive. I went on,

'After that there were various technical meetings and then a meeting in Frankfurt with three people from Forgemasters, the Iraqi representative and myself. That was when the contract was signed.'

'When you spoke to the companies about these contracts, what did you tell them the components were for?'

'A petro-chemical project.'

'They didn't ask you if it was a gun?'

'No.'

Riley jotted down a note and looked up at me again. His manner was formal but not threatening. He was anxious for me to cooperate.

'You've already said you wanted to place the order with the French, because there was no embargo on the movement of weapons out of France to Iraq.'

'Yes.'

'So you were aware that there could be problems in the exportation of these?'

'The problem we had was that everybody would *see* them as a weapon. In actual fact, they had no military capability. I mean, the full-scale was bigger than the Forth Bridge. Its weight was several thousand tonnes and it certainly couldn't be traversed or elevated. We didn't even know how to operate the charges. So it was essentially a pressure vessel. That's why it had instrumentation holes along all the sections, and that's why it was *made* in sections. If we blew up a section it could be easily replaced.'

'Why would you want to blow it up?'

This was Gaubert, butting in.

'Well you wouldn't, but in a development programme intended eventually to launch a satellite into space, you have to learn to make charges, that's where you'll have the most problems. If you don't get the charges right you keep blowing the vessel up.'

It was the first time I'd mentioned the ultimate purpose of Project Babylon. Gaubert and Riley exchanged a glance. They looked sceptical.

Gaubert said,

'So what you're saying is, this may start off in the horizontal plane, but the object was to put something in space?'

'Yes, but that could be five, six, seven years down the road.'

'So there is clearly an intention to supply elevation?'

'No. You would have to go to another design. The pipes supplied by Forgemasters and Somers are totally incapable of being elevated or traversed onto a target.'

Riley was now delving amongst the papers in the file. He withdrew a sheaf of A4-size papers.

'Can I ask you to look at these drawings?'

I said yes, and he began to slide the papers across the desk towards me. I stood up, as did Gaubert and Kevin Robinson, and we gathered round. The first set of drawings were numbered 8202002 to 8202014. Riley asked me if I would sign the drawings, to indicate I had been shown them.

'Yes, but I'd like to point out, I've never seen these drawings before, and I've had no opportunity to study them in detail.'

I knew what they were, of course. They were Forgemaster's copies of the drawings we had supplied, but rough machining copies. I could tell this because the internal diameter of the tubes was too small on these drawings. In their final form the tubes would have been machined to the exact specifications given on our own design drawings, finished by A.T.I. people – Iraqis and Brits – in Brussels and Baghdad during 1988.

After I had looked through this, and then a second series of similar drawings, Riley came back to the question which was most on his mind. He scratched his head, as if genuinely puzzled, and said,

'So why was it that the whole project was described as petro-chemical?'

'It was a decision made between the Iraqis and Bull. It was done to ensure that we were actually supplied with the tubes. If we'd described them accurately – as pressure vessels to undertake ballistic research – it's unlikely we would have got them.'

'I see,' said Gaubert, nodding his head sagely. Nonchalantly, he lit a cigarette, with the air of a man who'd just received the answer he wanted to hear.

Riley turned some more pages. He wanted to know about the supply conditions of the contract. I told him Forgemasters had insisted on an ex-works contract, with the Iraqis taking responsibility for the transport, shipping and paperwork, including insurance.

'Wasn't the idea to ship the goods to S.R.C. in Brussels, and so avoid a Department of Trade export licence?'

'I personally wouldn't have been aware that that was a way of avoiding a potential problem. Anyway, it was always going by sea.'

'Some components did go by land.'

'I know, but that's a year after I left the company. The intention, as far as I was aware, was to ship them to Aqaba in Jordan and from there by road to Iraq.'

Next Riley wanted to know about export licences and end-user certificates. What role did S.R.C. play in obtaining these?

'S.R.C. have no facilities for assisting people to get end-user certificates. They're a Belgian-based company, a software company. They manufacture nothing.'

Riley referred again to the papers in front of him, typed notes. He tapped the file.

'On 17 June 1988 there was a meeting with Space Research Corporation, members of Forgemasters and Mr Azzawi of Iraq.'

I told him I remembered the meeting.

'Can you remember Mr Cookson of Forgemasters asking you to reconcile the Space Research Company involvement in petro-chemicals, considering their brochure related only to defence and military equipment?'

'S.R.C. did many things which weren't directly related to the manufacture of guns.'

'Well, Mr Cowley, you were specifically asked—'

He was leaning back in his seat, with the box-file tilted towards him as it rested on the edge of the table. He referred to something in the file, prodding it with his finger, and said with a degree of deliberation.

'You were asked if the tubes are a weapon, and you said no, and that it's silly to fire from something 150 metres long and a metre in diameter. In other words, you claimed it was preposterous.'

'I don't remember making such a statement.'

66

He looked up at me, meeting my eyes.

'I would remind you, it's a minuted statement.'

It was a tense moment, because it would look bad for me if such things were indeed said. Riley must have sensed that I was about to ask to see this minute, because he suddenly backed off.

'We haven't got the minute, that's the trouble. I've been looking for it, I can't find it. The exhibit isn't around.'

Riley's ploy had failed. I got a tiny kick out of the petty victory.

'Well clearly Cookson was in doubt about the use of this thing, because he rang the D.T.I. several times to establish the need for a licence to export it,' he added, almost apologetically.

Now, as if forced back, Riley shifted his ground.

'About our friends Walter Somers, what was the difference in the contract with them? Was it also ex-works?'

'Whether it was done on Azzawi's instruction and paid for separately I don't know. But they helped to move the tubes from Walter Somers to Ringway Airport, Manchester. They were air-freighted out, those tubes.'

Riley seemed very surprised by this. Once more he and Gaubert looked at each other, then Riley said,

'Some of them?'

'All of the ones I was involved in,' I said, firmly.

He was of course thinking of the 350-mm tubes that had been stopped in Greece on the back of flatbed trucks.

'Well, I have seen some tubes mentioned in the papers recently. They look like replacements. They must have blown the original tubes up.'

Riley was smiling now. He looked chuffed with himself, as if *he'd* scored a point, though I had no idea what it was. Then he rubbed his face and looked around at the rest of us.

'We will now terminate the interview at this stage, while we put in a new tape. Okay, Mr Cowley?'

I nodded my head, as if I had some kind of say in the matter.

15

In all, the evening with the two Customs men lasted three hours. They filled four tapes with their questions and my answers, trying all the time to tie me into their version of the Supergun plot, to construct what they hoped would be a solid case against me.

I was tired. As they questioned me – first one, then the other – the shock of my situation was beginning to tell. From the outset I had made the decision to speak the truth, but was unsure how much detail would be appropriate. The interview was already difficult. This only made it worse because simplifications are often just as misleading as lies. However, I was beginning to realise that Riley and Gaubert lacked the technical expertise to deal with much of the detail – the properties of advanced metal alloys, the conduct of research into high-altitude ballistics and the chemistry of high-explosive propellants – and so were not prepared to listen to technical explanations. As I groped for ways to make them understand me, they kept interrupting, like two suspicious attack dogs circling and barking at a wounded prey.

It was clear they had agreed their respective roles before the session. Gaubert, nervously smoking, silent for long periods, then interjecting suddenly, was the more aggressive. Riley projected a more reasonable image. He was just doing a job of work, he seemed to be saying. Can't we get on with it and then all get off home?

Riley's reasonable, no-nonsense cast of mind couldn't believe that we thought we could get away with describing the pipe orders as belonging to a petro-chemical plant. He pointed out that one of the negotiators for Forgemasters – Cookson – was a metallurgist and head of their foundry subsidiary River Don. He would have been perfectly familiar with gun barrel manufacture. It was this Cookson, he suggested, who had asked me directly at one meeting if the tubes were really components of a gun barrel. Cookson's question wasn't at that time unreasonable for he knew the metal in our specification to be similar to that used to manufacture artillery.

But a gun barrel, I tried to explain, is only a kind of pressure chamber, and pressure chambers are used in other industries, the petro-chemical industry being one. If the tubes were to be used, say, in the manufacture of plastics, as the Iraqis would later assert, and a thin-walled pressure-chamber happened to be required, then similar properties to those of a gun barrel might very well be ordered. In fact at the time I knew nothing about the Iraqis' more elaborate cover-story about polyethylene and, as I knew nothing about the manufacture of advanced plastics any way, it was just as well: I'd soon have been out of my depth. Our own simpler story was intended as little more than a polite fiction, a euphemism. The pipes were for 'improvements in the efficiency of oil production', was what I'd told Cookson: as vague and as transparent as that.

The point being that I honestly believed everyone knew exactly what was really being done here. And that included several governments. Hadn't Luis Palacio, Bull's right-hand man and best friend, with Bull's son Michel, visited the State Department in 1988 with the express purpose of telling the Americans what S.R.C. was doing for Iraq? Hadn't they also discussed the Iraqi contracts in the presence of Chris Ohly, Bull's lawyer, and Joe Smaldone, an official in the Office of Ammunition Control? Hadn't Bull himself put a proposal for a 1,000-mm gun to the Pentagon, and even taken U.S. officials over the now disused Barbados test-site? Hadn't the Forgemasters chairman, Philip Wright, telephoned the British Department of Trade and Industry in June 1988 to discuss the Iraqi contract, in my presence? Hadn't Iraqi transports landed at a major British airport in 1989 to take away the whole of the 350-mm assembly? Hadn't the Belgian Air Force, a N.A.T.O. ally, connived in the movement of Supergun-assisted propellants? Hadn't several other major European com-panies, suppliers-in-chief of military equipment to their own governments, signed contracts as part of Project Babylon?

'Okay, so why the deception?' asked Riley again, scepticism etched into his face. 'If your company believed that this was the biggest secret since sliced bread, why the subterfuge?'

It was the Iraqis' deception, I told him. If, for their own reasons, they chose to call the pipes petro-chemical equipment, Bull wasn't going to argue. For him, this was the realisation of his dream. Too much was at stake, he believed, to argue about these unimportant details and, as I've already indicated, Bull was a man who carried you with him. Babylon was a great and worthwhile enterprise. It must go ahead. Period.

69

Bull's personal objective was clear: it was the same as he had outlined in his work on H.A.R.P. Okay, Project Babylon was a gun, but it was a *peaceful* gun. In the 1960s, H.A.R.P. had launched hundreds of his specially-designed Martlet projectiles into the upper atmosphere. Although limited in size and equipped only with the relatively primitive electronics of the time, these flights gathered very useful information about the physics of the upper atmosphere and about weather patterns. The system easily reached altitudes far beyond the capabilities of balloons, and operated at a negligible cost compared with rocket launches. Now, after another twenty years of advances in solid-state electronics, coupled with our increasing anxiety about the state of the upper atmosphere, this technology looked unarguably even more beneficial. What could be further achieved from orbit, once a Martlet attained escape velocity, was (Bull suggested) limited only by the scope of the imagination.

But the question which then plagued Gaubert was, what was in it for Saddam Hussein? He was an aggressive warmonger, wasn't he? Gaubert couldn't see him as a weatherman.

'Look,' I said, 'the Arabs have an inferiority complex. Everybody looks down on them. I think if an Arab state put a bag of dates into space, that would be a tremedous accomplishment for them. It would have been perceived in the Arab world as that.'

Gaubert was nonplussed.

'But why would Iraq spend seven million quid on putting a bag of dates into space?'

I said,

'Seven million is peanuts. You can't get the wings of a Mirage jet fighter for seven million.'

'So basically you're saying,' said Riley, 'that it's an ego-trip for the President of Iraq. Can you see, though, that the Iraqis *may* have perceived your project in a different light? That they may desire to make a military application out of it?'

'But there were many real military projects,' I told him. 'The 210-mm mobile guns, which Bull was supplying, for example. *They* had major military implications. They would make the British Chieftain tank look like a Volkswagen Beetle.'

I wished I could adequately get across the peculiar status of Project Babylon. It seemed so gigantic – physically, it *was* gigantic. But in money terms it was as nothing compared to the $60 million Iraq had been spending every *hour* during the war with Iran. It was an ego-trip that Saddam could well afford.

Finally Gaubert said,

'So, if we can sort of compress this interview into a sentence. Maybe the Iraqis allowed Bull to undertake this project to satisfy his own curiosity, whilst using him on projects having a military value?'

I supposed this was basically correct, although Bull was doing a little more than satisfying his curiosity.

There were many more questions, the implications of which would become very clear to me later. The Customs seemed to think that the 350-mm model could be elevated, aimed and fired. I knew it couldn't. There was no way to aim it; it would fall over or break up as soon as it was fired. We explored this and other questions, exhaustively and exhaustingly, until after eleven o'clock. Riley then decided to call a halt and indicated to Kevin that I would be free to go.

'I'd better check with London first,' he said. 'Hang on a minute, would you?'

He went away, and we waited. When he returned he looked regretfully at Kevin.

'Sorry, Mr Cowley'll have to be our guest here for tonight.'

'What's the problem?' asked Kevin.

'The problem is I can't get hold of whoever in London.'

'What do you mean, *whoever*?'

Riley shrugged with an embarrassed smile.

'Well, I gather the problem is, she's gone to bed.'

16

I hardly had time to take this in before I was taking my leave of Kevin.

'They'll let you go in the morning,' he said. 'Just don't panic. I'll be back early.'

To the left of the interview room was a corridor lined with doorways. These were the police cells. As the policeman led me between the first pair of cells, we heard a cry from our left.

'Light, boss!'

We paused. The door had a small observation hatch set into it. The prisoner had a cigarette poked through the opening and was holding it in place with his lips.

'Gizza light, boss.'

The officer produced a lighter and held a flame to the cigarette. Then from behind us, came the same cry.

'Light, boss!'

The lighter was used again and we walked as far as the second couple of doors. Here another prisoner was holding his cigarette out, in exactly the same way as the others.

'Light, boss!'

And so we progressed down the corridor, the officer lighting a cigarette at each door until we reached the end. There a stack of soiled foam mattresses lay haphazardly against the wall. The officer gestured at them.

'Take one of those.'

I picked the least insalubrious mattress, holding it in front of me defensively.

'And you'll need this.'

He passed me a grey blanket, small, thin and stained.

'Okay. In there.'

He was pointing at a vacant cell, with its door open. I walked inside. Before I could turn around, the heavy spring lock had clunked into its slot.

The 'bed' was a concrete plinth built into a wall with, screwed onto its upper surface, a wooden board. I placed the mattress on it, took off my jacket and shirt and looked around. The choice of storage was the floor or a table which abutted against the end of the bed and which was the only piece of furniture in the cell. Its top was smeared with grease and spilled food. I folded my clothes as small as I could and lay them on a patch that seemed less encrusted than the rest, the jacket underneath. Then I lay down on the mattress and tried to arrange the miserable blanket so that it covered me. But it was too small: either my shoulders or feet were exposed. The cell was by no means warm.

Concealed behind a square of reinforced glass recessed into the ceiling, a pitiless artificial light made sleep impossible. I could hear the other prisoners chatting from cell to cell.

'What you in for?' said one. I thought the voice came from the cell opposite mine.

'Mass murder,' shouted a voice from further away.

'That why they're letting you out on two-quid bail tomorrow?'

They seemed in a good humour, although I couldn't imagine why. I shut my eyes, but the lids were unable to exclude the harsh light. I turned and faced the wall, but the hardness of the platform through the emaciated mattress, made comfort impossible.

I rolled off and walked to the observation hatch. By pressing my face against it and tilting it sideways I could see two or three of the cells on the other side. The youth opposite, with his face similarly pressed, spotted me at once and called out.

'You in for mass-murder too?'

'No.'

'What then?'

'It's to do with the Iraq Supergun.'

This got him really excited. He jumped up and down and his voice cracked as he yelled to the others.

'Christ! Did you hear that?'

He thought for a moment.

'Hey. I say. Can it really fire five thousand miles?'

'Well you see it's not really a gun at all. Not in the normal sense.'

He seemed disappointed.

'What is it then?'

'It's a kind of a ballistics test-bed.'

'Oh.'

He reflected on this for a moment.

'It'd be better if it really was a gun that can fire thousands of

73

miles. You'd be more famous then. Even better than being a mass murderer.'

He must have caught my face. I have no idea what its expression might have been, exactly, but it moved him to kindness.

'Never mind, eh. You'll get bail. You'll be okay.'

After another moment I asked him why he was here.

'Stealing.'

'Stealing what?'

'A Mars Bar. I just got out of Hull Gaol after a month on remand for nicking food.'

'For a month? Couldn't you get bail?'

'No way. I got no fixed abode.'

'What about your parents?'

'My stepfather beats me up. He's usually drunk anyway. So I been living rough the last few months.'

'So why did you steal the Mars Bar?'

'When I come out of Hull Gaol I went to the dole office, but the Social Security said I'd not been available for work, seeing as I was in jail, so they couldn't give me anything. So I was hungry. So I stole a Mars Bar. Trouble was the shopkeeper caught me.'

So the second offence had been entirely preventable, and yet it would now condemn this boy to an extended period on remand, with no prospect whatever of bail. It was an obvious injustice, but he was remarkably philosophical.

'Oh well. At least in here I'm fed and I'm out of the weather.'

Later I lay on the platform again. I don't think I slept. To stop myself thinking about my own situation I dwelt on what the boy had told me. I hadn't seen this side of my country before, except perhaps to some extent during my childhood in Liverpool. I had thought these were more enlightened days. How outraged my father would have been. I had never been a socialist the way he was, but now I felt anger welling up within me at the whole degrading, futile system with which we try to deal with the poverty.

At seven in the morning we were released briefly by turns in order to wash at two basins plumbed into the corridor wall. They had no plugs, and the small tablets of soap supplied by the duty officer refused to lather. As a substitute for towels, rolls of pale blue tissue paper were provided, so flimsy that it disintegrated as soon as it came into contact with water, leaving small damp flakes of tissue adhering to one's face and arms.

74

At around eight o'clock room service arrived. The breakfast tray held a plate with a fried egg and two sausages swimming in a deep mixture of liquidised tomato ketchup, all entirely cold. The plastic spoon and fork provided had slid beneath the surface. Several slices of white bread lay beside the plate.

I retrieved the fork and spoon and settled for a cold sausage sandwich.

17

'Mr Robinson's here.'

The cell door banged open, and a new officer greeted me.

'You're going in to see him.'

I rose stiffly and put on my jacket.

'Hey!' The officer gave me a gentle nudge with his elbow as he ushered me through the door. 'You're lucky. We see a lot of Mr Robinson in the courts. He's one of the best.'

Kevin was waiting in the now all-too-familiar interview room.

'How are you, Chris? It's not too pleasant, is it?'

Kevin was a master of the understatement.

'No,' I said, trying to sound more cheerful than I was. 'Not very.'

'Right, well, Customs are back and they want to carry on with the interview. Afterwards they're telling me you can leave. We'll see how much weight we can attach to that.'

He looked at his watch.

'But I'm hoping it won't take too long. Got to be in court by eleven.'

After a few moments Riley and Gaubert trouped in. Suddenly I felt conscious that I was wearing yesterday's clothes and was unshaven. I had no toothbrush with me. I felt crumpled, while they looked fresh and full of bounce – no doubt the result of a good night's rest.

They wanted to know exactly when the contracts were signed and whether Somers and Forgemasters tendered jointly or individually.

'It was an individual tender.'

'So the contracts that were signed, would they be around the same time?'

'Yes. June 1988.'

'This is in *both* cases?'

'Yes. In the contracts I am aware of. It's apparent that other contracts have been signed and I have no knowledge of those.'

Had I been able to develop this thought, several months of subsequent confusion might have been prevented. Riley must have thought I was talking about contracts for further Supergun components, but I had in mind something quite different and which was making me increasingly uneasy.

It had begun when I'd seen the television and press pictures of Paul Ashwell's lorry, whose load was still being held in Greece. These clearly showed a slide assembly, of a type and size that could only belong to a major gun system. The trouble was, I knew it didn't belong to Supergun. So what *was* it? Slowly, from hints and odd remarks made by Riley and Gaubert in the course of the previous evening, something had begun to dawn on me. Maybe there was more than one big gun project. Maybe, behind Babylon, there was another Supergun, a *military* Supergun which I had known nothing about.

And, if that was the case, how the hell was I going to convince these two – or, for that matter, a court of law – that I'd had nothing to do with it?

But Riley was bustling ahead, seeming as eager as Kevin to get this business over with in the minimum time.

'Among the items that have been shipped are accumulator tanks. We believe they were from Walter Somers.'

I didn't know what he was on about.

'I know nothing about any accumulator tanks.'

'Would that be after you left the company?'

'The Somers contract I was involved in was for five pipe sections only.'

'What about Forgemasters?'

'Two contracts, each for 26 pipes.'

'Any ancillary parts, hydraulic systems?'

'No.'

Riley changed tack again.

'Can I go back to the question I asked you yesterday about a model? It has been suggested that there was, in fact, a desktop model of what was being built. Is this right?'

'Yes.'

He was sitting as before, with his boxfile open. He referred to something inside.

'Well, yesterday evening you said no, the term model means the 350-mm item.'

We had a problem in semantics. Riley was using 'model' in the sense of a small-scale representation of the outward appearance of something. We had indeed made one of these, to be displayed at the Baghdad Military Fair of 1989, a one-hundred scale of the full-scale Project Babylon system, complete with mini-figures and parked vehicles to give scale. But when Riley asked me about a 'model' the previous evening, I didn't think of this. I assumed he was using the word in the *engineering* sense of an assembly to model not the appearance, but the *behaviour* of a full-scale system. As such, 'model' was an accurate term for the 350-mm system, and we normally referred to it by that name.

Now that I was confirming the existence of a table-top model, one which S.R.C. had ordered for Iraq from a company called Amalgam in Bristol, Riley was showing intense interest.

'Which directors of Somers saw the model?'

'Nobody. Nobody from Somers or Forgemasters saw it.'

Riley leaned forward slightly, frowning.

'See, amongst the minutes of a joint meeting between the Halesowen company (i.e. Walter Somers) and Forgemasters, they talk of examining a model.'

I asked about the date of this, but Riley appeared not to know it. I said, 'If they saw that, they would definitely know what they were building. But to my knowledge they never did.'

'Can you describe the model?'

I did so: nearly two metres long, mounted on a perspex base, a complete mock-up of the full-scale assembly, all 26 tubes. Also represented were the charge bags, which in reality would be sacks of chemical propellant packed in a column behind the projectile. I had personally organised the model's construction and had it flown to Iraq. But I told the Customs men as little as I could about this. My own son had brought the thing out to us, and the last thing I wanted now was to get him involved with this.

So I didn't mention the Baghdad International Military Fair either. I just said, 'It went immediately from the manufacturers to Heathrow and was flown out. So, if they say they've seen it, this must have been in Baghdad.'

Gaubert now joined in the conversation. He wanted to talk about the grades of steel used to make the tubes, and whether these were exclusively military in application. They weren't of course, but he still hadn't grasped that *all* pressure chambers need metal with various special properties – measures of its tensile strength and impact values – and that a gun is only one type of pressure chamber, albeit with an open end.

We moved on to questions about the breech – the closed end of our gun/pressure chamber. They were trying to understand how this fitted onto the first section of the barrel.

On the 350-mm model we had designed a wedge breech which screwed into the first tube in the assembly. On the full-scale, a male thread on the first tube had originally been proposed, and it appeared that Customs had formed the idea that this was the final design of a tube section that had already arrived inside Iraq. I told them that anyone who thought it feasible to screw a breech block into a 1,000-mm barrel could have formed no real conception of the size of thing.

'That breech would probably be five metres by three by something similar. You can't treat that like a nut and bolt and just screw it together. The dynamics are impossible.'

'But if that section of pipe *had* a thread on it—'

'I don't think it has. I was involved in the design and there was no thread on it then.'

Actually I knew it hadn't. The 1,000-mm system also had a wedge breech, but the breech block was split in half, so that it was joined onto the first barrel section by being clamped together around it.

The customs men then asked me if I thought the breech had been made in South Korea. I didn't react. Certainly Korea *could* have made a breech for the 1,000-mm, although I knew it had been made by Terni, part of Italy's nationalised steel industry.

Gaubert now returned, like a crow to a carcase, to the question of why I had tried to deceive the manufacturers as to the nature of this order. But now there was a twist. He wanted essentially to hear that the manufacturers knew all along, by means of a nod and a wink perhaps, that they were making a gun and not a petrochemical pressure chamber.

'I'd like to ask my solicitor a question privately, if I may.'

'I don't think we'd like that. This is an important point to us, you see.'

'Well I would like to examine the question.'

I was allowed a three-minute conference with Kevin, while they stood in the corridor.

'There were visits to the U.K. people on my team,' I said in a low voice. 'They were very enthusiastic and got carried away, you know? Several times somebody mentioned something about the gun, or the breech-end, or something like that, in the presence of Forgemasters staff – and Somers people too. Should I explain this?'

'Yeah,' said Kevin. 'Why not?'

So I explained. The truth was, I didn't expect to deceive the steel makers. In meetings with them I myself maintained the fiction, without being particularly happy about it. However, amongst some of my younger colleagues, those who were sent to Sheffield and Halesowen at Bull's insistence to witness these phenomenal forgings for Project Babylon, enthusiasm overwhelmed discretion.

But when the words 'gun', 'barrel' or 'breech' were inadvertently used at meetings, the response was normally a deaf ear. On only one occasion that I recalled did a representative of the companies say anything. I was told at a meeting with Forgemasters,

'I don't wish to hear that word again, clear?'

By now, the Customs men had what they thought they wanted, at least for the time being. They packed up their papers, called in a police officer to take charge of me and left. Before he went, Barry Riley told me he would talk to London about my release. Kevin left too, hurrying to court, though not before he'd promised to be back soon. I was then returned to my cell.

Riley came in about lunch time.

'Afraid I haven't any good news for you. London won't countenance your release. You're to be charged.'

Quietly I absorbed this. Then I said,

'But I'll get bail?'

'You'll be up before a magistrate in the morning. I imagine bail will be a formality.'

So I was facing another night in the concrete box. It was all very discouraging.

Shortly afterwards Kevin arrived with the morning's papers. Supergun was still all over the headlines. Margaret Thatcher had deftly parried a series of hostile Opposition questions during Prime Minister's Question Time the previous afternoon. She had hinted that Government records about the matter were incomplete, but gave nothing away. Meanwhile, one paper was suggesting wildly that the West African state of Mauritania contained a supergun test-site.

We smiled over this and I asked Kevin what would happen next.

'It's unlucky you came in so late yesterday. If you'd appeared in the morning they'd have to bring you to court this afternoon. As it is they'll charge you in an hour or so, and bring you to the Magistrate's Court tomorrow.'

80

'And then I'll get bail?'

Kevin's face was serious.

'Look, in spite of what Riley told you, I'm not optimistic about that.'

'Well, can't we do something if the magistrate refuses bail?'

'We can make a second application, but I wouldn't do that just yet. Your opportunities to apply for bail will be limited and we must make the most of them. If you are ordered to be held on remand we'll keep our powder dry initially and await developments.'

Held on remand? This was all routine to Kevin, but to me it was horrifying.

'So am I kept here until— ?'

'Yes. This afternoon at two o'clock you'll be charged, which will give them a further 24 hours in which they can detain you before a court appearance. My information is they *will* oppose bail.'

'And then?'

He smiled.

'Let's wait and see. You might get a sympathetic magistrate. In the meantime, don't be down-hearted, okay?'

Kevin's prediction about my charge was accurate to within five minutes. At five minutes past two precisely, a Superintendent entered my cell, admitted by the duty officer. The door was closed behind him. He stood in front of me in his pristine uniform, blue, black and silver.

'You are Christopher Cowley?'

'Yes.'

He produced a piece of paper and read from it. I cannot remember the words, they were something vague about the illegal exportation of goods.

'Do you understand?'

'Yes.'

I understood all right. I was being charged. I was officially on the wrong side of the criminal justice system.

'Do you wish to see someone?'

'Someone?'

'We do have a lay preacher on hand, a counsellor.'

I shook my head.

'No, I'm fine.'

'Okay then.'

And he went out.

The charge of assaulting Justin Sutcliffe was never proceeded with.

18

The exercise area was little bigger than the bottom of a lift shaft. Three floors above our heads, as we shuffled round the short perimeter, was a heavy steel grille.

My companion was John. His arms, face and neck were covered in bandages and plasters. He opened his shirt to show further gashes and punctures, painted with a yellow disinfectant. His story was distressing.

John, as they say in Liverpool, has got a few of his pages stuck together. He also has a speech impediment, which makes him sound as if he's had a skinful, although he doesn't drink. John had been found astride a factory wall by a policeman with a guard dog. Ordered down, he'd been afraid of the dog, but the officer had promised him it would behave itself. It did. When John reached the ground, the policeman set the dog on him.

The police surgeon, treating the worst bites, told John to lay a formal complaint against the police. I was left wondering if he would be likely to get justice.

On my way back inside I noticed that the police cells were becoming crowded. I asked around. Many of the new arrivals, it seemed, were coming in from Strangeways Prison, Manchester, where an entire wing was currently being torn apart by riots. Police cells designed for single occupancy now contained two or three men, the floors used for sleeping. However, I was not allowed to share a cell.

Towards midnight I was offered a bath. The bathroom had abundant hot water but no plug, so I rolled some blue tissue in a ball and rammed it into the plughole. This served to contain an inch or two of water, but the soap still wouldn't lather.

I had no towel. Drying myself with disintegrating tissue, I found its blue dye had a tendency to run so that, by the time I was halfway dry I was standing in a snowdrift of wet tissue, with soggy strands of it stuck in my hair, and my skin tinged a dirty blue.

It must have been in the early hours, before dawn, when I heard a tearing sound, like continuous, accelerated vomiting. I went to the door and pressed my face against the hatch. It was coming from John's cell. I started slapping my flat hand on the steel door. I yelled.

'Hey, officer! Help needed here. Hey!'

There was no response. I took off my shoe and started hammering with it. The sounds from John's cell had developed into a ghastly, mucous throat-rattle.

'Help,' I shouted. 'Somebody needs help down here!'

I had my head canted sideways to fit as far as possible through the rectangular slot. The shelf below the slot bit into my breastbone as I strained forward.

'Help, somebody needs help!'

'What's the problem?'

A bleary-eyed young constable wandered into view.

'The prisoner in that cell. He's ill. I think he's having a fit.'

The policeman cocked his head towards John's door for a moment. Then he started to move away.

'No, he's not. He's just snoring.'

'No, no!'

I could hardly contain myself, I was jumping up and down in agitation.

'He's an epileptic. He's having a fit, I'm telling you.'

The urgency in my voice was just enough to make the officer peer in at John's peephole. Then he was off, running for keys.

When they opened the cell I could just see, by twisting my head at right angles, John lying on his side his face covered in vomit. By now he was also foaming at the mouth.

'Quick,' I called out. 'Make sure he's not swallowed his tongue.'

John was making spasmodic movements but the officers were strangely slow-moving and helpless, almost as if sleepwalking. I found myself shouting instructions to them.

'No, no, don't use your finger, he may bite. Use a pencil or something. And don't roll him onto his back, leave him like that. Get a doctor, get an ambulance.'

The spasms ceased and John slumped into unconsciousness. Shortly afterwards an officer brought a wheelchair and he was lifted, inert, into it. Then he was carted away.

In mid-morning I was due in court, but I looked like a vagrant brought in from the gutter. Fortunately Glenys had driven up in the early morning with some clean clothes and Kevin brought them to me.

'As I warned you, you'll probably be refused bail. If so, you'll be remanded to Hull prison.'

Kevin was following his usual policy of pessimism so that, when things went better than expected, it felt like a bonus. Such a prospect seemed a long way off now.

'Hull? But how's Glenys going to get over to see me? Can't I get somewhere near home?'

But Kevin wanted to warn me about something else.

'The press and T.V. are massing already. They've got the court under siege.'

I thought of my family struggling through the scrum of the media. On the other hand, the last thing I wanted was for the case to be swept under any Establishment carpet. I wanted my story told and the truth known. But again Kevin was doubtful.

'Reporting of the case will be severely restricted. Hardly anything of what is said will get into the papers.'

'Can't we apply to have the restrictions lifted?'

'As defendant, that is your right. The restriction is supposed to protect you, after all.'

'Then let's do it. Let's cause some embarrassment.'

Later, waiting in my cell, I had another visitor. It was Riley.

'I'm very concerned that you want to have reporting restrictions lifted.'

'Well I'm sorry, but I want to make a statement to the court and I want it reported.'

I could see the disappointment in his face. I followed up the advantage.

'I'm sick of being used as a football. I travelled all the way to Sheffield to make a voluntary statement. I was promised no charges were to be laid against me. Now I'm going to be slammed in jail in the back of beyond for God knows how long. You said you had authority over this case.'

'Yes.'

'Well I want to be sent to a prison nearer home.'

He thought for a moment, and then said.

'I might be able to arrange something. But will you do something for me in return?'

'I might consider it.'

'Will you agree not to ask the magistrates to lift reporting restrictions?'

I considered. It would be worth it not to be stuck in Hull, miles from anywhere.

'All right. But listen, if it doesn't happen, I'm going to kick up one hell of a fuss.'

It was peculiar to be standing up in court and treated like The Invisible Man. But that is the defendant's role at a remand hearing, when everything has been arranged before you arrive. It was an indication of how nervous the prosecution was that a senior Crown Prosecutor, Annabelle Bolt, had been brought up from London for this extremely routine affair. She formally opposed bail, on the grounds that I was likely to abscond and/or interfere with witnesses. She made this sound like a sexual misdemeanour.

The magistrate accepted her argument without question, despite the fact that I had gone to Sheffield Police Station voluntarily and cooperated with the Customers officers to the best of my ability. Which witnesses in particular did they think I would get at? And by what route was I going to escape from the country? With a tinge of cynicism in the air, I was accordingly remanded in custody for one week.

Now I was in handcuffs, being taken down to an underground car park beneath the courts. They draped a blanket over my head and told me to lie down on the floor of a car. I could feel throughout my body the thrumming vibration of wheels on concrete as we accelerated up a ramp. It seemed a less than dignified way to begin my life as an inmate of H.M. prisons.

I was under no illusions. I had spoken to several of the remand prisoners bussed into Sheffield from riot-torn Strangeways. Many had been waiting trial more than six months. One had been held as long as 18 months. It might be a long time before my situation was resolved.

19

You don't easily forget your first experience of the prison admission procedure. It is called being 'processed', which has just the right connotations. The whole idea of prison is to turn people into objects.

The Yorkshire Police, whether by order or mistake, first tried to deliver me to Pucklechurch, a youth custody centre for the under-twenty-ones which lies to the West of Bristol. Pucklechurch, not unreasonably, wouldn't have me and, after a long wrangle I was put back in the car and driven to H.M. Prison, Bristol. As I was brought into the reception area, prison officers were sitting around in various attitudes. The atmosphere was of bored indifference, which in retrospect sems surprising since, as I was shortly to learn, one of the prison's wings had just been destroyed by rioting inmates. The police handed over the paperwork on my case and custody was transferred with an exchange of signatures. Then the police departed. I stood looking about me, awaiting instructions. I noticed a printed card fixed on the wall:

> We, H.M. Prison Service, serve the public by keeping in custody those committed by the Courts. It is our duty to look after them with humanity, and to help them lead law abiding lives in custody and after their release.

This desideratum may have been a trifle pious, but its motive was unarguable. Within obvious constraints, my police minders had managed to behave with general courtesy and a meticulous observation of the rules. I was, after all, an unconvicted man with no previous record. I was innocent unless found guilty, and I expected my treatment in prison to be commensurate with this.

'Get your *fucking* clothes off.'

I hesitated. The officer behind the desk wasn't looking at me. So who was he shouting at?

He had been sitting sideways to his desk, perusing the court documents that had accompanied me. Now he raised his eyes and swivelled his body to face me. He spoke again, savagely.

'Yes, *you*! Think we got all *fucking* day?'

I began to strip. None of the others were taking much notice. The warders lounging here and there, smoked and conversed, their conversation larded automatically with repetitive foul language. Occasionally they grunted instructions to trusty convicts, who scurried about, with maximum servility, to do their bidding.

When I stood in front of him naked, the reception officer jabbed his finger towards an elderly trusty who was loitering by the wall.

'You. Get him a box.'

The trusty darted away and came back with a cardboard carton. He picked up a felt marker from the desk and waited expectantly for the officer to speak.

'He's number 4269.'

The number was scrawled on the box which was then deposited on the floor.

'Clothes in the box.'

With a forlorn attempt at dignity I folded my clothes as carefully as possible, turning the soles of my shoes to make contact with the inner surface of the box. It seemed important not to dirty the suit unnecessarily.

'Not the valuables. Give them here.'

My money, watch, wallet and wedding ring were handed over to be listed and signed for. As I began to slide the ring from my finger I suddenly felt an overwhelming reluctance. They had made me a number: this was my last link with my real identity.

'Can't I keep my wedding ring?'

He paused in his writing. He looked up at me.

'I decide what you *fucking* keep.'

I felt a flicker of resistance. What if I refused to hand it over? What if I defied him? By himself he seemed incapable of enforcing his order.

The trusty had manoeuvred himself into a position behind the duty officer. He frowned and gave a quick shake of the head. I immediately abandoned the thought, handed over the ring and, leaning across the desk, I signed my name under the list. The trusty then beckoned me away into a side corridor. He opened up a small store room where clothing was stacked on wide shelves. I stood outside at the hatch, while he brought me items of prison garb to try.

'Your first time, obviously,' he said. He was small and wizened, with quick, intelligent eyes. 'Don't worry, you'll be okay. Here, try these for size.'

He handed over a dun-coloured pair of denim trousers which, when I inserted my leg, jammed somewhere around the thigh. He clicked his tongue and selected another pair.

'They're all the same size, of course, but some are bigger than others.'

After several more attempts we found an approximate fit, although the cheap brass zip became stuck half way.

'Whoever orders this rubbish must be making a fortune on the side,' said the trusty. 'You probably didn't know we convicts are supervised by crooks at the expense of the tax payer.'

I ended up with an oversize jacket, two extra-large vests, two buttonless grey shirts, some shrunken odd socks and a pair of shoes so tight I could hardly cram my bare feet into them. The trusty noticed me starting to get dressed.

'Don't bother just yet,' he advised. 'You've got to see the quack.'

'The quack?'

'Prison doctor. I'll just fix us a brew, 'cos by the time you get over to D Block they'll be all banged up.'

It was seven o'clock in the evening by now. The trusty took me a little way to a small cubicle where he had his domain.

'Shouldn't take minutes.'

He switched on an electric kettle and then busied himself with tea and milk.

'Doing a fifteen stretch myself, for drugs. Just coming up to ten years now, so maybe I'll get out soon.'

The water had boiled. He spooned tea into a china pot.

'Belongs to the screws, this lot does. Not prison tea. Give you some advice.'

He looked at me shrewdly.

'Don't discuss your case with anyone, specially prisoners.'

'Why not?'

'Just don't. Sugar?'

'No thanks.'

'Doesn't matter here, but if I were you I'd take it when you're over there in D Block.'

'Right.'

I stood there stark naked, drinking my tea. But I wasn't embarrassed. I had the feeling that, in this little niche in the wall, I'd reconnected with humanity.

The trusty walked through the open door and said,

'Last one tonight, doc.'

He handed my personal file across the desk.

'Come back to the store when you're finished and collect your clothes, okay?'

He left us. It was a small, scuffed, uncomfortable cubby hole containing a desk, two chairs and a filing cabinet, which occupied almost all the floorspace.

I stood naked in front of the doctor, holding in front of me a cardboard box containing my prison costume. He took me in with one cursory glance then returned to a printed form in front of him. 'This won't take long. Have you ever suffered from cancer?'

I was taken aback.

'No.'

'Heart disease, lung disease, stomach, liver or kidney problems?'

I realised he was checking off the list. I began to say no to all of these, but he had already moved on.

'Epilepsy, neurological disorders, A.I.D.S., syphilis, any other contagious veneral diseases? Do you use drugs?'

Since he wasn't looking at me he missed my shakes of the head, but checked the items anyway.

'Any distinguishing marks.'

'Just this.'

He looked up over his spectacles at the scarred shoulder I was pointing to.

'Looks like it was done by a butcher. Any tattoos? If you have, we can take them off, if you like.'

He scribbled something at the bottom of the form and dropped his pen.

'Okay, you'll do. Oh, and a word of advice.'

He had begun to take off his glasses and he held them now, poised in the air.

'Don't talk about your case to anybody except your solicitor. Got it?'

'Right,' I said and left.

On the way across to D Block, my trusty suddenly said, quite casually,

'Like some marijuana? Help you to sleep, it really will.'

'No,' I said, smiling. 'No, thanks.'

20

I stood in the middle of the cell. I apparently had it to myself, although it contained a pair of beds, two chairs and two small cupboards. It also had a plastic window, a table and a powerful smell of urine.

A brown plastic bucket of poor quality swung by its handle from my fist. I had selected it, with the help of another prisoner, from amongst several stacks of similar buckets, at the far end of the Block.

'Let's try and find one with a lid,' he'd said, kindly.

No lid could be discovered, though the handle was a bonus. But where to put it? I chose the corner nearest to the cell door, as far as possible from the bed I now chose, which stood beneath the window.

I put my spare clothing in one of the cupboards and sat down, overcome by a sudden and very peculiar feeling. It was as if I had stopped being the man I knew I was. My name had been changed to a number. Free will had been taken from me. I couldn't use a phone, go for a run, make a sandwich. I was officially shut away – removed from my loved ones, from society – in a concrete box which stank overwhelmingly of stale urine.

Kevin had told me that I should be provided with a booklet entitled *Information for Male Prisoners*, but I had never seen it. If I had, I would already know that, as an unconvicted man, I was entitled to keep my own clothes. I was entitled to the wedding ring I had asked to keep. But, in prison, what you were entitled to and what you get are two very different things.

'Justice?' Kevin had said. 'Justice is a rare commodity in prison. The truth is, they can do anything they like in there, and you're going to have to get used to that.'

Now I could see why he'd spoken to me like that. And it would be no good bleating. The only thing that mattered was survival.

Suddenly I needed the lavatory. I made a reflex movement towards the door but stopped myself. Forget it. Banged up means for the night and they won't make you an exception. I looked instead at the dirty brown bucket.

Physically I was tired, I was utterly drained, but I couldn't sleep. Thoughts sped like tracers through my mind. Was this me, this person in here? Was this person really a criminal?

Whichever way I examined this, I couldn't see it. It all looked like a sham, a piece of clever politics.

Everybody had been working for Iraq, or trying to. And a lot were operating much closer to the margin of what may or may not have been criminal. I remembered a certain Colonel Kadoori. He'd dropped in on Azzawi to discuss a production problem for components for the Ababeel missile, an extended version of Scud. I'd met him once before, as a matter of fact, during a visit to the Al Taji missile factory, thirty-two kilometres north of Baghdad, where we'd gone to see if they could make projectiles for the 350-mm model.

On this occasion, in Azzawi's office, Kadoori was in great spirits. He'd just come back from Britain, he told us, where he'd been holding discussions with a company called Flexible Manufacturing Technology. I remembered the name – a subsidiary of Vickers, wasn't it?

'That's the one', Kadoori confirmed. 'We're negotiating a very nice little contract, only $5 million to start with, but our order may rise to $12 million if all goes to plan.'

'What's it for, then?'

'For the army. They're going to equip us to make our own multiple rocket launch systems.'

'But what about approval – didn't you have problems?'

Kadoori smiled broadly.

'No problem whatever. The D.T.I. love it. They love it so much that if we give this company the contract we will be permitted to acquire 35 per cent of its shares.'

'In F.M.T. you mean?'

'Yes, and the best of it is, it's a fantastic investment for us. The British Government are going to give the company £2 million in grants first!'

He rubbed his hands with satisfaction at a successful piece of bargaining.

'I must say, Mr Cowley, your embassy here in Baghdad was very good when we approached them about this. Even more helpful than the Germans.'

'But you'll need export licences on this equipment, won't you?'

'No problem! The head of F.M.T. wrote personally to Margaret Thatcher, and she passed it on to your trade ministry. The British know that, if they don't help us out a little, we won't place big orders with Vickers or British Aerospace at the Baghdad Military Show.'

In a few weeks' time Iraq was holding its International Military Fair. The table-top model of Babylon, which would later so interest Barry Riley, was scheduled to be on display there.

When we said good-bye to Kadoori, it was with assurances that we would all meet each other at the Fair.

21

'Good morning, all prisoners! This is your favourite station, Bristol Prison Radio, or B.P.R.!'

I twisted on my bed and listened. The voice was coming through the cell window from somewhere above me.

'And the time is six o'clock in the a.m. on Friday 27 April, and it's going to be another bright and sunny day.'

Except in the depth of night, prison is always a noisy place, full of clatter and cries, doors banging, feet stamping, voices singing or roaring. But now the ambient noise seemed to die, as prisoners throughout D Block tuned in their ears. The 'announcer's' voice rang out clear in the morning air.

'And B.P.R. extends its warmest greeting to our most recent and distinguished arrival. Currently residing in D Block in cell number seven – morning Topgun!'

I rolled off the bed and stood beside the window.

'Yes cellmates. Topgun, courtesy of Her Britannic Majesty, was eventually delivered here yesterday, following a total cock-up at Pucklechurch Remand Centre. You see, fellow convicts, they wanted to put Topgun into a youth facility. But Topgun is some-what over the maximum age of 18, and so now he's been sent to join us here. And now for the rest of the news . . . '

'Bristol Prison Radio' was so authentic that for a while I was fooled into supposing it was a real transmission. In fact, B.P.R. was 'broadcast' each day by a voice shouting out of the window, and doing it so well that he commanded a real audience amongst the prison community. No prisoner wanted to miss those well-informed, stylish and witty morning bulletins, which covered events both on the inside and from the world beyond.

The 'broadcast' went on for ten minutes and it was not until B.P.R. had signed off that the cacophony of prison sounds returned. Now I detected an increase in activity in the corridor outside the cells; a key was slotted into my own door and it swung open.

'Slop out.'

A line of prisoners could be seen shuffling past, each carrying a brown bucket and a plastic washing bowl. The prison officer waited beside the door as I collected my own receptacles and joined the line. Liquid could be heard sloshing about, the tart smell of urine permeated the air, and yet this was above all a social occasion. Prisoners called out greetings to each other and jokes were cracked.

The slowly-moving queue turned right into a white-tiled room which contained several kitchen-sized basins, two toilet stalls and a sluice into which we emptied our buckets and bowls. The floor was awash, the stench overpowering. It made me gag and I could hear other prisoners, perhaps newcomers like me, retching as they entered.

Carefully I watched the actions of the prisoner in front of me, following his example by refilling the washing bowl with water from a tap. Then we wheeled around and returned to our cells.

'Hey, Topgun, you're in the papers.'

The shout came from an unseen window somewhere above me and to the left. Another voice joined in.

'Yeah. Reckon Dennis is worried about Topgun's length. Why else would Maggie be so interested?'

From the yells of laughter and other comments I gathered the men of D Block were all at their windows, feeding birds with bread from their breakfasts, and trying to get what benefit they could out of the fresh air. The first voice came back.

'Topgun! What cell you in?'

I called out.

'Number seven.'

'Right, it's on its way down to you. Look out your window.'

I stood on my chair and craned round to the left. I could see the rolled-up newspaper hanging from a line. It was below, and some way to the left, of my windows, but straight away it began to move, swinging like a pendulum up and back past my eyes. I grabbed the line and pulled it in hand over hand.

'You got it, Topgun?'

'Yes.'

'Keep the string till you've finished reading, then send it back to me.'

I secured the end of the line to my bed-frame and opened up the newspaper. My remand hearing was reported, although necessarily only the bare facts. There was little attempt at any sensible coverage of Supergun. This was a tabloid daily whose stock-in-trade is sensation, and today's sensation was the revelation that Supergun was capable of firing a shell at New York City.

I sat there, realising these sensational perceptions would have to be dealt with. A jury would have to understand the truth of Supergun, its purpose, its expected performance and its limitations.

A gun is a throwing device. Assume, for the sake of argument, a fantasy gun, a gun with unlimited mechanical strength that won't blow up under any circumstances. The range of this gun is then limited by two factors: the projectile's aerodynamics (determined by design), and its speed leaving the muzzle. This muzzle velocity depends on the amount of gas pressure – caused by burning a propulsive chemical charge – behind the projectile. In theory, then, put enough of a bang behind an aerodynamically efficient shell and it'll go any distance you want.

Unfortunately a real gun, as opposed to a fantasy one, has operational limits. The maximum muzzle velocity achievable in any chemically propelled gun, however big and efficient, is in the range of three kilometres per second. In addition, after it has left the muzzle, the drag exerted by atmosphere on the inert shell causes immediate deceleration. Nevertheless ballistic calculations show that Supergun's rocket-enhanced shell, could have had a theoretical terrestrial range of 13,000 kilometres. The tabloid I was reading had, I suspected, extrapolated these facts from Bull's book on H.A.R.P. The distance from Baghdad to New York is only about 11,000 kilometres.

Supergun was a space-launch system; it was never intended to be a piece of terrestrial artillery. However, so conditioned are we to associate space exploration with rockets, a gun-launched space probe seems like a joke, a piece of Jules Verne fiction. I considered it had been so to the Customs men, Riley and Gaubert.

However, such a probe has real advantages over a rocket. Most of the weight of the rocket-launched system is in its fuel. In the American four-stage Scout D satellite launcher, for example, the lift-off weight was almost 21 tonnes. Most of this was accounted for by the contents of the fuel tank for the first stage, with the effect that the Scout's lift-off weight was 120 times greater than the satellite it placed in orbit. With a gun-launced orbiter, the vast preponderance of the missile's propellant would be left behind on the ground, so that in Bull's Martlet-4 – the space projectile Bull designed but never fired during H.A.R.P., and developed at the time when Scout was being used – the ratio of the all-up weight to the weight of the orbiter itself was only 10:1. This gives a huge cost advantage per launch. The cost of the rocket's disposable first stage alone would probably exceed that of one of Bull's Supergun barrels. But, unlike the rocket, our launch tube was reusable.

Nevertheless a gun does have an inherent problem; its maximum muzzle velocity is insufficient to effect orbit. The Martlet-4 would slow to around 2 kilometres per second by the time it reached an altitude of only 80 kilometres. The velocity needed to achieve orbit is four times this speed.

To overcome this inherent limitation, the Martlet-4 had to be more than a simple shell. It was, in fact, a gun-launched three-stage rocket. The engines of its first stage were intended to ignite at a height of around 25 kilometres, the second at 50 kilometres; and the third at 425 kilometres. But at these heights the atmosphere is so thin that the amount of power needed to boost to 8 kilometres per second and put the missile into space is relatively small. Compared once again with rocket-launch systems, the amount of fuel carried by Martlet was minute.

One reason the Babylon system was more than twice the size of Bull's 400-mm H.A.R.P. gun was that, even with its relatively small fuel load, the Martlet-4's fuel storage did use up valuable payload capacity. Fired from this new 1,000-mm system, it became capable of carrying a scientific payload of more than half a tonne, nine times larger than could have been achieved in the tests on Barbados using Betsy.

So what was the use of all this? Even now, Bull is still being ridiculed in the media for his 'pretension' in saying he could build a satellite launcher on the gun principle. Yet a cost-effective way to do scientific work on the upper atmosphere, and to use orbiters to monitor the earth's climate and environment are both looking more vital as each year goes by. Meanwhile rocket launching technologies are foundering on the rock of their cost. The old Soviet programme is dead and the Americans are cutting back. Satellite launching by rocket alone will one day, as Bull predicted, be the subject of ridicule, because it is so cost-ineffective. His proposal offered the only really viable alternative.

I rolled the paper and tied it back on its string. Such distortions and misunderstandings could be serious for me. I remembered how Bull had complained of something similar. One of his critics within McGill University – a 'theologian turned historian' was how Bull dismissively described him – had noted that the elevation of the 400-mm gun was, under certain circumstances, to be brought down from 90 degrees to 45 degrees. This would have been a necessary change for orbital, as opposed to high-altitude, shots but Bull's critics failed to understand the difference. As far as he was concerned, such an angle of firing was proof that the venture was of 'a military nature', and not suitable for University support.

The Supergun I had worked on was for peaceful purposes, but I had work to do if I was to convince the world.

22

By standing on the small table I could just see out of the barred plastic-panelled window and into the yard below. Here, every morning, was strewn a litter of newspaper parcels, posted from the windows of our Block during the hours of darkness. Whilst banged up, prisoners, by tradition, never use their buckets; these parcels contained the products of those men who could not wait until daylight.

A group of inmates were being herded towards the parcels by warders. They were shambling, pathetic figures in prison clothes, some pushing brooms, others carrying bin-bags, stooping to gather the balls of newsprint as they came to them. It was the dirtiest job in the prison, but the awkward squad detailed to do it were not criminals. They were former psychiatric patients who had, quite literally, nowhere else to go but here and no alternative employment but this. The scene was one of Dickensian awfulness.

But there was worse to follow.

Addressing one of that miserable cleansing crew, a warder was having trouble making himself understood. So he took hold of the man's hair and started to drag him around the yard, shouting abuse at him, wagging his finger and yelling as he yanked the man forwards and backwards. The prisoner's arms windmilled as he felt himself losing balance. He whimpered for the warder to let go, but was merely pushed and pulled with greater violence. Then, suddenly, the warder released him. The prisoner staggered for a moment and went down.

But the warder hadn't had enough. Viciously he began to kick out, still yelling and cursing, as the fallen man curled into a helpless, defensive, foetal position. The warder circled so as to aim a kick at the prisoner's head, and we all heard – and felt – the dull thud as his boot made contact. Now another prison officer, a dog-handler, ran forward and stood by. His Alsatian, excited by the scene, was snarling and snapping at the prone figure, who was now screaming like a hunted and wounded animal.

Some of the other psychiatric patients were crying by this time, pointing and gesturing or turning in circles in their distress. One of them ran and hurled himself bodily at the weld-mesh fence which surrounded the yard. A couple of warders sprinted furiously across to restrain him.

There were roars of rage coming, too, from the battery of cell windows which overlooked the yard and I found myself adding my own voice to this chorus of impotent anger. For these few moments, every prisoner was united in outrage at the squalid incidence of sadism being played out like some demonstration scene below us. We howled, we banged the glass, we shouted threats. Some prisoners found missiles to hurl, although none had any effect.

At last the warder, winding his fist into the man's hair once more, jerked him to his feet and began to lead him out of our sight. Slowly I got down from the table, sat on my bed, and started to cry.

The cell door opened.
'You want to work?'
'Yes.'
'Follow me then.'
A group of prisoners had been formed into a cleaning gang, which, with mops and buckets, was working its way along the landing. I joined them. One was a large man wearing an expensive though perfectly ordinary pin-stripe suit. As everyone else was wearing prison drabs, of a quality which reminded me of my time in China, this man's clothing looked bizarre.

'That's St Michael,' I was told later. 'They leave him alone and he leaves them alone.'

He didn't leave them alone when, finishing the portion of floor allotted to me I grabbed a rag and started to rub a table, one of several dotted along the corridor.

'What d'you think you're doing?' shouted one of the prison officers.

'Leave him be,' said St Michael, sharply. 'He's not doing any harm.'

But then he turned to me and said, with more kindness, like a teacher issuing a gentle admonishment.

'What's your hurry?'

I had yet to learn a golden rule of prison life: all actions outside

101

one's cell should be taken slowly. In a system which intends to turn minutes into days, any extra seconds spent on the wrong side of your steel door was a nugget of freedom pilfered back.

I was in the exercise yard, breathing deep and trying to move my limbs as briskly as possible. I had not been running for a week and was missing it. Besides, to adopt the sluggish pace of work-time is futile here. A prisoner's allotment of daily fresh air is 60 minutes, and no ploy can make it stretch.

I looked around. It was sunny. The general mood was good with even the prison officers acting more relaxed and tolerant. A group of them were assembled near the gate, allowing prisoners to go through in small groups to the prison shop.

'Hey, man. You Topgun, right?'

A Rastafarian figure bounded towards me. I had already noticed that the number of black prisoners was all out of proportion to their numbers in society at large. I refuse to believe that blacks are, to this extent, a more criminal sector of the population although, if legal discrimination against them continues, the fact may eventually match up with the prejudice. It is known that men who get custodial sentences are more likely to re-offend after release. I was beginning to appreciate how prisons perpetuate crime.

Prisons are also notably colour-conscious places, largely because the wardens (*white to a man*) never let the blacks forget they *are* black. Every prisoner is, to them a bastard. But blacks are always *black* bastards.

I said to this big man whose dreadlocks framed his face, yes, I was Topgun. He wore a smile which seemed to belong in a happier place than this. He nodded at my feet, limping in their unsuitable shoes.

'I see you wearing those high-class shoes. Get yourself some trainers, man.'

'Where from?'

'Order them in the Shop, man. Couple of days your feet will be raw liver wearing piggie shoes.'

'They already are raw liver,' I told him.

He leaned closer to me, and dropped his voice.

'Don't let them get to you. Walk tall, man.'

He touched me on the shoulder and left, rejoining a group of other blacks who had stretched out to enjoy the sun.

I had company in the cell. His name was Peter, and he had spent five months as a remand prisoner and was due, the next day, in court.

'No point in wasting everybody's time so I'll plead guilty.'

'What to?' I asked.

But Peter, although talkative about most things, would provide no details.

'I borrow other people's money without their permission,' he said vaguely.

Peter was a quiet, neat, self-possessed individual, on whom the squalor of prison life left little trace. He instructed me carefully in prison lore – such matters as not defecating into the bucket at night, and the importance of laying paper all around the toilet seat.

'Why must I do that?'

'Lots of them prisoners have A.I.D.S. You never know. A little nick is all it takes.'

He sat propped up in the corner of the cell, rolling a cigarette so thin that it was finished after two inhalations. He then told me where to get marijuana, if I should want it.

'Believe it or not, it's sold at the Shop. Screws all know about it. But it keeps us quiet. It's the perfect prison drug.'

'I don't use drugs.'

'Well, if you did you'd soon find out you can get any drug you fancy in here, from aspirin to heroin – at a price of course.'

Our conversation moved on to prison punishment.

'Governor has absolute power. He can give you twenty-eight days punishment without asking the Board. The worst is the Punishment Cell. It's a box within a box, it's total isolation. They reckon four to six hours is as long as a human being can stand it.'

I was informed, too, about the less official punishments.

'If a prisoner's got bruises or cuts, he might tell you it was done by the fluffy white rabbit. That means the screws did it. Or, otherwise, you might hear a prisoner say he fell down the stairs in his cell. That's the same thing.'

The next day Peter went to court, pleaded guilty to whatever it was he'd done and received a twelve month sentence. Now transferred out of the remand wing, he returned to collect his things in a philosophical mood.

'Only about six weeks to go, if I stay out of trouble. See you Chris.'

23

Prisoners do a great deal of writing, not just letters, but notes, queries, even essays and reflections. I spent some time elaborating an allegorical account of prison life as a new kind of Animal Farm, a factory-type farm and therefore more in keeping with our times than the one represented in George Orwell's fable. In my farm the animals are kept in battery stalls except for occasional visits to the stockyard for exercise. The owners of the farm are absentee investors, who know little about how the animals are treated by their professional managers, and appear to care even less. They even seem uninterested in the farm yield, just so long as the numbers of stock remain high and the running costs low.

But most of the time I continued to compile notes about my role in the creation of Supergun, moving on from the background to S.R.C. and my first few years there, to details of my life in Iraq.

To emphasise that it had a special place in his heart, as well as being distinct from all the defence-related work of S.R.C., Bull created a new company to handle Project Babylon. He called it, vaguely but rather grandly, the Advanced Technology Institute, and for the last year of my association with Bull, A.T.I. was my direct employer.

I put together a team with which to set up an A.T.I. office in Baghdad. It was initially a small design team, consisting of a graphics expert, John Heath; a draughtsman, Mike Clark; an aerodynamicist, Tony Slack; a mathematician, Graham Ingham, and myself.

We were to work in conjunction with an Iraqi team, under a senior engineer, Shabib Azzawi. Technically Azzawi was a Brigadier, but the rank didn't signify very much. Iraq has a military government in everything but name, and civilians in influential positions acquire service commissions as a matter of course. Azzawi's job was to represent the interests of the client at all meetings, to organise manufacture and delivery of Supergun's components, and to manage the development of the Iraqis' technical knowledge of the project. The entire scheme, not unlike our previous work with China, was aimed at giving the client the technology to maintain and operate these systems himself.

I had met Azzawi during my first visit to Baghdad, following the fateful meeting with Bull in his office in the spring of 1988. I came to like and to trust him. Always dressed in a formal suit and tie, always courteous to fault, he was hard-working, highly intelligent and extremely competent. Like the majority of qualified Iraqis, he had received higher education in England, taking his MSc at the University of Liverpool.

Azzawi's superior was Dr Amir Saadi, a chemist and 'General', who had a position of total authority over Iraq's new technologies, within the special projects ministry presided over by Kamil Hussein, Saddam Hussein's son-in-law. Saadi got on very well with Bull. Apart from being gracious and courteous to everybody around him – irrespective of rank or position – he was incisive and extremely well-informed, a technological polymath with an incredible grasp of subjects well beyond his own speciality. The combination impressed Bull powerfully, and the two men established an immediate rapport.

Saadi's clout was in keeping with his abilities. This was fortunate. We needed it to loot Iraqi draughtsmen and technicians from other departments, where such skills were already scarce. We also required test-sites, labour, transport and much more, often in very short order, and all at a time when Iraq was still fighting a bloody and exhausting war with Iran. Project Babylon might easily have become bogged down in a mire of bureaucracy and competing interests, but Saadi's unshakeable commitment put it in a fast-track, and kept the money flowing into it.

If Saadi's charm, knowledge and influence could open doors and locate resources, the ultimate stimulus in that society remained fear. You saw it in almost all interchanges between the powerful and those whom they ruled, but most obviously of all in any situations involving the family of the President himself. This authority was represented as far as we were concerned by Kamil Hussein. The Minister for Industries was a man in his mid-30s, an urbane individual, in many ways enlightened, quite well educated, even charismatic. His great interest was nature conservation, and on his private estates he maintained wild bird reserves and breeding herds of gazelles and antelopes with which he planned to restock the depleted deserts.

Yet to see this man in relation to his inferiors was to know the full meaning of the word grovel. Kamil Hussein operated a simple system for stimulating production in his factories. As he arrived on site he would be all smiles. He would make a swift tour of the plant and inspect the books, before suggesting that productivity was a trifle low. Perhaps new targets should be set, let's say at double or triple the existing output. He would then leave, promising to return in one month's time.

Once Kamil Hussein made a promise to come back, his return was a certainty. It was anticipated in agonies of fear. His ever-present team of body-guards always carried canes, as thick as a finger and over a metre in length. If, for whatever reason, the Minister found that the revised production targets had not been met, he would personally supervise the severe caning of the factory's senior management, just by way of a reminder. At one particular plant which made mortar tubes, productivity received a five-fold increase following the receipt of one of these reminders.

Paradoxically this treatment might be regarded as lenient by those who suffered. They might, after all, have been accused of Economic Sabotage, a catch-all charge which covered everything from laziness to theft. It was nevertheless a serious crime, an offence against the war effort, for which the penalty would be, at the least, immediate redeployment to a position forward of the front line.

To put this threat into perspective, it has been said that the slaughter seen during the Iran-Iraq conflict was worse than any since the western front in the First World War.

24

When I first came to Baghdad, the war against Iran was the most important fact of everyday life. Saddam had initiated it. In 1980 he had unilaterally revoked the joint treaty on the Shatt-al-Arab waterway, which divides the two countries at the head of the Gulf, and commenced an all-out invasion of Iran. By cowing his people, the endless misery served President Saddam well, no doubt. On Westerners in Iraq, the war had a different effect: it gave the entire Gulf region the character of a vast arms bazaar. To understand what happened over Supergun it is necessary to know what that meant.

Many people live under the illusion that arms deals are struck by shadowy entrepreneurs operating on the margins of the law. This may be true of light weapons, although virtually any competent government can now clone its own Armalites or Kalashnikovs and doesn't need to buy them. However, contemporary wars cannot be won with assault rifles, machine guns and grenades. The eight-year Iran-Iraq conflict consumed hundreds of advanced fighter aircraft and helicopters, thousands of battlefield tanks and artillery guns, millions of modern rockets, shells and bombs, and for most of these the only realistic source of supply are the state-regulated arms industries of the industrialised nations. For such nations the war was, at the same time, a major trading opportunity and a moral dilemma.

At this stage Iraq was more or less openly supported by Saudi Arabia and the Gulf States. However, western oil supplies were not in jeopardy, and the problem for the West was how they could cash in on the war without losing the high moral ground. The answer for Western governments, and the arms industries they controlled, was to operate *clandestinely*.

In its relations with the Ayatollah Khomeini's Iran, America had been roundly humiliated, first by the deposing of its friend the Shah, then by the 441-day American Embasssy hostage crisis and the 'Delta Force' rescue fiasco, which had left eight American servicemen dead in the desert. To the American public Khomeini was 'the mad mullah', and there were even those who called for a selective nuclear strike against him. However, once the hostages were released, and while Saddam Hussein seemed to be keeping Khomeini occupied, the Reagan administration judged it possible to lift economic sanctions against Iran. Within a week some 300 American and European companies had offered to sell goods to Iran, including arms, by changing labels and re-routing deliveries through third countries.

Take one such deal. For two years an American company made a regular shipment of tractor engines from Boston to Teheran. But one day a vigilant Customs official with a military background noticed something strange about these engines: they were fitted with superchargers. The engines were, in fact, replacements for U.S.-made M-60 tank motors. This consignment was stopped.

Officially America and her allies, as neutrals, were refusing military aid to both sides. But neutrality took many forms. It is now well known that, under the Iran-Contra scheme, members of the National Security Council, led by Admiral Poindexter and Colonel North, proposed to use Iran's need for sophisticated weaponry in a bid to release hostages in Lebanon, as well as (illegally) to shore up the Contra guerillas in Nicaragua. The obvious supply-route to Iran was through Israel.

Instability, and preferably war, between Islamic nations is an important plank of Israel's regional policy, and initially it was natural for the Tel Aviv government to be willing to supply the more hard-pressed Iranians. That the hardware fitted was an added convenience. Iran still had the Shah's old American-supplied arsenal, and Israel has always been equipped from America.

Iran's desperate need from the first was for ground-to-air and ground-to-ground missiles. Israel's Hawk anti-aircraft system fitted the requirement, and – even better – the new T.O.W. anti-tank missile. In discussion with the Americans, the Director General of Israel's foreign affairs ministry proposed a deal through an intermediary, the expatriate Iranian arms dealer Manuchuhr Gherbanifar.

On 30 August 1985 more than 500 T.O.W.s were shipped out of Israel, *via* the Cape, to Iran, arriving in mid-September. However permission to supply American arms had to be obtained from the White House. On 5 December President Reagan complied, signing a Presidential Order retrospectively authorising the sale. But on the following day Reagan, under pressure from the State Department, decided to reverse this policy: further Iranian sales would not, he agreed, be allowed. However, the C.I.A., the National Security Council and Israel were all unhappy about this. By 17 January Poindexter had convinced Reagan to do another about-turn and the President authorised the purchase by the C.I.A. of 4,000 T.O.W.s from the Defence Department for shipment to Israel and thence to Iran. In February and October 1986, further T.O.W. deliveries totalling 1,500 were made, before the 'Irangate' affair became public. Plans to sell Hawk ground-to-air missiles to Iran on a similar scale were by then well advanced, but these had to be abandoned by Israel.

But even after 'Irangate', secret Israeli support for Iran continued, with or without American connivance. The details of one of the biggest proposed deals, worth more than $1 billion, emerged when it was uncovered by U.S. Customs in a covert operation. The case illustrates the mechanism used. Iran was to have a number of aircraft – 16 F-4s, 12 F-5s, 46 Skyhawks and six C130 transports – along with assorted Hawks, T.O.W.s and tanks. These were to be drawn from the Israeli arsenal, shipped to Iran, and then replaced in Israel with technically more advanced systems from the U.S. It was a doubly attractive exercise, because Israel would have been upgrading its hardware at a profit. However, it happened also to be illegal, because the end-user certificates issued by the Israelis for all their American weaponry had renounced unauthorised onward sales. The chief Israeli negotiator arreted in this scam was Auraham Bar-Am, an allegedly retired General.

End-user certificates have been an important factor in all military sales since the mid-1980s, introduced, in principle, as a means of containing the spread of sophisticated arms. In practice the container is more like a colander, because nations subject to an embargo can so easily circumvent the system. It is not difficult to find another country willing to ship the required arms on your behalf, flouting the terms of the end-user certificate. Where this is too cumbersome, the third party – in return for a large commission – will agree to issue a fictitious end-user certificate for a consignment which may never approach their shores at all.

European countries that are flexible in their approach to the issue of certificates include Belgium, Spain, Portugal, Yugoslavia and Austria. Virtually all South American countries sell them, at rates of commission ranging from 10 per cent to 200 per cent. 'Quickie' end-user certificates are available over the counter in Pakistan or

Thailand, while there is a standing joke that Singapore would long since have sunk had it kept all the arms that its nationals had signed for.

'Neutral' countries such as Switzerland, Austria and Sweden all did well trading with Iran. But Britain did even better, becoming, in spite of E.C. restrictions, Iran's second most important trading partner. In a single year, 1983, British exports to Iran jumped 21 per cent to 56 billion Rials, and most of this was defence-related.

In spite of our lack of diplomatic relations, and the arms embargo in place, the British allowed the Iranian Air Force to have its principle international arms procurement office near Trafalgar Square in London. This remained in business until 1989. Meanwhile the extent of our own arms sales to Teheran justified the maintenance of a permanent office in Teheran, staffed by senior, technically-qualified staff from International Military Services, the sales department of the Ministry of Defence.

In justifying the highly lucrative trade, many economies with the truth were required. The supply of Chieftain tank engines was explained on the grounds that the motor 'did not form part of the tank's lethal weapon system'. The delivery of advanced radar defence from Plessey was authorised because it was to be used in the northern regions, 'close to the Soviet border'. Its positioning had of course little to do with the U.S.S.R., and everything to do with the fact that, from here, it could maintain surveillance over the whole of northern Iraq, where air force squadrons were based for strikes against the Iranian capital.

As late as 1990 one of Britain's leading aviation companies, Martin Baker, was supplying spares for Iran's F4 Phantoms and F5 Tiger jets, in a contract for ejector seats worth £50 million. The rationalisation for this was that the item formed part of the 'safety equipment' of the aircraft.

Officially Iraq was in no better odour with the West than Iran, both being classed, with Libya and Syria, as 'terrorist' states. Moreover, Iraq had for decades been a client of the U.S.S.R., and had been largely armed by Moscow.

However, Western 'non-intervention' was as permissive on the Iraqi side as on the Iranian. France was quite openly arming Iraq, which it subsidised to the tune of $9 billion. But French pragmatism found no hindrance to selling on both sides of the front line. In one instance the state-owned S.N.P.E. company delivered

450,000 shells to Iran, with a 4 per cent commission being paid into the coffers of the French Socialist Party.

Italy and Spain too played the double game. Italian defence industries did almost $3 billion-worth of business in the Middle East during the 1980s. Italy, for example, supplied nine million plastic anti-personnel mines to Iran between 1981 and 1985, whilst simultaneously filling an order for ten frigates to Iraq. Meanwhile Spanish ammunition was in use by both sides, Iraq receiving them through the intermediacy of Saudi Arabia. On occasions, the Spanish Air Force freighted the cargos, using its own C130 Hercules aircraft. These flew into Saudi airbases close to the road network which leads *via* Kuwait into Iraq, and along which military convoys of up to 200 vehicles were frequently observed to be moving north. This traffic increased markedly just prior to Iraq's offensive against Iranian positions in the early months of 1989, the push which effectively ended the war.

The Americans also used Saudi Arabia as an alibi for its assistance to Iraq. High-altitude and A.W.A.C. reconnaissance reports covering Iranian troop movements were comprehensively relayed to Saudi Arabia, in the knowledge that they would be passed direct to Iraq. There were, however, more direct dealings, as when the U.S. State Department authorised the sale of 60 surplus Bell UH-1 Iroquois attack helicopters to Iraq 'for agricultural use' – machines which had previously seen service with the 1st U.S. Cavalry Division in Vietnam, and which are normally fitted with 25-mm Browning machine guns. In another contract, a further 60 Hughes helicopters and 45 more Bells were supplied. I saw many of these 'agricultural' machines at various Iraqi airports, invariably fitted with air-to-ground missiles.

Then, in December 1983, Reagan sent a senior State Department official, James Placke, accompanied by a high-ranking Pentagon official, Edward Tixier, on a mission to the Gulf States. These luminaries informed Arab rulers that America would regard the defeat of Iraq as contrary to its interests.

In 1985 Stephen Bryen, U.S. Under Secretary for Defence with responsibility for military exports, successfully scotched a plan to export chemical weapons technology to Iraq. In the event, the Iraqis found an alternative, though rather more expensive, supplier in Germany. Bryen continued to campaign against such deals, although he knew that a variety of chemical and biological weapons installations had already been built in Iraq with American help. In 1989, after Reagan's term of office was over, Bryen wrote

111

an article for the publication *Moment*, in which he enlarges on the allegation that the U.S. Government and its N.A.T.O. allies abetted the development of major chemical and biological agents for military use by Iraq. Technical equipment for this and other purposes was routed through Frankfurt Airport, says Bryen, with the Chamber of Commerce constantly pressing the needs of hard-pressed individual companies over the official policy of the U.S. Government. The State Department found itself complying.

When still in office, Bryen believed he had found a way to prevent the export of sensitive equipment to the war zone. Hearing that a shipment of advanced microwave antennae had been author-ised for the Iraqi missile research base Saad-16, Bryen by-passed the Chamber of Commerce and appealed directly to the National Security Council. As a function of the President's office the N.S.C. can override cabinet secretariats. However, it took Bryen a year of intense lobbying to have this consignment blocked, during which time the Chamber of Commerce, its feathers ruffled, had authorised dozens of similar shipments without even referring them to Bryen. Under America's Export Administration Act, the Commerce Department has a right to keep its export licences secret for an unlimited period.

The Chamber of Commerce does not enjoy entirely harmonious relations with the Pentagon. As will be seen in due course, a not dissimilar situation between industry and defence appears to exist in Britain.

No Englishman, living as I was at the Al-Rasheed hotel in Baghdad during 1988, could fail to notice the amount of business being done there by Britain. Many particular instances – like the story Colonel Kadoori had told me – came my way and one feature of these stories was the enthusiastic backing available from our Embassy. The Al-Rasheed was always swarming with excited Brits – as well as Americans and Europeans – behaving almost like gold-rush prospectors. It was a Klondyke in which picks and pans were replaced by document cases and laptop computers.

I know a little bit more about the background now; about why, for instance, Kadoori was so confident of his share-buying proposal. In the 1980s the British Government found itself increa-singly attracted towards Saddam Hussein's regime. For years we wooed him. High-level ministerial visits had taken place on both sides; from ours, David Mellor went there in 1987. Later, govern-ment ministers like Tony Newton, John Wakeham and William

Waldegrave all made visits to Baghdad. Praise was handed out, costly gifts were exchanged, Saddam Hussein's ego was energetically massaged.

Hence Colonel Kadoori's confidence. Goods, military goods, allegedly the subject of a stringent embargo, were nonetheless at that time being copiously licensed for export to Iraq. Thorn-E.M.I. quite legally supplied the Cymbeline battlefield radar system, for detecting oncoming artillery and helicopters. R.A.C.A.L. Electronics supplied similar systems. In all, 69 British companies set out their stalls at the post-war Baghdad Military Fair in 1989, with the deliberate intention of selling battlefield kit. And in 1991, the D.T.I. provided the House of Commons with an A-to-Z list of items that had been licensed for export to Iraq between 1987 and 1990. This list included the following equipment: air defence simulator, aircraft, aircraft spares, armoured vehicles and spares, artillery fire control equipment, body armour, depleted uranium, ejection seats and spares, encoder/decoders, explosives, explosives detectors, fast assault craft, gas respirators, gun sound ranging equipment, helicopter engines, hostile fire indicators, jet engines and parts, laser equipment and parts, long-range surveillance equipment, mortar-locating radar, naval spares, night vision equipment, pistols, rifles and shotguns, plutonium, tank engines, uranium, voice encryption units, zirconium.

Apart from these shipments, there were also the usual train of goods finding their way into Iraq *via* third countries. One particular case came to the public's attention, pungent with the smell of scandal and cover-up.

It arose after Margaret Thatcher travelled to the Jordanian capital Amman in 1985 and signed an agreement extending a line of arms credits to King Hussein worth $275 million. Over the next four years, $125 million-worth of weapons could be accounted for as having been delivered directly to Jordan's defence forces. Weapons bought with the remaining $150 million seemed to have gone missing. However, not all went unaccounted for; some was later found to have been used against Allied Forces in the war which came to be known as Desert Storm.

In May 1990, Allan Rogers, a Labour Front Bench spokesman and M.P. for Rhondda, began to ask the Defence Secretary Tom King a series of questions, in the hope of establishing which proportion of the missing weapons had in fact been diverted to Iraq. Mr Rogers indicated to the House of Commons that he possessed documentary evidence of such diversions. Within a day

113

or two, Rogers's London flat had been burgled and documents relating to the Middle East tampered with.

In this case neither Rogers nor anyone else could prove Government complicity in the diversion of weapons. However, given a modicum of vigilance, British-made arms could certainly have been prevented from reaching Saddam Hussein. The will, the desire, it appeared, was not there. Nor was there a desire to stop Project Babylon when it was first initiated. So why was it stopped in the end?

Perhaps it was too visible, too sensational. Moreover, the British Supergun contracts reached completion at exactly the time when uncertainty in our relationship with Iraq had suddenly begun to be resolved. That was the real 'crime' of the Supergun. It was as if the whole world had been picnicking on a forbidden beach. But, when the tide turned, it was only Gerald Bull's rug and parasol that didn't float away to a safer place.

25

I began to appreciate that there were others in this prison with as little reason to be there as myself. Billy Proudfoot, for one. He was on a charge of attempted murder and, with a string of previous convictions, he was looking at a 15-year stretch. One day he wandered into my cell.

'You the Supergun guy? You can help me.'

'How?'

'Well, you know about guns, don't you? It's about my case. They fitted me up.'

Until now Billy had been out of trouble for five years, living with a woman who had told him that he must go straight or lose her. He didn't want to lose her.

'Well, if you mean small arms, I'm afraid I really don't know anything about them.'

'Come on, you must. It's about the ballistic evidence, and it's all wrong. I never had anything to do with a gun. I can let you have the prosecution evidence – just have a look at it, will you?'

A few hours later a bulky envelope was delivered to my cell. It contained details of the forensic evidence in the case. Billy was alleged to have shot the victim with an Italian handgun identified as a Titan, and having a calibre of 6.35 millimetres. Such a calibre, claimed the forensic report, was very distinctive and unusual in a handgun. Police had dug up the weapon in a garden in Cheltenham.

X-ray pictures very clearly showed the bullet lodged in the victim's pelvis and at once I felt it did not look right. To my eyes the diameter was obviously larger than 6.35 millimetres, although I had no way of measuring this. Quickly I looked over the rest of the evidence. It mostly concerned ballistic tests carried out with the gun, impresive scientifically-presented data. The odd thing was, there seemed nothing in all this to connect Billy with this, or any other, gun.

I copied out the report and sketched the X-ray picture of the bullet.

At final slopping-out, I saw Billy again.

'Did you get the forensic report?'

'Yes. It was very interesting.'

'It's all wrong.'

'I know. I could tell, and I'm no expert. Maybe I'll be able to find out more.'

There was a look of eagerness and hope of Billy's face and it was compelling. I made a resolution. If ever I got out of this place I would do something for Billy Proudfoot.

I had a new cell mate, John, only 17 years old, was a burglar, and another figure who had dropped through the net, or whatever system exists for catching the socially disadvantaged.

As a child his father had used him as a look-out while he stole cars. By his mid-teens his home was so broken that it ceased to exist, and John was thrown onto the world destitute. Without a home, assistance from the authorities was unavailable, and he now decided to help himself – to the contents of other people's cars and houses.

'It was funny really. This was a house near Swindon, middle of the evening, no one at home. I got a window open, and got in, and went upstairs. Bedroom's best place for finding stuff – money and jewelry, right? So I'm searching around in the dark when the dog starts barking down below. Bloody horrible noise it's making. So I stop what I'm doing and I go down again. Dog's still yapping away, so I think, I'll feed it. So I switch on the light and open up the fridge, and there's some cold meat in there, so I give it to the dog. Few minutes after that the police arrive: neighbours saw the light go on and they phoned 999.'

'So, if you hadn't fed that dog – ?'

'I'd have got clear away. Doesn't pay, being kind to animals, does it?'

But John obviously didn't entirely believe his own maxim. By the time we parted, he was negotiating with another prisoner to buy a mouse.

'Why?' I asked.

'I like them. They're good company, and they're easy to feed, aren't they?'

26

Sitting at the small table in my cell, I continued to scribble my notes. I was trying to explain how we came to choose the British steelmakers for the Supergun barrel sections.

As I told the Customs in Sheffield Police Station, the contract placement was done by Azzawi, but the contract specifications were drawn up by A.T.I., under guidelines laid down by Bull. Bull's contract philosophy was that, although we would consider possible contractors world wide, our bias should be towards large state-owned Western European forgemasters. An extensive list of companies were reviewed, including manufacturers in Korea, Japan, Russia, China and North America. From Europe we compiled a shortlist: Sheffield Forgemasters and Walter Somers (U.K.), Terni (Italy), C3F (France), Von Roll (Switzerland), Tysen Kruppe (Germany), V.E.W. (Austria) and Renosa (Spain).

Renosa was crossed off early. There were also doubts about Von Roll and Somers, because they were not state-owned. Saadi and Azzawi both felt that nationalised companies would offer greater cost concessions, because of the huge amount of business Iraq was already doing in Western Europe, particularly with state-owned companies in Italy and France.

Eventually I convinced Bull to include both Von Roll and Somers. The former manufactured heavy artillery for the Swiss Army and, under licence, much of the Leopard II battletank. Somers, a company that had existed for over a century, had produced heavy ordnance in the past. They were currently making large marine drive-shafts for the British Admiralty, in diameter not unlike the 350-mm barrel of the Supergun model.

Although I admit to a bias towards British companies, both in myself and throughout S.R.C. and A.T.I. (about 80 per cent of the staff were British), I initially fancied the French state steelmaker for the job. Back in 1987, when the Pentagon had commissioned Bull's feasibility study for a reopening of H.A.R.P., C3F, a Creusot Loire subsidiary, had actually been approached about making a 1,000-mm gun barrel. They were undoubtedly capable of fulfilling a similar order for Iraq, and would do so without objections from Paris. However, in the event, the French put a prohibitive cost on the job and were ruled out. It now looked increasingly as if the contract for the metal tubes – the first Super-gun manufacturing orders – would come to Britain.

In negotiations it was decided by Bull and the Iraqis to define the contract as a 'petro-chemical installation'. Although not entirely honest, it is common in industry to camouflage an order during contract discussions. This is especially true in defence, where commercial confidentiality is often so vital that secrecy is a contractual condition of employment. When, in the previous year, we had sounded out C3F over the 1,000-mm gun-barrel tubes for America, these had been described then as a 'particle-physics testing facility'. With hindsight, I accept that the 'petro-chemical' deception used for the Supergun tubes was, in the long run, a blunder. At the same time we made no attempt to disguise the client, and Azzawi represented Iraq in all major discussions with Walter Somers and Forgemasters.

Design work had begun even before Iraq agreed to Bull's proposal but, as technical discussions with steelmakers progressed, modifications were being made. It was clear that conventional thinking – at Sheffield Forgemasters in particular – was making it difficult for the manufacturers to accept that they could create steel with S.R.C.'s required impact values, a measurement of material toughness. There is a somewhat inverse relation between a metal's impact strength and its ability to withstand stress and, as far as Forgemasters were concerned, the material properties S.R.C. was asking for were incompatible with one another. I was sure, from experiments I'd carried out in China, that the S.R.C. specification was not unreasonable and, in the end, an unconventional contract was signed, whereby we agreed to accept whatever values would be achieved following correct manufacture of the material.

In the event, both Somers and Forgemasters excelled themselves. The steel tubes were of such quality that, in toughness and strength, they often surpassed by a good 50 per cent even the values I had expected.

Similar, hidebound attitudes at S.R.C. in Brussels were hindering the outline designs, on which my own team in Baghdad was waiting to work. Designs for the 350-mm test model were not too difficult, since this is approximately the same as a conventional (if old-fashioned) 16-inch gun, and could be based on the experience from H.A.R.P. However, we also required two 1,000-mm designs, the first to be mounted horizontally for full-scale tests; the other in an inclined position for operational firing. When they did calculations of the recoil loads for this gun they couldn't believe how large they were, and (wrongly) assumed a mathematical error. Such recoil forces had never been tackled before. The designers' initial reaction was to increase the mass of Supergun so as to absorb more of these loads.

As soon as the first drawings for the full-scale assemblies began to arrive, we could see that they wouldn't do. S.R.C. was thinking in terms of scaled-up versions of conventionally-sized artillery systems. These ideas looked reasonable on the drawing board but showed no appreciation of the difficulties in handling materials of such immense mass and weight. One design, for the superstructure of the gun, would have meant building the equivalent of a Royal Navy destroyer from welded plates of alloy-steel plates 150 millimetres thick, and attaching it to the side of a mountain.

I almost hit the roof with frustration when I saw this. Azzawi himself then got onto Brussels and explained that there was no question of Iraq being able to construct something like a shipyard in the middle of the desert, just to build this thing. Increasingly thereafter we originated our own designs in Baghdad, with the Brussels team, as the 'Design Authority', rubber-stamping them.

The five 350-mm tubes (each ten metres long) for the horizontal test model were a priority and in May 1988 Walter Somers, without a signed contract but with an advance guaranteed payment of £150,000, began work. The total value of the job was fixed at £350,000.

Final agreement was reached with Forgemasters on 7 July 1988 for the manufacture of the 1,000-mm assembly – the Supergun. Here was a contract, worth £7 million. It called for two sets of 26 five- and six-metre long sections of flanged tubes made from alloy-steel, and varying in weight (prior to machining) from 136,000 kilogrammes to typical weights of 95,000 kilogrammes reducing to 80,000 kilogrammes in the lower-pressure sections of the barrel. The wall thickness of the barrel varied from 250 millimetres in the high-pressure region to 50 millimetres in the muzzle area, where the pressure would be lower. Studs, each with two nuts, were to be used to fasten the flanged ends of the tubes together. To lift the largest of these bolts required two men.

This seems – and was – a gun on an enormous scale. Nevertheless I was happy to have agreed to a significantly lighter assembly than we had at first contemplated. True, the problem of recoil would still have to be faced. The lighter barrel's acceleration rate, on recoil, would be significantly greater than that of the heavier one, but this seemed less problematic than the other difficulty, of containing the much higher energy that would have resulted from the use of a barrel with thicker walls and a resulting much higher mass.

27

I was awoken at five in the morning by the sound of the warder's key.

'Your police escort's waiting.'

I sat up and swung my legs over the edge of the bed. I had not seen this man before. I looked at him warily.

'Get everything together, will you? Bedding included. You can wash over the other side.'

I rolled my bedding and assembled the few belongings I'd accumulated. Then I followed the prison officer as he wended his way back, past the rows of locked steel doors, out of D Block and towards Reception. Before we got there he paused and allowed me to catch him up.

'You'll feel better when you've had a wash.'

Just to be outside D Block was a considerable relief, though the warder must have thought I looked the worse for wear. Nevertheless, his tone surprised me. Instead of the usual bark, it was soft and considerate.

We arrived in a small washroom off the reception area. He handed me my clothes and a razor.

'I'll try to get you something to eat,' he said as he left me.

Dressed in my own things, and properly shaved in warm water, I certainly did feel a different man. The prison officer reappeared with a tray bearing two fried eggs, bread and a large mug of tea.

'Sorry, best I could do. The kitchen's not open yet.'

But I took the tray gratefully. After a week of prison catering, two hot, freshly-fried eggs were a luxury – the more so because this officer must have actually cooked them for me himself. I nodded to him and smiled.

'You're proof that it's possible to do this job and still behave in a reasonable manner. Thanks.'

He smiled back, pleased by the compliment.

Later I was introduced to a couple of policemen with Yorkshire accents. After I had signed for my personal belongings, and slipped my wedding ring back on my finger, I was handcuffed to one of them and led out to their car. But even the cuffs did not dispel the sense that I had had my identity returned to me, if only temporarily. To be outside the prison, breathing free air, was in itself an intoxication.

I found myself directing the policemen through the streets of Bristol and towards the M5 motorway. As soon as he could the driver put his foot down.

'Can't hang around or we'll catch the traffic round Birmingham,' he said.

I remember the anxious wobble of a motorcyclist, himself travelling well in excess of the limit, as with a touch on the siren we left him for dead.

'Useful things, sirens.' I commented.

At an average speed of more than 160 kilometres an hour we were off on the long drive to Sheffield, where a magistrate was due to review my remand in a court hearing later in the morning.

I had been back in the familiar cell at Sheffield Police Station for only half an hour before I was extracted once again, escorted down the corridor and into the interview room.

'Hi, Chris,' said Kevin with a broad smile, shaking my hand. 'Good news at last.'

On a visit to Bristol a few days earlier, and in his usual pessimistic style, he'd told me that we would as a matter of course be reapplying for bail, but I wasn't to get too excited. Now it was different.

'Bail's been organised. I talked to Barry Riley, and he won't oppose the application. You'd think he *wanted* you out. In fact, I *know* he wants you out.'

And once in court, I found it was all over in a few minutes. I had endured a couple more hours of suspense in the police cell, after which the hearing passed in a flash. Bail was fixed at £25,000 and I was free to go.

After the intensity of the past two weeks, the rapid succession of bewildering experiences, confrontations, anger, tears, the thing was done almost casually. Before we parted Kevin shook my hand again and said,

'Take a week's holiday. Forget the whole thing. Now go.'

Instead I spent the next week consulting my own diaries and filing cabinet, and writing feverishly.

Forget the whole thing? Some chance. I still had a charge hanging over me, I was awaiting trial at some future unspecified date. More than anything else I wanted to continue with my record of the events surrounding Project Babylon, the record which would be the core of my defence. Not, I now thought, that I would limit myself to my own experience. The whole affair had grown too big and too threatening and now I was free, I was determined to start digging into all the things which I didn't know about this case, or hadn't understood. What was the breech slide on Paul Ashwell's lorry in Greece? What were the extra tubes, whose drawings Barry Riley had shown me during my interrogation? Who had tipped off the Customs about the Teesport tubes, and why? Who were the men in the Cavalier? Were they the same people who had threatened me; the same, even, who had killed Bull?

My ten days in jail had felt like 15 years. I wasn't going back there. I wanted those answers.

I remembered from the Customs interrogation that one of the most important bones of contention was the development and use of the 350-mm test model. It was something I would have to make absolutely clear. After the first weeks of design work in Baghdad I began to be particularly concerned about the breech-block. The term *breech* is from an Old English word meaning 'buttocks' – the part covered by your breeches. At some point in the early days of gunnery, however, it came to be used to refer to the closed hind-part of the gun. The breech-block is the closure, which is needed in any breech-loading system to shut the aperture behind the projectile and propellant when you want to fire.

There are often times when you must, if not re-invent the wheel, then subject it to fresh scrutiny. However, still rather labouring under ideas derived from smaller guns such as the 155-mm one, Brussels had designed for the Supergun an enormous, if entirely conventional, screw-breech. This, I believed, would prove to be a non-starter. It was too costly and too difficult to make on that scale, and probably impossible to operate, especially in the sandy desert conditions prevailing in any place where we were likely to set up our firing site.

In Baghdad we therefore re-attacked the problem, eventually coming up with a completely new concept, a *split-wedge breech*. We had a working-scale model of the design made at the Nassr Establishment, north of Baghdad, which we fitted to a 122-mm Russian anti-tank gun. At an Iraqi army firing range to the south of the capital, the gun was mounted horizontally on railway bogeys to allow it to recoil along a section of railway track. As the breeh was such a radical and untested departure from convention, the wise precaution was to fire the gun by remote control. We therefore loaded a small test-charge and retired behind a sand mound some 60 metres distant.

'Fire!' shouted Azzawi.

We were peering over the top of the sand mound and saw the puff of smoke followed almost immediately by a BOOM. But the gun didn't move; no recoil had taken place. Apart from the wedge itself popping up vertically like toast from a cartoon toaster into the sky, little else had happened.

We discovered the simple error: a device holding the wedge in place had not been screwed down. We refixed it, reloaded and retired once more.

'Fire!'

BOOM.

This time the gun recoiled gently down the track. When we examined our invention, we found no indication of any gas leakage through the breach. The thing had functioned well. In spite of my cautious protests, Azzawi immediately decided to try a much larger, three-quarter-size propellant charge. This was loaded, the wedge breech was closed and we retired a third time.

'Fire!'

Nothing happened. We clicked our tongues with frustration.

Following a misfire, the normal precaution is to wait at least an hour before approaching the gun, and I thought I would go for a walk to fill up the time. But Azzawi's imperturbable deputy Colonel Shaki was already walking towards the gun.

'Inshallah!' he called back cheerily over his shoulder. Several Iraqi soldiers were walking with him, then one or two broke into a run.

What I saw in the ensuing moments left me with no doubts about the courage of the Iraqi squaddie. The first to reach the gun peered into the mouth of the barrel to see, as he said later, if the propellant was still burning. In the meantime a second soldier had seized the electrical ignition cables near the breech and was waggling them about to see if they were loose. If the misfire had been a loose connection, this action ought to have fired the gun and blown his comrade's head off.

They came back to us in triumph, Colonel Shaki smiling broadly.

'We found the problem,' he told Azzawi. 'Just a loose wire.'

Azzawi now told his men to load a full charge, into the breech. The revolutionary design, with just one tiny firing to its name, was about to be tested to the limit. I protested that we ought to do more small-scale firings first.

'No problem, Chris,' said Azzawi firmly. 'It will be O.K., I am sure. *Inshallah.*'

I now found myself peering over the heap of sand for a fourth time.

'Fire!'

BOOM. CRACK. CRASH.

The gun blew itself to pieces. In one direction the barrel reminded me of a Highland caber, cartwheeling down the range. Meanwhile the breech block assembly, our loving invention, had shot backwards out of the barrel like a 500-kg champagne cork, flying and spinning through the air for 20 or 30 metres.

Thinking of Kamil Hussein and his cane-wielding bodyguard, I may have turned a whiter shade of pale. But Azzawi seemed unconcerned. He patted me reassuringly on the shoulder.

'Don't worry, Chris. One should expect a few setbacks with a project as big as this.'

Back in Baghdad we had welcomed the arrival of the newest member of the team, the young mathematician called Graham Ingham. Graham was unattached and, though in his mid-twenties, he was an innocent abroad with the appearance and manner of a teenager. One evening he had been picked up by an extrovert and attractive young woman called Bernadette, who worked at the Belgian Embassy. She and Graham soon developed what looked like a very close relationship, seeing each other two or three evenings a week. Twice I had dinner at the Al-Rascheed hotel with the two of them, and found Bernadette undeniably charming and well ahead of Graham in sophistication. Apart from her native French and Flemish, she spoke fluent English, Spanish and German.

'What do you do at the Embassy?' I had asked with casual interest.

'I am only a clerical worker, you know,' she had said, with a shrug and a pretty smile.

A clerical worker who spoke five languages and was provided by her employer with the exclusive use of a driver and car. No ordinary clerk, I thought.

Azzawi too had noted the relationship, or had it reported to him.

'Chris, it is not good for one of your staff to be going out with someone from an Embassy. Such Embassies are here for only one reason, to collect intelligence.'

I tried talking to Graham, but he wouldn't take my point.

'Look, it's nothing serious. She's just a friend. And anyway, it's my business, isn't it – what I do in my spare time?'

A few weeks later, Graham begged a few days off to go with Bernadette on a camping trip into the desert, down near the Kuwaiti border. Several other diplomatic staff were in the party. When they returned Azzawi called me into his office.

'Mukhbarat are concerned, Chris.'

Mukhbarat are the Iraqi Security Service – Saddam Hussein's secret police.

'Oh, why?'

'Graham's camping trip. There was an American with them.'

'I see.'

Americans of any description were regarded with the deepest suspicion, and now Graham's social life was beginning, from an Iraqi point of view, to look increasingly dubious. I asked Graham about the American, but he just said,

'What American? Everybody was talking French.'

The next day Azzawi told me that Mukhbarat had made the decision to pick Graham Ingham up. I was horrified.

'What'll they do? Deport him?'

Azzawi did not try to minimise the trouble our young genius had got himself into. He shook his head.

'No. They'll place him under arrest and hold him until Project Babylon is finished.'

'When are they going to do this?'

Azzawi shrugged and looked me straight in the eyes.

'Some time.'

I could take a hint. The same day I invented a pretext, a job in Brussels which only Graham's unique talents could fulfil. As I handed him his ticket I almost told him the real reason he was going away, but then thought better of it. When he got back to Brussels and realised there wasn't an urgent job requiring his attention, he would work it out for himself. I don't think he ever forgave me for separating him from his girl, though.

Several months later, after my departure from S.R.C., Bull wanted Graham to go back to Iraq. He reported at the Iraqi Airways desk at Frankfurt Airport to pick up his ticket in the usual way, only to be turned away. He was now, said a telex from Baghdad, *persona non grata*.

28

Released from prison I was living back at home, reunited with Glenys and our sons. But my freedom was constrained and conditional under the terms of my bail. I reflected on all the varieties and relativities which exist within that term 'freedom'. Had it been an abuse of freedom to trade with Iraq? Bull certainly had not thought so. He was an old-fashioned free-marketeer, sharing with Margaret Thatcher a hatred of bureaucratic regulation. Bull reserved the right to market his skills where he wished and to decide for himself the moral issues.

On the whole, as his employee, I had agreed with the philosophy and been loyal to it. S.R.C. was, in my opinion, an admirable outfit. It was small, flexible and accountable to itself. Its activities were guided by the excitement of new ideas rather than the dead hand of balance sheets and profit margins. If Iraq was the only country with, in Bull's terms, the vision to invest in S.R.C.'s revolutionary concepts, then I for one (and there were many others, as I've said) was prepared to work with that country. Iraq's human rights record is certainly very bad, but if intolerance of opposition, even cruelty towards it, were a bar to trade, American and European dealings with the rest of the world would be at sharply-reduced levels.

In any case, Bull was not impervious to the interests and policies of North American and Western European governments. In beginning to deal with Iraq, S.R.C. happened to coincide with these policies, as Bull took care to verify. Subsequently he remained in touch with representatives of Washington, London and Brussels, but, by the time the 350-mm model had reached the stage when it could be tested, the political atmosphere had changed. Iraq was no longer the bulwark of Western values against the tide of Islamic fundamentalism. This left Bull in an uncomfortable dilemma, albeit one that he was familiar with, for it was a repeat of the predicament he had found himself in over South Africa. Then the advent of the Carter government had left him high and dry, a scapegoat with a criminal record. Now the same thing was happening all over again.

But there were other things I should think about, now that I was out of jail. I might have a charge still hanging over me, but I still wanted to deal with some more immediate unfinished business – the case of Billy Proudfoot.

I went to the Bristol Public Library, in the hope of educating myself about handguns, and asked for the best reference books they had on the subject.

I was expecting to find little information about guns of the 6.35-mm calibre, since forensics had suggested this was a very rare gun. In fact, to my surprise, the list of handgun manufacturers which I now read showed that virtually all of them made, or had made, automatic pistols of this size. Far from being an unusual calibre, the 6.35-mm was quite a common weapon.

I walked back to the enquiry desk.

'Would you have a reference book on small arms ammunition?' I asked, innocently.

When you come out of prison, even after a relatively short time, you're conditioned for some days into thinking your every movement is watched and evaluated. There was, however, no raised eyebrow or sense of surprise in the librarian, though if he had known I was on bail for the illegal export of weapons, perhaps he might have wondered. After a few minutes he returned to me, carrying a second thick reference book. I leafed through pages of illustrations, showing every type of bullet available. There were scores of 6.35-mm bullets, but none of them matched the shape of the bullet in the pelvis of the victim.

Billy's defence lawyers had not apparently worked this out. They should be told. The police had the wrong gun, and (there was every reason to assume) the wrong suspect.

As I'd told Billy, I hardly had the authority of an expert. But I knew a man who had. I packed up the copies and sketches and sent them to Liep Sie in Amsterdam. Liep, who had worked for S.R.C. on the design and development of ammunition, confirmed what I had found out, and wrote it out in an impressive-looking report for the benefit of the court.

I was, of course, not the only one arrested following the Supergun barrel seizures at Teesport. On 10 April, the same day that the barrel sections were detained, the offices of Walter Somers and

Sheffield Forgemasters had been visited by the Customs and Excise. The house of the Managing Director of Forgemasters, Phillip Wright, was searched under warrant.

Five members of Forgemasters management were held for thirty hours under questioning. All five were released without charge but on police bail. This meant that possible charges against them remained pending. Three men from Walter Somers were also arrested and interrogated, although only one, Peter Mitchell, was ultimately charged with the illegal exportation of goods.

But now the Customs investigation was stalled. They were having trouble making sense of the information they'd gathered in their various raids, and the manufacturers had refused to answer any questions. I became sure this was the reason why they wanted me out when, the day after my release, our telephone rang.

'Hello, Chris, it's Barry Riley. I was wondering if we could meet.'

'Oh yes? Why?'

'There are various technical points we couldn't cover at Sheffield Police Station.'

I told him I'd think about it and phoned Kevin. His advice was pragmatic.

'They've obviously got problems. It could be quite useful to meet him. It would be helpful to find out what the problems are.'

'And if it's an unofficial meeting they can't use what I say in court, can they?'

'In legal theory, they can't. But it's been known to happen in practice. Go ahead and meet him. Just be careful and for God's sake don't sign anything!'

Six days later, shortly after noon, I collected Riley from Temple-meads Station in Bristol, and we drove to a café in the Clifton district to eat. I found myself worrying about the protocol of the situation. Riley had asked for the meeting, and furthermore he was a H.M. Customs case-officer with the duty of trying to put me behind bars for a very long time. On the other hand Bristol was my home territory, placing any hospitality obligation on me. So who should pay for lunch?

A little probing elicited the very strong hint that the civil service meal allowances for day-trips out of Birmingham were about enough to pay for a cheese sandwich and a cup of tea. The hospitality convention prevailed.

Riley and I were about the same age and I found that I couldn't help liking this chunky, super-fit, ex-S.A.S. man. Before going to Kenya I had worked for the International Nickel Company in Hereford, England, the town most famous as headquarters to the Special Air Services. There I'd climbed with and taught the soldiers and got to know some of them well. They had in common intense motivation, courage and discipline and were generally open and good-humoured. Riley was all these. He was also, like me, a marathon runner.

After eating, we drove the mile to Leigh Woods. I said I would show him my favourite training ground, but there was another reason. I didn't think my house was secure. We needed a place where we could talk without fear of eavesdroppers.

Riley started to discuss the five members of the management of Forgemasters who had been so fruitlessly questioned. He compared their stony refusal to answer questions with my own openness in the same situation. What he needed, he was telling me, was someone to stand up in court and answer particular questions from the prosecution, questions which would assist the prosecution's case. Riley turned to me and said,

'If *you'd* do it, we could do certain things for you.'

I was curious.

'Like what?'

'Like arrange a quick, low-publicity trial. You plead guilty, but we get the sentence deferred. Once you've given evidence against the others, the prosecution can have a word with the judge, explain how you've cooperated and you only get a suspended sentence. Two years, max.'

A suspended sentence – it offered a guarantee against the one thing I dreaded the most, a return to jail. The fear of prison was such that I took Riley's suggestion seriously, as he knew I would. It wasn't that I accepted any measure of guilt. I could never do that. The fear was, could I *prove* my innocence against the prejudice of a judge and jury?

'But what if it went wrong?' I asked. 'Suppose the judge didn't play ball?'

'They always do. It's routine, Chris. Just trust me.'

After I'd dropped Riley at the station I called Kevin.

'Forget it, Chris. Don't even think about it.'

'But he guaranteed a suspended sentence. Wouldn't it be better to take the uncertainty out of it. At least I'd know I wasn't going to jail.'

I could hear Kevin's sigh.

'The prisons are full of those who assisted the police, Chris. As they lead you away Riley will shrug his shoulder and tell you he did his best. So forget it, will you?'

I forgot it.

29

Two days later Riley was on the phone again wanting my answer to his proposal.

I wasn't going to put my head inside Riley's noose. But Kevin and I had decided to keep him guessing. I said,

'It's early days yet. Kevin Robinson says I can't commit myself to anything of the kind at the moment.'

There was a momentary pause as he pondered whether to try further persuasion. Instead he said,

'Well look, can you help us on another matter? It's about Anwar Saadi.'

'What about him?'

'Can you tell us everything you know about him?'

So I told him about the multi-talented Iraqi who had charge of his Government's special industrial projects.

A weekend passed, and the Customs were back on the telephone, this time in the person of Ray Gaubert.

'These tubes, Mr Cowley. Their internal bore dimensions are all slightly different, aren't they? Now why was that?'

This was becoming a Helpline service.

'We're quite clear we've got a gun but the thing is, we're not sure if we've got *one* gun or several.'

I said I could see his difficulty. One would normally assume a gun to have a uniform bore but, in this as in so many other ways, Project Babylon was different. With Forgemasters still adamant they had supplied pipes for the petro-chemical industry, Customs' inability to assemble the tubes into a gun had become increasingly embarrassing for them. It was a jigsaw that refused to fit together.

The explanation for the differences in bore between the tubes was our need to minimise barrel-erosion. With each firing of the gun the ultra-high temperature gases from the propellant, combined with friction, would eat into the internal surface of the barrel. Computer modelling had indicated that – with temperatures inside the chamber reaching 2,800 degrees Celsius – the bore diameter immediately forward of the propellant charge would increase by 3 millimetres per shot. If the problem was not resolved, the Supergun's operational life could be measured in just a handful of firings.

Our solution was the fitting of a replaceable lining inside each of the high-pressure sections of the barrel. These tubular linings would be made out out of a suitable nickel- or cobalt-based heat-resisting material. In order to accept them, and in varying thick-nesses, the steel tubes had been machined to slightly differing bores, depending on their proximity to the chamber area.

All this I told Gaubert, and he hung up, satisfied.

A few minutes later, Riley rang me again.

'I just wanted to ask if you'd reconsider giving evidence for the prosecution. It really would be in your own interest, you know.'

He was implying that he would have me anyway, so I might as well turn Queen's Evidence. Saying once again a firm no, I was emboldened by my horoscope in *The Daily Mail*: 'Other people may imagine that they have you cornered, but how wrong they are!'

Next day, Riley rang yet again.

'Thanks for helping Ray out yesterday. I appreciate it. It's really helped.'

'I suspect my phone's being tapped,' I told him. 'What do you know about it?'

There was a slight pause before Riley responded cautiously with,

'What makes you think it's tapped?'

'There's a lot of interference on the line. Can't you tell? The reception's terrible.'

'I agree, it isn't very good. Well if anyone *is* tapping you, it's not the Customs. I'll have a word about the problem, though. I'm not saying it *is* tapped, but still—'

'Improve the reception, at least. And if whoever-it-is wants to know anything about Supergun, tell him to come and ask me.'

'OK, Chris, I hear what you're saying.'

I was already beginning to track down documents and contacts which would help to find out more about the Iraqi Government's later orders with Walter Somers and Forgemasters – the 350-mm tubes which Customs had shown me, as well as the breech slide on Ashwell's lorry. I was also trying to establish as much background

Saddam Hussein

Paul Ashwell, after his arrest in Patras, Greece, in April 1990

April 1990: Greek police officers inspect one of the steel tubes believed to be part of the Iraqi Supergun

Sir John Cuckney

Above: Gerald Bull (left), in1965, at a test-site in Quebec for a 21-metre projectile gun

André Cools, former Deputy Prime Minister of Belgium, murdered in Brussels in July 1991

Sir Hal Miller, MP, outside Buckingham Palace after being honoured
with a knighthood

Iraqi Airways jet departing from Manchester Airport with sections
of the 350mm horizontal gun aboard

One of the steel tubes forged in Sheffield. These tubes were to have been transported to Iraq for the building of the Supergun

Two of the finished tubes in Sheffield, prior to shipment. The size of the tubes (5.5 metres long, 32 tons in weight) can be gauged from the relative size of the engineer joining them together

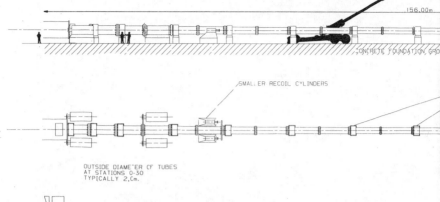

156.00m

CONCRETE FOUNDATION, GROU

SMALLER RECOIL CYLINDERS

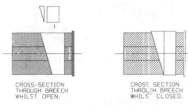

OUTSIDE DIAMETER OF TUBES
AT STATIONS 0-30
TYPICALLY 2.0m.

CROSS-SECTION
THROUGH BREECH
WHILST OPEN.

CROSS SECTION
THROUGH BREECH
WHILST CLOSED.

Above: Design drawing

Below: An artist's impression of a 600mm gun,
showing its scale

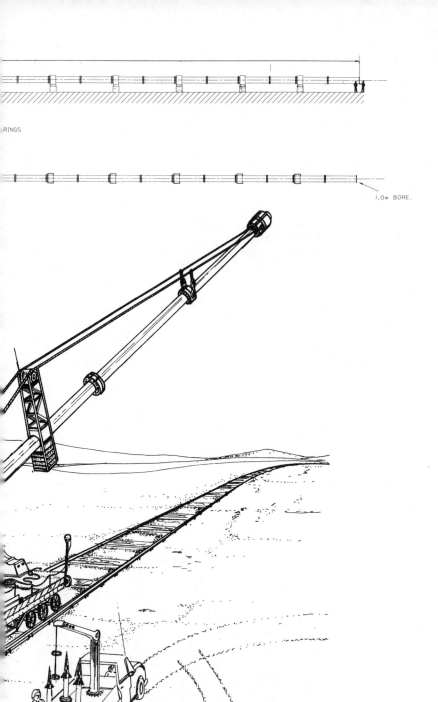

RINGS

1,0m BORE.

Left: One of the so-called 'Paris Guns', showing how the brace-system allows elevation of a large gun

Below: A test-firing in Barbados of Gerald Bull's HARP gun

as I could – in particular, about the scale of government assistance to British traders in Iraq since 1988. I hoped this might eventually lead me towards proof of the British Government's prior knowledge of Supergun.

C.B.S. Television had sent a producer, Claudia Rader, to research the death of Bull, and she had approached me for an interview. At this point, I was negotiating with her in the hope that C.B.S. might prove a conduit for U.S. documents, available to American citizens (but not to me) through the Freedom of Information Act.

One one recent occasion, during a phone call to Monique Jamine, Bull's former assistant in Brussels, the suspicion of a phone tap blossomed into near certainty. As we talked there had been a sudden and noticeable change to the background hiss on the line and a voice had said,

'This line is tapped.'

That was it. The line returned immediately to normal. The message, whoever it came from, was delivered calmly and succinctly, as someone might say 'This car is black' or 'this bread is fresh'. I wondered who it might be, imagining perhaps some left-wing British Telecom worker, carrying out a small act of subversion.

A phone tap would, of course, give an excellent idea of my contacts – whether in Britain, Brussels or the United States. But it was a situation that concerned me less and less. In fact, I realised, I could use it to my advantage, I could use it to leave 'whoever-it-was' in no doubt that I was telling the world what I was doing. I therefore started to speak over the telephone in a deliberately garrulous fashion, sharing my knowledge with anybody who would listen. It seemed, after all, better to be loudly repetitive than quietly assassinated.

At the same time I was creating multiple copies of the documents in my possession, and distributing them to various safe locations. I created one document which I regarded as very important. This was a memorandum of a conversation I had had one night in late 1988 with an Englishman I met over dinner in the Al-Rasheed hotel.

First it is necessary to recall how the atmosphere inside Iraq had completely changed by this stage. Months earlier, in August, I had been awoken in the dark by a rapid series of popping noises, sharply penetrating the hotel's double-glazing. Coming drowsily awake I lay for a few moments and listened. It sounded like gunfire.

I got up and pulled back the drapes on a truly extraordinary spectacle. My view embraced the rooftops of the blacked-out city, a city where each tall building had its emplaced anti-aircraft unit. Now I could see that in every one of these the guns was firing, continuously and hysterically into the wide night sky. This sky was not dark, it was alight with tracer bullets, streaking arcs of fire at every angle as far as the horizon. I looked down. People milled everywhere, packing the streets. Most of them seemed to be brandishing AK47 automatic weapons, and discharging them upwards, shouting and screaming. Bullets were ripping vertically upwards past my head.

Pulling sharply back, I scanned for signs of an air-raid – burning buildings, explosions. There were none. Yet the gun crew on the nearest rooftop, which I could see quite clearly, were working frantically to throw shells into the sky with all the ferocity at their weapon's command.

I picked up my phone and called the desk.

'What's going on out there?'

The desk clerk was laughing. I thought he was intoxicated, and I was right. But it was not with alcohol.

'Oh yes, sir, come down. Come and shoot a gun.'

'Come and do what?'

'The war, sir! The war is over.'

For more than an hour I sat at my window and watched how Iraqis traditionally celebrate a ceasefire. Every single weapon in Baghdad had been converted at a stroke from an instrument of death into the means for joyful, and utterly uncontrolled, celebration. Millions of rounds were being expended, and the shooting continued without interruption until ammunition and people were exhausted. That took about two days.

The evening covered by my memorandum was one when things had returned to something like normal. The capital was still blinking in this new light, like a long-term prisoner suddenly released. The people had difficulty believing that their eight-year war was over, they were free of the war at last. They could not, however, have denied one piece of compelling evidence of change: the sudden increase in foreign commercial interest in their country. Tonight I was dining with a man who had flown to Iraq in the confident expectation that – now hostilities were ended – the now-legitimised Baghdad arms bazaar would boom with even greater energy. I had seen him in the hotel several months previously in the company of Gerald Bull.

He now introduced himself to me as working for one of the London clearing banks.

'Oh? Which one?'

'Midland.'

'So what brings you down here?'

'Trade. Setting up deals, financial packages, loans, that sort of thing. I'm actually talking about a loan worth something like a quarter of a billion dollars.'

He beamed at me, full of satisfaction at the prospect.

'That seems strange,' I said, 'coming from a banker.'

During negotiations with our steelmakers, I had become very well aware of Iraq's poor credit-rating. The companies were so suspicious they would only proceed on the basis of cash-in-the-bank or irrevocable letters of credit.

'How,' I asked, 'can a major bank possibly do business with a country that reneges on its debts as much as Iraq does? Won't you eventually go bankrupt, piling up bad debts on top of bad debts?'

'Oh no,' he said airily. 'We do everything possible to finance business between this country and the U.K.'

'That sounds almost masochistic.'

'Not in the least.'

He leaned forward, frowning in concentration, an enthusiast for his subject.

'You see, before we advance monies to a company, we always insist on any funds being covered by the H.M. Government's Export Credit Guarantee Department.'

'I see. So the British taxpayer is underwriting the risk?'

'Yes. That's how E.C.G. works. We can't lose. After ninety days, if the Iraqis haven't coughed up, the company gets paid instead by the British Government. Either way we recover our loan, plus interest of course. It's beautiful.'

'What sort of contract is this one, then?'

'Arms. That's my speciality. I work for the Midland Bank International Trade Services, M.I.T.S. for short. You must have heard of us?'

I shook my head. The man was being remarkably candid.

'We do mostly arms, though other things as well. Suppose Dr Bull had a client who needed funding, we could arrange it – always providing we had the necessary approval.'

'Who gives the approval?' I enquired, innocently.

'We apply through our Government connections.'

'You mean International Military Services, M.O.D.?'

'Yes. But also J.I.C.'

'What's that?'

'Joint Intelligence Committee, Cabinet Office. We have a good contact on that. Previously worked for the Midland as well as I.M.S. Actually we've just completed a deal with Malaya. Worth £1 billion, that was, just to give you an idea of what we're talking about. Maggie signed the contract herself, though M.I.T.S. put it together working with the M.O.D.'

'Sounds like a close relationship,' I said, but was thinking, or the old-boy network.

'We're pretty hush-hush. Lord Armstrong, an ex-M.I.5 man, set us up originally. Many people even in the Bank don't know about us, and that includes senior executives.'

'What about the shareholders?'

He seemed not to hear this.

'It's very much in line with Government policy. The Prime Minister feels we must do more to link the British defence industry to arms sales around the world, and especially to this region.'

'Isn't it a problem, having to work through the approval of politicians and bureaucrats? That's what I like about our company. Bull hates officialdom.'

'No, no, I can assure you we operate in a completely different environment. Our people have military or intelligence backgrounds, and if we need to talk to the Government, we go right to the top. Maggie hates bureaucrats too, you know. Given the chance she just steam rolls over them. And besides they do what they have to – they all want to keep their jobs.'

A little later, a vaguely familiar name came up.

'Do you know Wafic Said?' the banker asked.

'Heard of him, never met him though. Bull mentioned his name a couple of times. Saudi, isn't he. Originally Syrian?'

'Right. A very important Saudi. He looks after the King's business interests. Furthermore, he's a friend of young Mark Thatcher.'

'Well, I can see that would be useful,' I remarked.

'That's where I'm going next, Saudi Arabia. Thankfully only a few days. It's a hell-hole.'

I began to tell him about S.R.C.'s recent development work in Saudi, test-firing Bull's 155-mm gun in the hope of selling it to their army. He seemed very interested in this, eager to get

M.I.T.S. into the deal somehow. I supplied him with the number of S.R.C.'s Brussels office and he left me, saying he'd probably be getting in touch with Bull directly.

The conversation was to have its own repercussions for me later on. For now, it just served to illustrate once again the position the U.K. had got itself into *vis-à-vis* Iraq. Like an incautious bank we'd permitted Baghdad to run up an overdraft with us of £750 million, through our over-generous Export Credit Guarantee system. This had, in effect, turned the U.K. into a large *de facto* investor in Iraq's ruling Ba'athist party. So even when the commercial banks – in Britain and elsewhere – had found Saddam's regime a mite too untrustworthy, Whitehall went on recklessly pouring money in. After eight years of war, the Iraqi exchequer was virtually bankrupt, and the pile of unpaid-for goods was a mountain. Some officials in Thatcher's Government had the queasy feeling that we were getting in too deep. One day we might find our foreign policy constrained by the need to recover the money which Saddam owed to us. Others, of course, remained bullish. We were selling British excellence on the open market: what could possibly be wrong with that?

30

Peace in Iraq eased our own task somewhat. The tubes from Walter Somers for the test-model had arrived shortly after Christmas, as had the breech block from the Swiss company Von Roll. Then it was necessary to do a trial assembly over a period of several weeks, on four tank-carrying bogeys at the Iraqi Railway Workshops in Baghdad. This was one of the few places equipped with the necessary heavy lifting gear. In theory, the A.T.I. staff were then in a supervisory capacity. In reality, just to meet our planned firing date, we did much of the heavy work ourselves while several of our Iraqi colleagues stood at a distance and watched, disdaining to get their hands dirty.

I remember in particular Faris Major, as we called him, one of the better-qualified engineers at our disposal. Generally he was to be found standing for most of the day, staring into space. Someone, or thing, must have been looking after him though. On one occasion he moved fractionally from a position he'd previously occupied for several hours. Seconds later, our overhead crane accidentally dropped a 500-kg piece of steel from a height of about five metres onto his previous location.

We were now anxious to get the gun dismantled and moved up country for re-assembly at the test-firing site as soon as possible. We had already decided on the place, although it had not been easy to find. What was required, after all, was a firing range about 900 kilometres long.

I had explained to Azzawi that H.A.R.P. had solved the problem in the past by siting its long-range testing facilities on Barbados, beside the Atlantic Ocean.

'Iraq's ocean is the desert,' he had remarked. The trouble was that the desert wasn't extensive enough for Supergun, and it became clear we would need permission for projectiles to be shot into Saudi territory. This, remember, was only two years before Desert Storm broke. Yet at this point, Iraqi relations with Saudi Arabia were such that permission to fire Supergun test projectiles into the vast and empty Nafud Desert was given within a few days.

The test site for 'Baby Babylon' was determined by the needs of the full-scale 1,000-mm system. These were for a slope, somewhere in the north of Iraq, to which the gun could be fixed, at an angle of approximately 45 degrees and aiming south. The only suitable area was in the hills to the north and west of the town of Mosul, up in Kurdish territory, and it was here that we eventually located a suitable site. The place was called Tal Uwaynat.

After a laboured journey north we all arrived on the site, five tank-transporters for Baby Babylon, together with the A.T.I. team including Azzawi. On this site, if all went well, the 350-mm test model would be assembled in its horizontal position on 200 metres of railway track. Alongside it the horizontal 1,000-mm system would be placed for purposes of full-scale testing. On a stony slope nearby, pointing up at the sky above the southern horizon, would be fixed the operational 1,000-mm system – the Supergun itself.

The site was more than 500 kilometres from the industrial workshops of Baghdad, on which we had so far relied for the machining or manufacture of small components. Initially we took comfort in the fact that the magnificent Saad-16 missile research base was nearby, equipped as it was with incomparable workshops and all the most modern machine tools, many of them British. Unfortunately the magnificence of Saad-16 proved delusory. Simple re-machining tasks proved to be beyond them and eventually we were forced to look for an alternative. This we found, in the shape of a privately-owned machine shop, ina run-down area of Mosul which had some of the oldest, worn-out machinery I have ever seen. Nevertheless the elderly owner managed to do all the work we brought him, and to a standard far higher than anything available from Saad-16. For me, that contrast sums up all the best and the worst of Middle-Eastern industrial life.

While assembly proceeded at Tal Uwaynat, Saad-16 was at least managing to make the test slugs for us. These resembled squat, thick-walled, open-ended aluminium cans. They were not intended to fly very far down the range, for their only purpose was to test the barrel's integrity, and the effectiveness of the charge propellant. And now a first consignment of this propellant had arrived from the chemical plant at Al-Qaqa – the place that later proved the nemesis of Farzad Bazoft. At last we were ready for the first firing.

141

We began the loading of the first slug. It stuck half way up the chamber. For hours we struggled to withdraw it, until it became obvious somebody would have to be persuaded to go up the barrel in order to fasten a rope to the base of the slug. A Filipino worker seemed to have the right bodily proportions and he accepted a bribe of ten Dinar to do the job. Quickly, before he had time to change his mind, he was thrust into the breech with a line tied around his feet. He did change his mind, however, just a small way in. He begged us to pull him out because, he said, he was frightened. Gradually the bribe was increased until it stood at 50 Dinar, a sufficient sum to overcome the Filipino's claustrophobia. He struggled on, fixed the rope and was pulled out followed by the recalcitrant slug.

A new test slug with its propellant charge was inserted into the gun, and the 350-mm system was made ready for its first firing. We had cleared the area and were just about to drop the wedge into place and close the breech. Bruce Smith, another ex-H.A.R.P./ S.R.C. employee (and now on loan to us from Belcan, a subsidiary of Poudreries Réunies de Belgique) was the gun captain. It would be his responsibility to make the final checks and give the order to fire.

I sat astride the breech block, three metres off the ground. Smith was facing me, straddling the barrel. Underneath us was over one ton of propellant charge. Protruding from the breech was a thick bundle of electrical wires, and Smith was completing the final connection. It was through these wires that the 24 volts required to fire the propellant would soon be passed.

It was time to proceed very cautiously. Had the gun gone off inadvertently, we would both have been killed instantly. To avoid accidental firing through the build up of static, we had carefully earthed every part of the propellant and gun. We'd checked with voltmeters that there was no energy running through the circuits which connected the charges to the command bunker some 500 metres away.

Smith's head was bent over one of the last electrical connections when I smelled the unmistakeable aroma of Turkish tobacco. At the same moment, Smith looked up and pointed over my shoulder. A tribesman in his djellaba, cigarette dangling insecurely from his lips, had heaved himself onto the breech block and was craning round me, trying to see what was going on.

We persuaded this fellow to retire to a discreet distance. Then everybody, apart from Azzawi and myself, was sent to the underground bunker which stood to the east of the firing zone. Here the instrumentation which monitored the tests was located. Azzawi and I walked to a vantage point about 250 metres distant from the gun. He held in his hand a portable radio. He looked at me.

'O.K. Chris?'

'O.K.'

He gave the order, in Arabic, over the radio.

'Fire.'

I had seen guns fired before, but never anything like this. Flame belched from the muzzle, and the 52-metre barrel began to trundle backwards along the railway track. We looked down the range. There were several spurts of sand to show where the slug was bouncing off the desert floor before coming to rest. Suddenly Azzawi turned to me with a cry of triumph and a wide smile. He held out his hand. In his grip I could feel the measure of relief he felt. The gun had fired and we were on our way.

31

Only eight months before we test-fired what was probably the largest gun in the world, detailed mechanical drawings or specifications of it did not even exist. We had completed the design, commissioned the manufacture of components, solved unexpected problems as they arose and, from scratch, had built a ballistics test-bed in the bare desert, all at a total cost (for the 'Baby Babylon' system) of around £1 million. Congratulations and celebrations, we felt, were in order.

Bull, for his insistence on a lean design team, for his determination to avoid bureaucratic interference, for his daring solutions and sheer infectious confidence, must take a great deal of the credit. I am convinced that a corporate defence contractor in a developed country could not have done what we did.

If that seems like an exaggerated championship of 'the little guy', it would be good to remember the SP70, the abortive 155-mm self-propelled gun which the British tried to develop over eight years with Germany and Italy, and which I'd mentioned to Mike Napier at the Irwin Mitchell 'safe house'.

There is a perfectly good reason why Bull's designs were so comparatively low in cost. He insisted that they should be. He considered that large defence contractors thrive only in conditions of near-monopoly where they can foster the myth that, compared with all other industries, defence work is intrinsically expensive. This myth enables them to operate on a cost-plus basis, which fundamentally means that they can rig the market, write their own cheques and have them signed by the governments for whom they work.

Bull had fallen foul of this before – for example, over his highly original extended-range, full-bore artillery shell. Bull's design, produced at the same time as his GC45 gun, was a low-cost solution to the problem of how to stretch a gun's range. Because of its obvious effectiveness he had hoped for large N.A.T.O. orders, but Bull soon found himself struggling in competition with the

144

'official' U.S. arms industry, which had itself been developing an extended-range shell. The new American ammunition, it turned out, was neither worse nor better in performance than Bull's. The primary difference was that the American system was rocket-assisted and its development and unit costs were thousands of times greater than Bull's. N.A.T.O. procurement, however, favoured the big contractors and they duly ordered the American rocket-shells.

So, suppose Babylon had been the project of a British corporate outfit – say, the British Aerospace subsidiary Royal Ordnance. How much expenditure, in money and time, would have carried it as far as the test-firing of a model such as 'Baby Babylon'? I would suggest eight years instead of eight months, and probably a hundred times more than the actual cost to the Iraqi exchequer of our own 350-mm test model.

Not everything had proceeded smoothly with the design of the 1,000-mm full-scale Supergun, but at this stage I was pleased about a number of things. Initially, much of our effort had been concentrated on the barrel assembly. Now, at last, the barrel design was fixed and other aspects of the gun were being worked out around it. One thing in particular told me we were on the right track.

The initial design drawings, done in Brussels, had shown ugly lumps of metal protruding along the length of the barrel, like the legs of some giant centipede. In the original design these legs were planted on slide-bearings which allowed the barrel assembly to recoil backwards. I had never liked this arrangement. It is not widely recognised that there is a strong aesthetic element in mechanical engineering: an ugly or ungainly solution is never a good one, and the Brussels design was ugly. I was determined to change it.

I was convinced, too, that the proposed design would not function. Brussels seemed unable to appreciate the energy generated by 1,500 tonnes of metal recoiling at 8 metres per second. The loads are so enormous that they would cause the barrel not only to move backwards, but to twist and lift violently like a 1,500-ton steel whip being cracked. Only cylindrical bearings fastened around each alternative tube section would contain forces of these magnitudes. So, despite howls of dismay from Brussels, those ugly centipede legs disappeared. I was delighted. The new concept looked right. Now the final design iterations of Supergun could be drawn with near certainty.

The design of these new recoil cylinders was well advanced, as was the steel support-structure and deep concrete foundations into which the recoil load would be dumped. Many hundreds of design drawings were still required, but I felt growing confidence that the major design difficulties had been resolved.

During the mechanical design stages of Supergun, Tony Slack, an aerodynamicist, was with us in Baghdad working out designs for a whole range of projectiles. Using computer modelling in conjunction with Bull's earlier H.A.R.P. work, Tony studied projectile behaviour at the hypersonic speeds applicable to Supergun, i.e. Mach 5. But at three metres per second, the behaviour of a projectile is not easy to look at and, when the computer had taken Tony as far as he could go, Bull used his Chinese connections to secure the use of the hypersonic wind-tunnel facilities at Beijing's Institute of Technology.

One of Tony's objects was to establish the most appropriate type of fin control, or guide, to the projectile. The projectile's ability to change course, even slightly, was crucial to the effectiveness of the launcher, since fairly precise orientation is needed to achieve orbit. However, it was not Tony Slack's work in this area that was causing me concern, but the design of the inboard electronics, and the external tracking system, both of which would be needed in order to guide the projectile from the ground. Delays in this area were causing concern from the end of 1988 right up to the time I left A.T.I.

Almost daily, throughout June 1990, Barry Riley was on the phone to me. He wanted information about the A.T.I. personnel; he wanted to fix a meeting in Birmingham between me and his boss, Nesbitt; he wanted more and more technical information.

'What can you tell me about a "T" fitting at the muzzle end of the 1,000-mm barrel?'

Usually I was able to give him information to order, but this time it took me a minute or two to realise what he must be referring to. At one time, very early on, consideration had been given to the fitting of a 'muzzle-brake' on Supergun. This is a fairly standard device fitted to the muzzles of artillery and tank guns in order to reduce recoil loads. After some thought, the idea was given up, as its benefits would have been negligible. But in the meantime – at one of our meetings – I had asked Forgemasters about the possibility of fitting the end tube with a special flange to

146

which such a device (of which I did not give details) might be fitted.

This flange might actually have been used in connection with another bright idea which came to nothing. Initial studies had suggested that the range of Supergun could be extended if the projectiles were fired from within a barrel at extremely low pressure or – even better – a vacuum. This would have entailed fitting a membrane of some kind over the muzzle, and for this a flange would have been necessary. In the event, I decided that the thing was unworkable. There seemed no way to allow the projectile to pierce the muzzle membrane without damaging, or even destroying, itself.

Anyway, the idea of a special T-shaped flange on the end of the last 1,000-mm tube in the assembly had been mooted once with Forgemasters, and then dropped. Riley's 'T' piece must have been recovered from a minute of that meeting. Clearly, he was now in possession of much relevant Forgemaster's paperwork.

32

My son's friend unscrewed the cover of the phone. Once the inner workings were exposed he placed an instrument on the table beside it which looked like a pocket calculator, though with dial-and-needle rather than a digital display. Two delicate wires, one red, one black, and with small crocodile clips at their ends, were attached to this instrument. Delicately he placed the clips on terminals within the telephone. We all saw the needle jump into position on the dial.

'It's a potentiometer,' he explained, 'a very sensitive voltmeter. Phones use a small amount of electricity, just 28 volts. In the moment when your line is connected to another phone, there's a slight voltage-drop, O.K.? It's just momentary. The voltage dips and then rises to the normal level again.'

We all stood around like an audience, me and my family. The young electronics buff went on.

'Right, so suppose there is a phone tap. The line will connect first with the person calling you and, almost immediately after that, with a second terminal – the tapper – and that second connection gives a second voltage drop. So the voltmeter tells the tale: one voltage drop, you've got a normal call: *two* voltage drops, you've got someone listening in. And that's how to tell if your phone's tapped.'

We all nodded. Without replacing the telephone cover, our friend balanced the receiver on top of its cradle.

'So, if someone would go down to a public call-box and dial this number, we can check it out.'

Ian, my son, left the house and walked to a payphone a few hundred yards away. We waited. I felt curiously excited, like a fisherman expecting a bite.

The telephone rang. I hesitated, allowing two rings, then picked up the reciever. Immediately I noticed the voltmeter needle flick down and back through the arc of calibration.

'Hello?' I said.

And there! There it was: another twitch of the needle, as quick as the first. I hung up, and waited. I'd instructed Ian to repeat the exercise several times, but to say nothing.

We waited. The phone rang again and I picked up, watching the dial. It was unmistakeable. The needle flicked once, and then, perhaps a second later, it flicked again as the second, unknown listener clocked on.

It was a sobering moment. We stood still, absorbing the fact. Then someone said.

'Right. We're tapped. What about the mail?'

I created a series of three-page documents relating to Supergun and placed them in manilla envelopes, whose flaps I sealed. I addressed them to myself, stuck first-class stamps in the corner, and then placed them inside a second envelope which I addressed to various friends in different parts of the country. In a covering note I requested each friend to mail the enclosed item straight back to me.

In each of these mailings I had inverted the second page of the Supergun document before folding it and placing it in its envelope.

The first two envelopes came homing back 24 hours later. In one case I found nothing amiss, but when I withdrew the second and unfolded it, I saw that the second page was now the correct way up.

On the next day the balance of the envelopes arrived. Some of the documents came out as I had put them in. In others the document had been taken out, read or copied, and put back with page two the right way up. One of the envelopes contained even more striking evidence. Inside it I actually found, not the original document, but, by some clerical error, a photocopy.

Bull, had he been there, would have been intensely interested in this. He was fascinated by the intelligence world, as I was to become aware after my conversation in Baghdad with the M.I.T.S. man. My memorandum of the meeting has appended to it an account of a conversation I had with Bull at his Brussels office a few weeks later.

'Yes, M.I.T.S. has been in touch. I'm seeing a guy called de Carmoy from S.G.B. I know him. He's a Belgian, used to be with Midland – he was Chief Executive, actually.'

S.G.B. was very big potatoes. The initials stood for Société Générale de Belgique, which, with more than 1,000 subsidiaries, was the largest company in Belgium and wielder of extraordinary influence over every aspect of that country's life. This is quite apart from its enormous stake in the economy of a former Belgian colony, Zaire. Bull had been connected years earlier with one of S.G.B.'s subsidiaries, Poudréries Réunies de Belgique, an explosives company with which he had worked on his extended-range, full-bore ammunition in the 1970s. In 1988, P.R.B. had been contracted to supply the propellant for Supergun, a deal negotiated by Azzawi.

'When you met this guy in Baghdad, you didn't mention the Babylon propellant contract to him, did you?'

'No, never said a word about it. I didn't know of any connection between Midland Bank and S.G.B., so I had no reason to. I talked about the Saudi 155 gun, which he seemed keen to get in on. But M.I.T.S. knew quite a bit about us already, it seemed to me.'

'Well somebody must have told them about Babylon, because de Carmoy knows all about it. I just can't decide if it came from his contacts in P.R.B. or his friends in Joint Intelligence Command.'

He paused and then asked.

'Was Sir John Cuckney mentioned in your conversation?'

'Only in passing. Who is he?'

'He's Chairman of 3i, the industrial group. Big man in British industry. Was Chairman of Westland, and of I.M.S. for 11 years. And he was a Director of the Midland Bank at the same time. He was also high up in the Crown Agents – you know, supplies to Third-World countries.'

Bull got up and strolled over to his bookshelf, crammed with technical reports and print-outs as well as books. He hooked the spine of a thick hardback, pulled it out and threw it on the desk in front of me. It was *Spycatcher*, the memoirs of the ex-M.I.5 man Peter Wright.

'Cuckney gets a mention in that.'

Given Bull's interest in intelligence matters, I wasn't a bit surprised to find he had *Spycatcher*, a book so 'explosive' that the British Government spent millions of pounds on legal expenses trying unsuccessfully to have it injuncted.

Yes, there was an element here of boyish delight in cloaks and daggers. But Bull also had a serious reason for keeping tabs – as best he could – on what the various intelligence networks knew about him. In 1975, through a retired Brussels-based U.S. Air Force Colonel called Jack Frost, the C.I.A. had put Bull in touch with the South African defence industry, Armscor. The C.I.A., as usual, was working to its own policies in preference to those of Washington. It was worried about the pounding South Africa and her allies – the 'democratic' Angolan forces – had been taking from the Cubans with their 122-mm Soviet rockets, and wanted Armscor to have Bull's extended-range shells. The result was that Bull went ahead and dealt with Pretoria, on the understanding that he was in accord with 'real' American policy in southern Africa. By the time Carter came to office, and cracked down on covert C.I.A. support for South Africa, it was too late for Bull to extricate himself.

In 1978 the British overseas intelligence service, M.I.6, played a vital part in tracking the route taken by Bull's embargo-busting shells. It was not until 1982, however, after he had served his prison sentence, that Bull learned how even the C.I.A. itself had betrayed him. Jack Frost, their Brussels agent, had been a shareholder in S.R.C.'s Belgian subsidiary, and was officially controlled by C.I.A. Headquarters in Langley, Virginia of everything Bull was doing in Europe. Frost, it turned out at a Congressional hearing on U.S.-African relations, had also informed the Office of Munitions Control about S.R.C.'s South African deal – the same office, incidentally, visited by Michel Bull and Luis Palacio when they travelled to the United States in 1988, to inform them about Project Babylon.

Bull therefore had learned from experience that the intelligence services are not to be trusted, and that it is advisable to try and stay one step ahead of them. During my time with him, Bull claimed one very powerful government contact which he may have found useful in this regard. His name is George Wong, a Westernised Chinese businessman based in London, whom Bull had met in 1978. Wong has extensive and varied Far-Eastern business interests and, in the course of time, the two men had become very close friends. Even as late as February 1990, Bull had travelled to China with Wong.

George Wong was of considerable importance to Bull in his dealings with the Chinese Government. Officially George attended Bull's meetings with the Chinese Minister of Defence as Bull's translator. However, it soon became apparent to me, as I listened to their conversations, that his role extended far beyond translating and explaining the idioms of the Chinese language.

But Wong is not an ordinary international businessman. Through his extensive contacts he was surely in the ideal position

151

to keep Bull informed of various British attitudes towards Project Babylon.

33

One fact, however, was miserably apparent. All his attempts to keep tabs on the intelligence services, and perhaps even to second-guess them, had not saved his life. I was haunted by the murder of Bull, and its connection (or otherwise) with the sudden, last-minute impounding of the Supergun tubes. I was also desperate to know more about the breech-slide mechanism carried by Paul Ashwell's lorry, and about the drawings which Riley had shown me for a tapering 350-mm gun barrel made by Walter Somers. A visit to Brussels, I hoped, would make some of these matters much clearer.

On the way to Sheffield, where I was to apply to have my passport returned, I stopped off in Birmingham for my meeting with Nesbitt, Riley's boss. It was, in part, a replay of my first interrogation in Sheffield Police Station, although of course this was an unofficial, unattributable and entirely deniable meeting. In particular, Nesbitt was extremely puzzled as to how I knew that Forgemasters were aware of the true purpose of the tubes. Hadn't we presented them throughout as components of a petro-chemical plant?

I told again about the time a representative had heard Mike Bayne use the phrase 'the breech end' at a meeting and had told us not to use the phrase in his presence.

'I don't expect the remark was minuted though, do you?'

Nesbitt looked grave.

'Were there any other occasions, in spite of what you were told?'

'Yes there were. I remember another occasion, also at Forge-masters.'

Nesbitt looked up from his notepad.

'Yes? We're *just* as interested in them, as you know.'

'Well, we had Tony Slack and his colleague and girlfriend, Caroline Henry, over from Brussels. One of the people asked them what they did in S.R.C. and they said, "Oh, we're aerodynamicists." '

Nesbitt sucked his pencil.

'I see. A profession not normally associated with oil pipes.'

'Not unless these were flying oil pipes.'

'Exactly. So I still don't understand what these two aerodynamicists were doing at the steelworks.'

I took a deep breath. How many more times would I have to cover this ground?

'We wanted them to see the forgings, the size of them. We wanted all our people to understand the scale on which we were working. No one really appreciated that. They kept thinking they were working on some scaled-up field gun while this was something completely new and different, and *that*'s what I wanted them to grasp.'

I could see Nesbitt's eyes, and they were vacant. He hadn't *really* grasped it, either.

The court returned my passport in return for only five thousand pounds surety, a bargain rate which, I was given tacitly to understand, was due to my 'special relationship' with the Customs. Thank you, Barry.

Within a few days Barry Riley had done me another favour. He contacted on my behalf a Belgian policeman called Patrick Renoir, the man in charge of the anti-terrorist department. Renoir telephoned me to say he thought a meeting between us might be very beneficial and proposed to meet my flight at Brussels Airport. I gave him the flight number and arrival time.

The Sabena flight took off an hour late, bringing back unfond memories. It was still the worst airline in Europe. However, at last I stood on the arrivals concourse in the Brussels terminal, trying to look conspicuous and expectant. But no one approached me to enquire if I was Monsieur Cowley. After a while I went to the enquiries desk and asked if a policeman called Renoir had left a message. No, sir. No message from a Monsieur Renoir. I decided to give him a little longer, left my name at the desk and went for a coffee.

An hour later I telephoned his office.

'Monsieur Renoir is very busy today, sir. Would you mind making your way here?'

Oh, I don't mind at all. I had just flown hundreds of kilometres at my own expense to see this man, so what was a little extra inconvenience? Besides, he had just afforded me a valuable insight into the value *he* placed on our acquaintance. I took a taxi down-town to the Palais de Justice.

The Palais is just that – it's enormous – and Renoir's office, room 238, took some finding. When I did, I was told to wait outside. I looked up and down the narrow corridor. There were no chairs, nowhere to sit. I propped myself up against the wall, watching the traffic to and from the great man's office. Occasionally I sent in a reminder that I was waiting.

After two and a half hours of waiting, I sent in the information that I was leaving. I didn't feel any obligation to leave word as to where I would stay.

I had arranged to have dinner with Monique Jamine, to discuss the affairs of S.R.C. and A.T.I. between my resignation and Bull's death. But I wasn't due at her place for two or three hours. In the interim I visited a lawyer friend, Bernard de Witt, whom I knew to be very well-informed about the ramifications of Supergun in Belgian political and legal life.

'I'm not surprised to hear this about Patrick Renoir, Chris. He's the policeman in charge of the murder enquiry. Forgive me if I laugh. There *is* no enquiry!'

Bernard described an upheaval in the anti-terrorist office, with the suspension of Renoir's boss a few days ago, and some kind of investigation into the conduct of the Ministry of Defence.

'There's a corruption scandal brewing and it's connected with Bull. Several investigative journalists have been threatened, phones have been tapped.'

I laughed and told him about my recent experiences. Bernard shook his head, wondering.

'It sounds as if events in Belgium are unfolding in parallel to those in Great Britain.'

Société Générale de Belgique, the giant conglomerate which had owned Supergun's propellant supplier P.R.B., was a very sensitive and secretive company. Nor did it take unnecessary risks. Bernard told me I should meet Serge Dumont of the respected newspaper *Le Vif/L'Express* who had been following the affairs of S.G.B. and P.R.B. Serge had been investigating, in detail, the Supergun propellants contract, and he was a tough operator.

Bernard telephoned Serge, whose office was nearby, and he joined us. It seemed that following Bull's death the Belgian police had raided the offices of S.R.C. and A.T.I., and had taken away most of the paperwork. They would, in any event, already have had in their possession much of the most crucial documentation because, as I told Serge, Bull always carried these around with him, in a bulging black canvas bag. But now they had the vast bulk of documents and they seemed in no hurry to release them.

But Serge had found out one very important fact.

'The Belgian Government actually approved the supply of propellants, Chris. More than that, the Office Nationale du Ducroire agreed to underwrite any loss – that's the equivalent of your export credit guarantee scheme.'

This information had excited Serge greatly, but it didn't surprise me.

'Well, since the Belgian Air Force transported the stuff—'

'I'm sorry? The Belgian Air Force did what?'

Both Serge and Bernard had reacted to this remark of mine. I looked from one to the other.

'You didn't know? *They* moved the propellant. They flew it in their own Hercules transport planes to Amman in Jordan. It went on, from there to Baghdad, by road.'

Serge and Bernard looked at each other in astonishment.

'This is new information about the Air Force, Chris. This is very important. Can you prove it?'

'There were plenty of other people who knew about it. We had to pay a heavy premium on the price, but it was the only way to get the stuff out there in time.'

'What sort of premium?'

'Oh, it involved a certain amount of *baksheesh*.'

'*Baksheesh* for whom? Belgian officials?'

'For whoever greased the path. We had $25,000 in gold taken to Amman from Baghdad. There were people to pay off in Amman, and in Brussels too, and they all insisted on gold. We also needed the Belgian Government's cooperation in other things. There was an agreement for Iraqi people to come here to P.R.B. from their Al-Qaqa chemical plant. They were to learn how to make propellant charges, because eventually Iraq wanted to be self-sufficient. So all of those guys needed the relevant approvals and residence permits and so on. That's why I wasn't surprised to hear that Brussels guaranteed the payments. They were obviously supporting the Supergun contract all the way.'

It was time for me to keep my appointment with Monique Jamine. As I left the two men were beginning to talk through who might have been in receipt of the bribes and kickbacks. I had given them much to chew on.

On 22 March 1990 it was Monique who had driven Bull home from his office in Rue de Stalle to the nearby Avenue François Folie, dropping him at the door of his luxury apartment block. Seconds after climbing out of her car, and passing through the external door of the block, he was shot dead. Monique now gave me the most detailed account of the killing I had yet heard. There were no witnesses to the event, but it must have happened something like this.

Bull was shot as he inserted a key into the door of his flat, by an assassin who had been hiding around a corner of the corridor. The killer stepped silently up to him and fired five times into the back of his head and neck. Bull was thrown forward and slid down the door to the ground, where he lay in a crumpled, untidy heap. He cannot have known anything about his death.

Only a few minutes later Bull's friend Hélène Grégoire, who had her own key, arrived expecting to go on a date with him. It was she who found Bull. She thought he'd had a heart attack, and in spite of her great distress opened the flat door, stepped over his body, entered and picked up the phone. Monique lived around the corner and Hélène was Monique's friend. She dialled her number. Monique immediately called the cardiac arrest emergency ambulance team and then hurried back to the Avenue François Folie. When she arrived, Bull was still lying beside his own threshold. The ambulance arrived seconds later, the doctor bending over to examine the body. He looked up at the two anxious women.

'This is no heart attack,' he told them. 'There's a lot of blood. I'm afraid he's dead.'

The killing of Gerald Bull was no mere opportunist act. It was a professional hit. Bull's movements from country to country were unpredictable, and to kill him efficiently, his movements must have been tracked over an extended period. But the murderer had not followed Monique and Bull from the S.R.C. office to the apartment block – there would scarcely have been time for him to get ahead of Bull and be waiting for him as he approached his door. The killer was therefore already waiting or getting into position when Bull left his office. He must have been in contact with an accomplice, by cellphone or radio.

Bull's telephone number was ex-directory and his name appeared nowhere in the lobby of the apartment building. The building itself was fitted with a high-security lock at street level, and the apartment had a similar lock. Yet Bull's flat had been entered by unauthorised people on at least two occasions during the year prior to that Thursday evening in March 1990. On one occasion, a video cassette inserted in Bull's V.C.R. had been re-wound, ejected and put back in its box. Even more strangely, a set of tumblers had been removed and replaced with a completely different set. Bull had the impression that he was, in some oblique way, being warned, or frightened, off.

The previous November two men, described by the property company as businessmen from Israel, had rented an apartment on the same floor as Bull's. Six months' rent was paid in advance and a bank bond (against damage to the property) was lodged with the owners of the building. The new tenants were handed a set of keys and the apartment was duly signed over to them. But it never was occupied and it later transpired that false names and fictional banking details had been used. Once the all-important keys had been handed over, the mysterious businessmen never reappeared. In the killers' scheme of things, six months' rent had 'bought' a key to the building.

Monique's eyes filled with tears as she told me how Bull had died with $20,000, in cash, in his pocket. The money was never even touched as the murderer made his unmolested retreat.

In an entirely circumstantial piece of evidence that turned up, a man answering the description of one of the 'businessmen' boarded an El-Al flight out of Brussels within a couple of hours of the murder.

34

Monique and I talked late into the evening and I had had no time to check into a hotel. So she offered me the use of her spare room and I went to bed, full of renewed sadness over the death of my friend.

Just before breakfast the next morning, the telephone rang. It was for me.

'Hello, Monsieur Cowley? It's Patrick Renoir here. I'm very sorry about yesterday – too much business, you know. But can you by chance come here today to talk?'

How the hell did Renoir know where I was? I hadn't told anyone.

'Yes, I can come down. What time?'

'Will 12 o'clock be convenient?'

I said it would.

'Good. I'll be waiting in my office.'

Before leaving Bristol I had also arranged to visit Mike Bayne. Mike was the principal gun designer at S.R.C. Previously he had risen to a senior position in the Royal Armaments Research and Development Establishment, but had become disillusioned after the SP70 fiasco and – like most of us – found Bull's set-up infinitely more congenial.

I thought, once I'd spoken with Mike, I'd be in possession of all the facts of the case, as he was in the best position of all to clear up the mystery of Somers's military gun barrel and the breech-slide mechanism found on Paul Ashwell's lorry. I now used Monique's phone to call him.

When I'd first spoken to Mike from the U.K. he'd been highly enthusiastic about meeting me. He said Martin Hughes and Tony Slack felt the same, and would undoubtedly be coming along too. But this morning, there was a change. Mike sounded cagey, and at once I knew the trouble. He'd thought about the possible consequences of talking to me. He was going to pull out.

'Sorry Chris. It'd be really good to get together. But it turns out

I'm fantastically busy today. I'm just not going to be able to make it. Sorry again.'

As I put the telephone down, a quote from Shakespeare's *Timon of Athens* came to mind: 'I am not of that feather to shake off my friend, when he must need me.'

I now telephoned Amilicar de Costa, an old friend who had worked at the library in S.R.C.

'Hey, Chris! Come and spend the weekend. I got plenty of room.'

'Sorry, I'm due in Amsterdam tonight. I'm going to see Liep Sie.'

'Go tomorrow. I'm having a party tonight. All the guys will be there, Mike, Martin, all the S.R.C. people.'

'That's funny. I've just been speaking to Mike. He didn't mention it.'

'Well he's coming. Why don't you?'

I thought about it for a moment, but then dismissed the idea. A party did not seem like a conducive atmosphere to the kind of conversations I wanted to have. I said good-bye and went through to have breakfast with Monique.

On Saturday it is difficult to gain entry to the Palais de Justice. Eventually I got past a concierge and made my way, via darkened staircases and corridors, to room 238. I knocked at the door.

It was a large office, and Renoir was sitting alone at a desk in its far corner. He was in his early 40s, neatly dressed in a fashionable check jacket. He was smoking a Gauloise cigarette.

'Ah! Monsieur Cowley. Welcome.'

But, as a matter of fact, he spoke brusquely, not making me feel particularly welcome.

'I'm afraid I can't tell you much about the murder of Dr Bull. He was killed with a pistol using soft-nosed bullets. It was a professional killing. We will probably never find who did it.'

We talked inconsequentially for five minutes longer. Then, with a certain finality, he stubbed out his cigarette, rose from his seat and stretched out a hand. I was astonished. He had dragged me across Brussels on a Saturday morning for *this*? From me, Renoir had learned nothing that he didn't already know. For my part, I had gleaned just one fact about Bull's death: the Belgian police were not much interested in it. This was an important and relevant fact, certainly, although it carried me no nearer to my own personal goal. And it begged the question: why? This was not some

160

backstreet mugging. Bull was a well-known man, killed in cold blood in the corridor of a luxury apartment block, and apparently for political reasons. It surely did not reflect credit on the police to leave this event without adequate investigation.

The reason, I suspected, was not unconnected with S.G.B. I remembered my friend Bernard's remark from last night. The smell of some great scandal was in the air, although its substance had been effectively suppressed by means of threats and contrivances.

I knew enough about S.G.B. to put nothing past them. When I'd lived in Brussels, everyone was aware of rumours that this company had been involved in plans by a right-wing terrorist group to destabilise a previous administration. The present Belgian Government, it appeared, was more amenable to the needs of industry, and especially to the dictates of Belgium's world-famous arms manufacturers. Huge quantities of Supergun propellant charge had been flown to Jordan, *en route* for Iraq, by Belgian Air Force Hercules transports. Through whom this was arranged? Was it unusual?

I would have liked to have asked these questions of Renoir, but he was already hustling me out of the room.

In Amsterdam I found Liep Sie and his wife anxious to know about the British end of the Supergun affair, and about my experiences of prison. We repaired to an Indonesian restaurant to talk.

For my part, I particularly wanted to pick Liep's brains about the murder of Gerald Bull. He had a sound knowledge of the world's arms industry, and had worked inside S.R.C. as an engineering consultant for several years. Knowing about Liep's interest in handguns, I asked what he thought could be learned about the gun. Was it a revolver or an automatic?

'An automatic can be efficiently silenced. On the other hand there are problems. If, as Renoir says, they really took the trouble to use soft-nosed bullets, then it was probably a revolver, because they can jam inside an automatic.'

'Why use a soft-nosed bullet?'

'To make the gun untraceable. The soft-nosed bullet mushrooms on impact and then breaks up inside the target, so you can't tell anything from that. A copper-jacketed bullet remains more or less intact, and can be matched to the gun; if it is found. If you use a soft-nosed bullet all you then have is the cartridge. Now, automatics eject their cartridges with considerable energy, and the killer fired five shots. Would he have risked wasting time looking for five cartridges from all over the corridor? Someone might have come. So the only way to be sure you take the cartridges away when you leave the scene is to use a revolver. The disadvantage of using a revolver is that you can't silence it easily as you can an automatic. So, it's pros and cons, isn't it? Mossad hit-men often use revolvers.'

'You think it was the Israelis?'

'Maybe. But I don't think Babylon was the reason.'

'No. Not by itself, I agree with that.'

'If they'd wanted to smash Babylon, they only had to stop the manufacture of certain critical components – the recoil cylinders would do it. Or the propellant.'

'Monique told me Bull was being watched.'

Liep smiled.

'That could have been by a number of agencies, of course. Just the fact that he worked for China would have attracted the attention of several intelligence networks.'

'Yes, but they would have been in favour of that, wouldn't they? Putting pressure on the Soviets and so on. The Chinese deal started long before the massacre of Tiananmen Square.'

'Yes, the Americans approved Bull's original Chinese deals. But did you know that Bull had just been back to China with George Wong, only a couple of weeks before he was killed? Ostensibly they went to look at progress on the manufacture of the 155. But there was more to it. I think Bull's death may have been connected to that visit.'

'Why?'

'Because of the Scuds, you see.'

'You think he was killed because of Scuds?'

'Yes, among other things.'

The Scud missile became famous throughout the world during the build-up to the Gulf War. It acquired a notoriety which now seems out of proportion, given the weapon's ineffectiveness against Israeli cities and the American Patriot missile. However, before Desert Storm, Saddam's Scuds were his only ballistic missiles and, as such, they had to be taken seriously.

The reason Liep made the connection between Iraq and China was that Iraq's Scud-Bs, although Soviet-designed, were a Chinese product which had been sold throughout the Middle East. It was, however, a missile with limited range and Saddam wanted to do something about that. Saadi had asked Bull to help him, and Bull

162

already had useful connections in China.

Bull hadn't worked on missiles – apart from his hybrid Martlet projectiles – since Velvet Glove the air-to-air missile project of the 1950s. But he knew a lot about nose-cone design, and he had access to plenty of scientists who could help with other parts of the programme. In Belgium he'd recruited a physicist to examine the feasibility of producing an extended-range Scud-B missile using Iraq's own resources. This programme would, of course, have been a matter of very real concern to Israel. Their anti-ballistic missile capability is poor, and a longer-range Scud, which could be sited anywhere in the hinterland of Iraq, would be much more difficult to locate and eliminate on the ground. This consideration, coupled with what we now know about the Iraqis' nuclear weapons programme, makes it certain that Bull's Iraqi interests had taken a highly dangerous new turn.

Monique had given me another piece of information which only served to emphasise Bull's vulnerability over the Scud deal. Early in 1989 I had dismissed John Heath from the team for frequently disappearing from Iraq on an unscheduled holiday. Back in Brussels, and with typical generosity, Bull had rehired Heath and put him to work on the Al-Fao, the new 210-mm self-propelled gun. When Bull's death caused the companies to be speedily wound up, it was Monique who'd arranged for the staff to be paid off with whatever limited funds were available and, during this painful process, Heath had approached her and said that he knew a lot about the Scud programme and he could always 'tell what he knew'. This was dismissed with contempt by Monique. When I told Liep about this, his response was interesting.

'I wonder if Heath took the files.'

'What files?'

'At some point – I don't know whether before or after Bull's death – three files went missing. They contained details of contracts between A.T.I. and Iraq, and between A.T.I. and China, new contracts pertaining to the development of missile technology.'

'Where are they now?' I asked.

'Good question,' said Liep.

35

Why had Bull stepped out of his usual sphere of activity and into missiles? I believe his decision was driven by the overriding need to keep Project Babylon afloat because there began to be real concerns over its future once the test-firing of the horizontal model was completed. I had frequently mentioned my concern about the slow progress being made on the guidance and control systems for the Martlet projectile. Now, from Liep, I understood the difficulty had continued long after I left A.T.I.

The guidance control, or telemetering, system was a vital component of the new Martlets, and on it rested the whole credibility of the Supergun idea. In itself it was a highly complex and difficult problem. First of all it entailed an electronic system built to a very high standard, the efficiency of its on-board element being required to withstand the thermal and mechanical shock of the launch. But that was only one reason why the system had to be unusually reliable.

The purpose was to use a radio beam to control the flight of the projectile. The Martlet's fins and other trajectory-control surfaces would be adjusted from the ground to achieve the required flight-path, but the problem lay in the very short period of time available in which this could be done. After the launch of a Supergun projectile, ionisation would mask all radio signals. Communication would eventually be established, but only four seconds before, as the control surfaces ceased to be effective, the projectile left the upper atmosphere. So in those brief four seconds, all the critical flight adjustments – involving highly complex command functions – had to be made, or they could not be made at all.

I had wanted to build a test rig for such a system and I believed we had the facilities to do this at Saad-16, near the test-bed in Mosul. However, I did not have the necessary scientific input, which Bull had placed under the control of an East German electrical engineer, Klaus Urbatzka. It was my belief that Klaus was out of his depth.

I knew that the non-appearance of the work on telemetering would eventually drive Azzawi to cut his payments under the Babylon contract – by as much as 20 per cent. This would result in salaries not being paid and would ultimately put a question mark over Iraq's commitment to the Supergun itself. Bull at first was difficult to convince of this. I tried to get him to allow me to renegotiate the part of the contract covering guidance and control, which I had always felt was under-resourced. But Bull would not accept that his original estimates on the cost of this contracted element was too low. His way of dealing with such problems was, as ever, to ignore them until they forced themselves on him.

Documents from A.T.I. which I have since studied show that, as late as March 1990, just a fortnight before his death, Bull received a memo which told him that the electronic designs had still not been delivered. I wondered if this technical delay with a vital part of Project Babylon was forcing him to offer the Iraqis help in areas he would not normally get into.

If this was so, and his death was provoked by the new departures, the reason for the murder still, after all, came back to Supergun. To Bull, Babylon was sacrosanct and, anyway, he had come much too far to turn back now. He would promise anything, I considered, if the alternative was a second destruction of his life's work.

Sound political judgement had never featured amongst Bull's virtues, but Supergun was an obsession which drove him into wilful indiscretion.

36

Back in Bristol I had much drawing to do.

Having kept no graphics or detailed specifications from Project Babylon, I was dependent on Riley to supply the component drawings he had gathered from Walter Somers and Forgemasters. He was happy to do this because the assembly drawings on which I was working would show him exactly how the individual tubes and other components, for which they had unearthed such a bewildering array of drawings, fitted together. There were also other component parts, such as the recoil cylinders, for which Customs did not have drawings. I had been trying to recreate these, or obtain them from elsewhere.

Now, as June turned into July, these hundreds of drawings, with the help of the C.A.D./C.A.M. computerised drawing programs I was writing, were beginning to shape themselves into the various Babylon assemblies; the horizontal and inclined Superguns, and the horizontal 350-mm model. In addition I had a thick bundle of drawings which still made no sense at all in the context of these three systems and, jigsaw-wise, I was trying to put these together as well.

Meanwhile I was being courted by another television company, the B.B.C., whose 'Panorama' team wanted to make a programme about the Iraqi arms trade. I had found my relationship with C.B.S. disappointing – more or less entirely one-sided and unproductive. But I agreed to meet the B.B.C., in the spirit of the strategy I had worked out with Kevin Robinson – that of keeping a high profile during the weeks or months leading up to my trial.

The B.B.C.'s interest must have been heightened by a notable development in the Gulf region. In a speech on 18 July the Iraqi Foreign Minister, Tariq Aziz, had made a violent attack on Kuwait. He accused them of having stolen Iraqi oil valued at $2.5 billion, and of conspiring to wreck the Iraqi economy by deliberately creating an oil glut.

I remembered during my time in Iraq that there had been considerable resentment towards Kuwait from many sections of the population. The average Kuwaiti hates Iran just as much as the Iraqi does, but there was always much muttering during the war about how the Emir of Kuwait sat back while Iraqis did all the fighting and all the dying. The fact that Kuwait loaned Saddam billions of dollars to finance the war was not a source of gratitude: Iraq was now in effect bankrupt and Kuwait seemed disinclined to cancel the outstanding debt.

The accusation against Kuwait centred on oil wells in the *Rumaila* field, the tip of which extends across a border that had for years been the subject of dispute. The statement by Aziz was belligerent, but the Kuwaitis tried to pacify him with a proposal for talks. Meanwhile troops were beginning to mass. The Kuwaiti army – a pathetic 20,000 men – faced Saddam's overwhelming strength, as it deployed into prepared positions along the Kuwaiti border. Saudi troops hurried north. Israel, Egypt and Syria put their forces on even greater alert than usual.

Iraq had at that time a million men under arms, and was, in manpower twice as strong as its two nearest military rivals – Syria with 400,000 troops and Iran with its own battle-sore force (many of them in fact only boys) of half a million. It was the Iraqi army's equipment, however, which showed the true degree of military imbalance which had developed in the region. The Saudis, for all their wealth, and with a population only a little less than Iraq, could deploy 550 tanks and 189 combat planes. Iran had 500 tanks and 185 aircrat. However, in 1990, Iraq was estimated to have ten times as many tanks as these countries, and between four and five times as many aircraft. In addition it had Scud B missiles in both fixed and mobile launchers, mustard gas and other chemical and biological weapons, and was developing a nuclear capability which, on various estimates, was between two and seven years away from completion. In weapons technology, only Israel was superior.

The execution of the *Observer* journalist Farzad Bazoft, the attempt to buy nuclear triggers and discovery of the Supergun tubes, as well as the memory, now rekindled, of Saddam's use of poison gas against his own Kurdish population a year earlier, had combined to build up the Iraqi President, with great suddenness, into a bogey of the British media. Previously Saddam Hussein had been perceived as unsavoury but of doubtful international significance. Now he was portrayed as a dictator to surpass even Libya's Colonel Ghaddafy in viciousness. Previously, he had been

167

viewed as the General Franco of his day. Now he was seen as a latter-day Hitler.

With this new Kuwaiti adventure, Saddam's revised status was about to be confirmed – and in spades. This undoubtedly raised the significance of my own case and I became more determined than ever not to be dragged down as a scapegoat.

On the day that Iraq chose to move several armoured divisions up to the Kuwaiti border, Barry Riley telephoned me in Bristol. He asked if I would come to Birmingham to meet some Swiss officials investigating the part played by the Von Roll company in the Supergun affair. I agreed to come the next day, after Glenys and I had kept some appointments in Bristol. Among other things, I had decided to visit my local solicitor and renew my will.

In the morning, Barry phoned again to cancel the meeting.

'The Swiss have had to leave, but they've drawn up a list of questions they'd like you to think about. Can I dictate them?'

'Look, can I call you back? I've got to see someone now. I'll be back after lunch.'

'O.K. Call me then.'

We left the house and reached the meeting with my solicitor by nine. My new last will and testament complete, we did some shopping in Bristol and returned to the house around three o'clock. Postponing my call back to Riley, I immediately sat down to continue with the compilation of detailed background notes to the case.

The previous day I'd been referring to documents I had variously acquired which covered the activities of the Ministry of Defence, the D.T.I., and the American State Department during the preceding two years. They were pretty sensitive documents and ones which, I knew, I should copy and distribute abroad quickly. This afternoon I was surprised to find that these documents, bound into an orange-coloured file with a transparent plastic cover, were not on the desk where I thought I had left them. I looked on the floor behind the desk, then got down on my hands and knees and looked under it.

Thinking I must have replaced the papers in the filing cabinet, I opened the metal drawers. They were not there.

At this point the doorbell rang. Two reporters from *The Western Daily Press* stood there.

'Good afternoon Mr Cowley. We were just wondering about your moving house . . . '

'Moving house? What are you talking about?'

'We were wondering about *that*.'

They turned and pointed behind them. A furniture van was parked opposite the house. It had been delivering, rather than removing, some furniture to the ground-floor flat in our building.

'And, as your bail conditions don't permit you to leave the Bristol area, we just thought it was sort of interesting.'

I was dumbfounded for a moment.

'Look, the van's got nothing to do with me, and I have no plans to move house.'

I didn't even ask where they got the tip-off. I firmly closed the door and returned to the search for my orange file. It was very strange. Someone was monitoring my movements. And now a file, which I had been looking at yesterday and seen that very morning, had gone missing from my desktop. It gradually dawned on me. During my absence in Bristol that morning, my house must have been entered. I had been burgled.

I telephoned Redlands Police Station.

'Is Detective Sergeant Evans there, please?'

Evans, I thought, knew something about my case: I could do worse than to report this to him.

'Sorry, sir. Sergeant Evans is off duty. Can I help?'

'Well, I wanted to report a break-in.'

'A burglary, sir? I'll just take the details.'

Slowly and with infinite patience the policeman led me through the form he had to fill in. I mentioned that the missing property was documents but not, at this stage, any detail. He seemed fairly unexcited and ended by giving me a pessimistic summation.

'We get more and more break-ins reported, Mr Cowley. We'll have a C.I.D. team round as soon as we can, but it won't be for a day or two. And, I should add, invariably they do find there's little they can do.'

'But there are special circumstances here—'

'Yes, I'm sure there are, sir. But it's best to be realistic, isn't it?'

He disconnected. Who had known I wouldn't be at home yesterday? Barry knew, of course. So did anyone who happened to be listening in to my telephone calls. I picked up the phone and dialled again.

'Barry? I've been burgled. Some important documents about the M.O.D. and the Americans have gone. And on top of that the local press were here telling me they'd been tipped off that I was moving house. What's going on?'

169

Barry said it was all news to him. I was inclined to believe him. It seemed more likely that I was the victim of tactics designed to unsettle me, and this wouldn't have been in Barry's interest at the moment. I was being too helpful to him.

I thought with apprehension of what Monique had told me in Brussels. Bull's flat had been entered; things had been rearranged. This had been done as a warning.

I decided to inform Kevin, and he was extremely indignant.

'But they must investigate this, Chris. We'll make them. I'll get onto it.'

It took two days, but eventually I was invited to Redlands Police Station where I met Woman Police Constable Ashton, a member of the Serious Crimes Squad. W.P.C. Ashton and her sergeant had apparently been taken off a murder enquiry to deal with my 'petty' burglary: it looked as if the police were now seriously over-reacting, following Kevin's intervention.

W.P.C. Ashton visited the house, but there was little enough to see. Entry had been undetectable, the missing file had been the only item taken. As she left I told her what I thought: the documents were important background material to the events of my case. They were being treated as of national significance. Some of the documents were of exceptional sensitivity. I added that my telephone line was being tapped and I was under surveillance. W.P.C. Ashton's lips were tight and her eyes expressionless.

'So,' I finished, as she stood looking impassively back at me. 'I believe this burglary was committed by 'the Authorities' – in one form or another. I am convinced of it.'

She snapped shut her notebook and said, briskly.

'Well, Mr Cowley, I'm hardly in a position to discuss that possibility, am I?'

But she knew the background to Chris Cowley. She knew I was awaiting trial in the Supergun affair. And if I had been burgled by M.I.5, or anyone else in the murky world of British intelligence, I don't suppose it would have surprised her a bit.

37

Among the documents which had disappeared from my house was a Ministry of Defence contract proposal, through the then-nationalised Royal Ordnance, to build a gun barrel factory for Saddam Hussein. It was just one of the many examples of secretive defence and business links between the U.K. Government and Iraq which I had been collecting for the use of my legal defence.

I had also been accumulating evidence of the Belgian Government's role in the Supergun affair. Like their British counterparts, Belgian politicians had initially denied knowledge of Supergun. Having surprised Bernard de Witt and Serge Dumont with the news that the Belgian Air Force had flown propellant charges from P.R.B. in Belgium to Amman. I now decided to set down on paper the whole story of the propellant charge.

I had had some experience of the theory and practice of artillery propellants during my time working on the Chinese 155. The size and type of charge is naturally determined by the projectile – its weight and the distance it is expected to travel. Most solid propellants are based on nitrated celluloses or nitro-glycerines, the latter (known as 'double-based propellants') having the advantage that they can be easily made in tubular form, or in grains, to specific sizes. The actual charge material is a paste of gun cotton and nitro-glycerine grains kneaded with acetone before being extruded through a specially-designed die.

Unfortunately, in this case, like everything else associated with Supergun, a whole series of new manufacturing and production technologies had to be developed specially for the project. Difficulties were encountered in the production of grains of large enough size. More importantly, the physics of the situation required very great care.

Ignition of the Supergun propellant would have been achieved by using a specially designed 'electronic squib'. Firing the 'squib' would result in the propellant burning at a controlled, but extremely fast rate. A wave of burning gas at a temperature of about 2,800 degrees Celsius would move across the exposed surfaces of the propellant, the design of the charge having taken into account the need to expose the greatest possible surface area to the hot gas. The effect would be a sudden rise in pressure within the gun's chamber area and thus the discharge of the projectile at a velocity of 2.5 to 2.8 kilometres per second.

However, if Supergun was to be a success, this stable and highly uniform burning process had to occur throughout the entire charge. Lengths of propellant in sticks 50 millimetres in diameter were bundled together to form cylinders one metre in diameter, and there were twelve of these cylinders, each weighing about a tonne. A harness of electrical wiring ran through all parts of the propellant, and was ultimately connected to the initiating current source. If something went wrong in the distribution of the current, if the propellant failed to burn properly, the result might be the destruction of the whole system. All this meant that the design of the squib was of overriding importance.

A physicist, Dr Jim Chan, had the responsibility of doing the necessary calculations for the production of the squib and the charge itself. During this period, Jim Chan had been making regular visits to Nobel's Explosives Company, a subsidiary of I.C.I. at Stevenston, Scotland. He was convinced that Nobel were the best company to assist him in the development of the electronic squib, a crucial component of the propellant ignition system. I had previously authorised payment of forty thousand pounds to Nobel, a down-payment towards research and devleopment costs. The final design given to P.R.B. was for a tubular charge 1,000 millimetres in diameter. To maximise the surface area, the tubes' interiors were honeycombed and their exteriors corrugated. Incidentally, the shape and dimension of the charge meant that P.R.B. could be in no doubt what these propellants were for: a 1,000-mm diameter charge of this type could be used only in a 1,000-mm gun.

The total amount of business for P.R.B., had the Babylon propellant contract ever been completed, would have been $30 million. The money was much needed, because by the end of 1988 P.R.B. was in financial difficulties. The conflict between Iran and Iraq had been gradually scaled down since mid-1988, and their sales to Iraq, on which the company had become heavily dependant, had slumped.

One obvious problem, with Azzawi pressing for an early delivery date, especially on the 350-mm charge, seemed to be that of transportation. Specialist propellants are a very expensive and potentially dangerous cargo, and commercial airlines understandably regard them as risky. Jourdain, P.R.B.'s principal negotiator, however, didn't see this as presenting any difficulty.

'We'll use the Air Force,' he told us.

'Which Air Force – the Iraqis?' we asked.

'No, our own. The Belgian Air Force.'

'How can you get permission?'

Jourdain simply shrugged with Gallic expressiveness.

'I just ring my friend the Minister of Defence and he gets it all organised. We often do it. You would pay a bit extra, but the stuff will get here in time.'

In March 1989 the stuff did actually arrive at Amman. It was then that we had to pay 'the little bit extra' – the $25,000 for each delivery, which I had mentioned to Bernard and Serge. Faris Major was selected to take the money to Amman and hand it over in exchange for the cargo. But when he got there he was told that they had no use for cash – they wanted their $25,000 in gold.

Faris returned on the first flight and explained the hold-up. Azzawi immediately sent him down to the *souk* to obtain a special waistcoat fitted with enough pockets to hold the required amount of gold. Meanwhile he had the Central Bank convert the dollar bills into gold bars. The unfortunate Faris then travelled back to Amman carrying two kilogrammes of gold, which was duly handed over and the propellant released for carriage to Iraq. This opulent *baksheesh* was split between Jordanian officials and certain people back in Belgium.

If Jourdain had really contacted 'his friend the Minister of Defence', then the claim that the Belgian Government knew nothing about Bull's contracts with Iraq looks false. In any case, officials in Brussels were well aware of the fact that Iraqi technicians were coming to P.R.B. to be trained in the design and manufacture of propellant charges, as well as in other aspects of Project Babylon. From time to time, as many as 20 Iraqi engineers and scientists could be found working under S.R.C. supervision in Brussels. They could not have come without the necessary residence and work permits, not granted without much official paperwork and investigation by the Belgian police.

When I was still working on Babylon I knew little about the Belgian connection. I assumed that certain individuals had to be 'squared' to ensure official cooperation, but did not know through whom this was arranged, and how much information was given to explain the need for it. In fact this was something of a bombshell and was eventually to trigger a series of dramatic developments in the Supergun story.

But a more immediate drama was just ahead. I was still wrestling with assembly drawings, and trying to write down everything I knew or could discover about Gerald Bull's disparate dealings with Iraq when, like a defective nuclear reactor, events in the Gulf suddenly went critical. By the end of July, it was already clear that the Iraqis were playing a game of poker. They indulged in a lot of bravura stake-raising during some ultimately futile summit talks with Kuwait. Then, on 2 August, 1990, they went for broke and invaded.

38

August passed in an atmosphere of rising tension. Saddam Hussein first set up a puppet government in Kuwait, and then proceeded to full annexation of the country, declaring it Iraq's nineteenth province. He also instituted a reign of terror. Stories were filtering out of the hunting down of Kuwaitis, of street beatings, rapes and summary executions. The predicament of Western nationals was also grave. They were to be held hostage against air attacks from the Americans, British, Saudis, or anyone else who had supported the United Nations call for Iraq's withdrawal. They were concentrated at the Al-Rasheed and other hotels in Baghdad until being gradually moved into accommodation at places like Saad-16 and Al-Qaqa, there to act as the infamous 'human shields'.

The worsening situation intensified my hunt for supporting evidence to show that Babylon was essentially peaceful and that I had not been involved in the deliberate export of military equipment to Iraq. In this quest, increasing numbers of documents were beginning to come my way.

I was especially anxious to get more S.R.C. material – not a particularly straightforward task. Monique Jamine, Amilicar da Costa and others were a great help, but certain key S.R.C. people, such as Mike Bayne, Martin Hughes, and Tony Slack, continued to avoid talking about S.R.C.'s affairs. Prior to my visit to Brussels I'd had friendly chats with Mike on the phone, but as soon as I started to ask about the breech-slide stopped at Patras or the 350-mm gun barrel made by Walter Somers, he clammed up.

'I'm sorry Chris. These are covered by commercial confidentiality. I can't discuss them.'

Commercial confidentiality? Five months after S.R.C. and A.T.I. had been wound up and gone into oblivion? Forgive me, but I didn't think so.

On top of that, British troops were preparing to go to war. As Riley said to me, 'to hell with commercial confidentiality'. I agreed, and the thought gave an added impetus to my own quest for information.

Ideally what I would have liked were copies of the S.R.C. monthly reports covering the period from my resignation on 31 May 1989 until Bull's death the following March. These reports were submitted to Bull by his senior engineers – by me in my time, and then by the likes of Bayne, Hughes and Slack. Bull's copies were no doubt in his filing cabinet, still being held under seal by the Belgian police. It was the originators' copies I wanted access to, but the originators didn't want to play ball.

Nevertheless, I was getting fragmentary bits and pieces, some of them from sources of whose names, even now, I am unsure. One document was of particular interest. It was the A.T.I. 21st Monthly Report, drafted by Tony Slack and C. Kossioris, an engineer who worked out of S.R.C.'s Athens office. The report was dated February 1990.

From this report I gathered that the final firing programme of the horizontal, rail-mounted test model of Supergun (now being designated System 350 or just S-350) had been carried out satisfactorily. The firing was followed by a dismantlement, with most components now being transported to another site, at a large quarry in the Jabal Hamrin mountains some sixty kilometres north of Baghdad. There the gun sections were to be reassembled on a 45 degree hillside ramp, pointing into the sky.

This was a complete surprise to me. The purpose of the 350-mm system had always been to fire horizontally, modelling certain characteristics of the Supergun. I couldn't imagine how the original design could be inclined and still function. The method of loading the chamber would have to be completely redesigned, for a start. Then I noticed something else. Martin Hughes had been in attendance at the last of the horizontal firings. Hughes was a design engineer at S.R.C. and, if *he* was there, it must have meant that new designs were being evaluated at this firing.

At first, I couldn't understand why they thought an inclined 350-mm test would materially assist the Babylon programme. But then I took out the drawing I had been working on, the assembly of the second Walter Somers gun, the one with the 350-mm barrel. Yes, the 350-mm Supergun model might be very useful for testing another system, something with the same barrel diameter as the test-model itself, although this second system was a piece of engineering very different, and separate, from Project Babylon as I had known it. All I had so far was a drawing. I didn't know anything more about the deal.

The February 1990 report contained another reference of some interest – a new type of projectile, known as S-32. This was to be fitted with a carbon-fibre sabot, offering a much improved range. I remembered the fiasco of the Lear Fan factory, by which Bull had intended to acquire much-needed advanced carbon-fibre technology. That sale had been blocked in 1989 by the British Government, but Bull had clearly found an alternative supplier for this material. It was a fact which would not, I thought, have escaped the attention of his enemies.

I had also gleaned further very telling information about forward plans to test-fire the new, inclined 350-mm configuration. The first of these firings was scheduled to take place on 20 March 1990, a date which looks particularly significant when you remember that, in Brussels two days later, Bull was shot dead.

The next document of importance I acquired was a status report prepared by John Heath. It was also dated February 1990. Item one concerned what was described as the 350-mm, 45-degree 'fixed system', which I took to mean the test model in its new inclined position. I looked down the page for item two. It was about another 350-mm system, an 'elevating system'. At last I was on the track of Somers's tapering military-style gun-barrel.

For, apart from the test-model assembly now transferred from Project Babylon, S-350 required *two* sets of tubes. One had already been delivered and a second was due for shipping from Walter Somers on 9 February 1990. There was also mention of the two cradles or slide assemblies being made by Forgemasters. Again, this order was nearly complete and planned for despatch by air freight from Ringway Airport, Manchester (although in the event they went by road). A further set of completely new components were detailed: 500-mm recoil cylinders, tube slide bearings, breech assemblies, buffer yokes and hydraulic systems – all items unnecessary to the horizontal 350-mm test model which I had taken part in designing.

When I used to write status or monthly reports for Bull, they always appeared under the general title of 'Project Babylon'. Neither of these documents, dealing with the inclined fixed system and the elevating system, used that heading. Instead there was a new name, and in these documents dated February 1990, I was coming across it for the first time. They called it Project 839.

As the possibility of war in the Gulf began cautiously to be

177

discussed, legal proceedings against Peter Mitchell, myself and others was beginning to worry the British Government. In particular, politicians were wondering what damaging things Sir Hal Miller might say from the witness box.

Shortly after the Supergun tubes were seized at Teesport, Miller had told the House of Commons of the warnings he had conveyed (at the company's request) in 1988, 1989 and early 1990 about the Somers contracts. These warnings were issued in person to the Department of Trade and Industry, the Ministry of Defence and the intelligence services.

'I told them,' Miller said, 'of the company's offer to withdraw from the contract, to meet the contract and enable it to be traced, or to carry on with the contract.'

The Department of Trade issued a denial that any record of the warnings was made. Miller disputed this. He had seen, he said, written records of his conversations with the D.T.I. Then, when Nicholas Ridley, President of the Board of Trade, told Parliament that 'the Government has only recently become aware in general terms' of the Supergun, Miller exploded, 'Never before have I come across so much lying in high places'.

Later, when charges were laid against Peter Mitchell and me, Miller promised to appear as a witness for the defence, adding that 'it is inconceivable to me that the Government would want my evidence to be given in open court'. Miller was making it clear that he was capable of being much more specific about his contacts with the Government – the individuals he had spoken to, what had been discussed, and what final decisions had been taken. Under oath in the witness box, he implied, he would be a good deal more candid than he had been in the House of Commons, and would be submitting documentary proof to back up his story.

At Cabinet level, Miller was now being seen as a danger to the Conservative Government. At some point in the summer Bernard Ingham, Margaret Thatcher's Press Secretary, swung into action. Ingham's political power was at its height at this time. For years he had used Downing Street's unique system of 'unattributable' briefings to shield politicians who had attracted the Prime Minister's favour, whilst discrediting those who had fallen from grace. As Miller later told Paul Foot of The Daily Mirror, the Press Office began to circulate a series of unsubstantiated rumours about Miller.

'I was told by several lobby correspondents that they had been briefed that I'd been duped and bribed. I was asked by one of them to confirm that I'd been seen in a hotel in Brussels with Iraqis and an export licence application waiting to go through. I told him that I was happy to confirm anything put about by the Government disinformation services, but there were three slight problems. I haven't been to Brussels for 40 years. I have never met an Iraqi. I have never made out an export licence.'

Meanwhile a tabloid journalist knocked on Miller's front door and enquired of Lady Miller if it was true that Sir Hal had a particularly close woman friend in Brussels, or that he had visited call-girls there.

39

Now that Saddam was the Western world's number one figure of fear, any hope that my case would recede in the public mind had been scotched. On 2 September 1990 I attended the Sheffield Magistrates Court for a remand hearing and the television cameras were out in force. They captured my arrival, and they pursued me as I left.

I actually turned up at the courthouse with Barry Riley. We'd met at Kevin's office, so that I could hand him my assembly drawings for the complete horizontal 350-mm model, showing the gun mounted on its railway bogeys. On the office floor I also unrolled a very long drawing, the barrel assembly of the full-scale gun itself. It extended almost from wall to wall. They were suitably impressed.

'I'm still working on the details of the 1,000-mm system's recoil cylinders and other appendages,' I explained. 'But I'll probably have those in a week or two. Then you'll be in a position to appreciate the full assembly of Supergun.'

I added that progress was being made with that other, mysterious 350-mm gun, made by Walter Somers in the autumn and winter of 1989.

'It'll be two or three more weeks before the assembly drawing is complete. Then you'll see it in all its splendour.'

After a convivial lunch with Barry Riley (it was getting increasingly difficult to reconcile this genuine friendliness with the fact that he was trying to put me behind bars) we went to court.

The place was in its usual chaotic state. The entrance hall looked like a venue for a rock concert, with hundreds of people milling around in ragged jeans, T-shirts, decayed trainers, long and unwashed hair. One particular individual had chosen to test the court's patience by wearing a one-legged pair of jeans and a T-shirt with the legend 'HATE – KILL ALL PIGS' on it.

Feeling severely over-dressed in my suit, I stood around chatting with Barry and Annabel Bolt of the Prosecution. The appearance itself was brief: the Crown Prosecution confirmed its agreement to existing bail conditions and the date of my next appearance. My defence, in the shape of a junior standing-in for Kevin Robinson had 'nothing to add'. I stood dutifully to attention in the dock.

Despite being corrected more than once, the Chair of the Bench kept referring to me as 'Mr Mitchell'. By now I knew that Peter Mitchell of Walter Somers was – apart from myself – the only one yet charged in connection with Supergun, and had presumably been appearing regularly in front of the same Bench. I wondered if the slip was significant, or just evidence of creeping forgetfulness in this elderly lady.

Three weeks later I again visited Barry, this time in Birmingham. The purpose of the visit was to meet a Ministry of Defence official and to show Barry more drawings.

Over coffee I first presented a drawing of the 1,000-mm system assembly. Barry was excited seeing, for the first time, a full representation of the assembled Supergun. It was not, of course, particularly reminiscent of an artillery piece, consisting as it did of 26 flanged barrel-sections bolted together. Fourteen cylindrical bearings secured the barrel to its deep concrete foundations, while four massive recoil cylinders and two not insignificant buffer cylinders – six cylinders in all – were shown at the breech end, slung like on either side of the barrel. In a bubble drawing, the cross-section of our unique wedge breech was detailed.

The gun had huge dimensions. The external flange diameter was two metres and the whole assembly would have weighed as much as 150 London buses. However, the assembly, in both plan and section, was made to look pencil-slim by virtue of its great length: 156 metres, the equivalent of two football pitches joined end to end.

I now unrolled the second set of drawings. These had been so much more difficult to recreate, since I had no personal involvement, no memory to consult, but they clearly showed a very different piece of engineering. This was the 350-mm assembly, whose breech was designed to lie in the cradle found on Paul Ashwell's lorry, found in Greece, *en route* from Sheffield Forgemasters. Just over 30 metres long, it was a classically-shaped tapering artillery barrel. At one end the lipped rim of its muzzle could clearly be seen. Stumpy pins protruded horizontally on each side of the much thicker breech end so that, on the drawing, it resembled the base of a bayonet-type light bulb. The gun would

181

pivot on these bosses as it elevated.

We were all still poring over the drawings when a tall, well-groomed man entered Riley's office.

'Oh! This is Mr Monkbridge, Chris,' Barry said, getting up and shaking the newcomer by the hand. Monkbridge extended his hand to me and I shook it.

'I'm from the M.O.D., Mr Cowley. As you know we have recently developed a new interest in dispositions inside Iraq, and I wondered if you might be able to share some of your expertise with us.'

Monkbridge was provided with coffee and, for the next two hours, he questioned me in an entirely friendly and low-key manner, writing down my answers in a notebook. He was particularly interested in where I had worked during my time in Baghdad – the Special Projects Office. In that building was the A.T.I. drawing office.

'It was just opposite the Tomb of the Unknown Soldier,' I told him. 'That monument was an incredible piece of sculpture, a gigantic opened-out oyster with its pearl inside.'

'So where exactly was that located, Mr Cowley? Could you show me on this street-plan of Baghdad?'

He unfolded the map and I showed him where the monument was, and then put my finger on the spot where I had spent so many hours with my team, arguing over design iterations, running ideas through the computer, and producing drawing after drawing, often late into the night. Azzawi's office was there too as was, higher up, Dr Saadi, and – at the very top – there was the suite reserved for the use of the President's son-in-law, Kamil Hussein himself. Monkbridge seemed very satisfied with my answers. I detected no hostility from him, just the desire to work together on a question of international importance.

He asked me about other places I'd visited, installations and plants, and I described some of these.

'Can you tell me some more about Saad-16?'

This was the high level research facility, located near our test-bed in northern Iraq, and where we'd failed to get a variety of simple machining jobs carried out to my satisfaction. It had certainly been built without regard to expense. The design was by an Austrian firm called Consultco, and it was constructed by a German engineering company, Gildemeisters of Biefelt.

'It was said to have cost many millions of dollars just to put up. I always enjoyed going there. You got the chance to view some of the most modern machine tools and scientific equipment in the world. They couldn't always operate the equipment, though.'

'And they were carrying out research into missile development?'

'Oh yes. I remember seeing a very unusual hybrid computer there. They'd got hold of components from two U.S. firms, Gold and E.A.I., and also from a British computer outfit, Scientific Computers. They put them together to make a very effective ballistic-missile flight simulator, a very good piece of equipment it was.'

I smiled then, because I remembered Klaus Urbatzka standing in the room as we'd admired the computer, observing in his loud, aggrieved voice.

'Of course, in *Germany*, they'd have placed these light switches higher up the walls.'

But Monkbridge was moving onto another subject.

'I gather you had quite a lot to do with the Baghdad Military Fair – in May 1989 wasn't it?'

'Yes, actually we had a display there. We had the one hundredth-scale tabletop model of Babylon, and a lot of sketches and visual material about the project—'

'Yes, but I'm interested in what else you saw at the Fair. Other weapons systems, that kind of thing.'

I told him about the Fair – as much as I could remember, though it was little enough at that distance in time. Among other things, I told him it was for this event that Bull's still-unfinished 210-mm self-propelled gun-howitzer – the Al-Fao – had been rushed to Baghdad from northern Spain in a Soviet Antonov AN-124.

This aircraft, the mighty 'Condor', hired from the Soviet Air Force, had not been seen outside Russia except for a visit to the Paris Air show in 1985 and a subsequent appearance at Farnborough. It had the world's largest wingspan and heaviest permissible payload, and its trespass on West European airspace had required the coordination of the entire N.A.T.O. alliance's air defence system. In fact the whole aviation pattern of the region had, it seems, been bent to accommodate the giant as it lumbered through the skies of Europe, from its Soviet Air-Force base near Moscow to the Victoria airport near Bilbao and thence to Baghdad. Subsequently, of course, knowledge of the Antonov charter was conveniently 'forgotten'. I told Monkbridge this story. He did not comment, but smiled. Then he rose and shook my hand again.

'Perhaps I'll get back to you, if I may. We might have further queries.'

I said I would be happy to help and the interview was over. I reflected that Monkbridge had made me feel like I was doing something useful, something in, rather than against, the national interest. I compared this with the behaviour of the prison-officers, their coarseness and brutish behaviour, with the briskness of the police and the idiocies of the court. Funny world.

The Customs officer who had been detailed to drive me down to the railway station was chatty.

'How d'you get on with the Major, then?'

The Major? I tried not to show how intrigued I was. No one had mentioned that Monkbridge had a rank. I said, trying to sound casual,

'Seemed all right. Nice bloke. Do you see much of him?'

'No, we don't usually have much to do with these Intelligence guys.'

Of course, in general terms I'd already worked it out. Monkbridge wasn't interested in Supergun itself. Monkbridge was one of the many 'Intelligence guys' who were spreading their net throughout the land, to gather up remnants and crumbs and scraps of information. These would be taken back to somewhere such as the Empress State building in Fulham, or Stuart House in Soho Square, there to be heaped into a computer and sorted and collated until they formed as complete a picture as possible of Saddam Hussein's military capability.

The conversation about the Fair had been especially revealing. It had been Baghdad's first Military Fair and invitations had been sent out to virtually every international weapons manufacturer. Since the Middle East forms the largest market for arms in the world, most of them came and, consequently, the Fair had been a magnet for the Military Attachés of every Embassy in town, most of them being resident intelligence officers. But these gentlemen would not necessarily be allowed to see everything at the Fair – there would be a number of sections open 'by invitation only'. They might also be unqualified to appreciate the significance of certain details even where they did spot them. Other pairs of eyes, other perspectives to augment the Military Attachés' reports – that was what Monkbridge was after.

Monkbridge would naturally have paid calls on British companies which exhibited, but these might be of limited value to him. A good many of the companies later put up smokescreens, pretending to have been anywhere other than the Baghdad Military Fair.

Alternatively, they said they had exhibited, but not intended to sell, or had sold, but for civilian uses only. I felt such protestations were just so much nonsense. As I knew from my own experience, in the atmosphere of early 1989 the hunger for arms sales into the Middle-East arena had grown more biting than ever. No company had been willing to hold back while others stole the plums, but they often used subterfuge and half-truths to protect their backs. The uncertainty of the whole situation made them unreliable witnesses.

We were drawing near to Birmingham New Street Station and I was thinking of the U.S.-made helicopters I'd seen at the Military Fair, fitted with air-to-ground missiles and labelled 'For Agricultural Use'. My driver then related another classic of the same genre. H.M. Customs, he told me, recently discovered that the D.T.I. had authorised exports – to Iran this time – of spares for the C130 Hercules military transport plane. The declared grounds were that the C130 was a civil aircraft.

I boarded my train, reflecting how innocently I had first become involved in the Middle East. I had sought to do a job with a man I respected, and it was a job which had seemed to chime in with my Government's own policies. I had little appreciation of just how two-faced those policies had been.

40

Within a few days of my trip to Birmingham I had received two further, cryptically informative documents about Project 839.

One was a memorandum from John Heath who, while not himself a competent engineer, had become an administrator of sorts within A.T.I. Heath wrote to Bull on 9 March 1990 that the inclined gun was 'almost ready for firing'. He also asked for an urgent meeting to talk about the establishment of 'an isolated communications office for liaison and reporting. The need for such a secure office is becoming increasingly apparent,' he said.

The second document which had come into my possession was part of an A.T.I. monthly report entitled *Annex 6 – Manning Effort*. It provided a comprehensive overview of individual tasks being carried out in Iraq and Europe and gave me, for the first time, the chance to see Project 839 in terms of its personnel. Straight away, however, I noticed an anomaly. Tony Slack was allocated 'preliminary work on S-600. Liaison with design engineering staff.' What, though, was S-600?

At first I thought it was simply a misprint for 'S-350'. But when I found the designation repeated on the second page I discounted the idea. Now the report was talking about a 'concept design for a 600-mm launcher'. If S-600 was a new launcher, what kind of launcher was it? If, as was almost certain, the figure 600 referred to the internal bore diameter, then we were talking about something very big indeed. Not, I knew, a space launcher, as even at 600-mm, it would not have the necessary performance which the 1,000-mm system could offer. The only possible conclusion was that this was to be a military weapon, like S-350. The profile of Project 839 was becoming clearer now.

In the last week of September I went again to Birmingham at Barry Riley's request. We discussed a number of matters, including whether I had changed my mind about becoming a prosecution witness. My answer was still the same – no decision, because Kevin says it's too early to decide. As I left, Barry played what he thought of as his last card. He told me that the case against me was now more or less complete and suggested that it wouldn't be long before I found myself on trial. He then placed in front of me a file of documents.

'What's this?'

'You may need it for your defence. It's a series of those A.T.I. monthly reports you talked about wanting to look at. I got them from the Belgians. But I'd like you to look first at that date on there.'

I glanced at the cover. It said *Project 839 – A.T.I. Monthly Reports and Annexes. From February 1989.*

I saw the implications at once. In February 1989 I was still an employee of Bull. If Project 839, which was all too obviously a military programme, had started as early as that, then they could put me in it, and deep. Could it have started then? February was the period in which I spent time in Iraq on the firing programme. Could anything have been developing without my knowing about it, either in Baghdad or Brussels? I felt a sinking feeling within me. It if had been, I was now in dire trouble.

It wasn't until I was sitting on the train that I had the chance to look at this damaging file. I opened it up with some trepidation, not at all sure what I would find. Progressively the papers described the development of the S-350, from its initial concept, through design iterations, contract proposals, and finally manufacturing and delivery schedules. I read how, on 1 February, Heath reported that the tubes had arrived from Somers. The seals were to be fitted by a British firm called Destec. On 14 and 15 February the horizontal test model was successfully fired. On 18 February an aerodynamicist, Paul Bottomley, itemised all the gun parts still to be delivered, some of them from Somers. Next was Heath's report of 9 March, which I had already seen. Then, on 14 March, Tony Slack reported that the inclined 350-mm fixed system would be ready for firing on 20 March. And so on.

I sank deeper into depression. How could I possibly defend myself against such comprehensive and damaging evidence of a full-scale development programme, by a company in which I was a senior officer?

Then I looked once more at the dates. The papers all related to February and March. One of the Monthly Reports was the one I had already seen, and it was dated February 1990. Immediately I saw what they had done. I flipped the cover of the file over and read again the date Customs had inscribed on the label: *February*

1989. It was a straight mistake, a transposition. For 1989 read 1990. I almost cried out in triumph and relief. If Customs tried to use this to prove my involvement in Project 839 they'd be laughed out of court.

Later, when I told Kevin Robinson, he agreed. He also told me not to correct the mistake with Riley.

'No point in handing them our defence on a place,' he said. 'Let's keep a few surprises back.'

Kevin was by no means as sanguine as Riley about my imminent prospects of coming to trial.

'Some cases drag on for years, especially where there's a so-called political dimension. And with the Gulf Crisis still unfolding, I doubt anybody wants to hurry this one up. They'd rather pretend to continue their investigations, do nothing and then, after several yeras have passed, quietly drop the case as if it had never been.'

The thought filled me with dread: to have this hanging over my head for *years* would be horrific, a sentence in itself.

A great deal of my time was still being spent clarifying the nature of my work for Bull, the separateness of Project 839, and the range of British interests, both legitimate and otherwise, in Iraq. But I was now beginning to think beyond the case and to develop some new business interests. The main one of these was an engineering consultancy which I planned to set up in Thailand, and it was now time to arrange to visit Bangkok and explore the possibilities. I again paid in a £5,000 bond and got back my passport. In early November Glenys and I would fly to Bangkok, and then follow up with a weeks' much-needed holiday in Penang, Malaya. Just the thought of this, the planning of it, gave us pleasure.

In the meantime a small article in *The Daily Express* caught my eye. It described how several directors of a company called Matrix Churchill had been arrested. I imediately called to mind Colonel Kadoori and his share-buying scheme for Flexible Manufacturing Technology, a deal that had ultimately fallen through. With Matrix Churchill, on the other hand, something very similar had actually been put into practice, and now, in the glare of publicity around the Gulf Crisis, it was coming to light.

Matrix Churchill had been in the vanguard of the British machine tools industry but by the mid-1980s the company's owners wished to dispose of it. Then, in 1987, the Iraqis, through their British company Technology Development Group (based in Chiswick and run essentially by Iraqi intelligence) stepped in to finance a management buy-out. The deal went through, although it meant that, through Matrix Churchill, and with the British Government's approval, the Iraqis now controlled a huge slab of what was left of Britain's machine-tools industry.

I knew about Matrix Churchill; that it had done, and was continuing to do, millions of pounds worth of business with Iraq, selling engineering machinery such as high-technology lathes to be used in the manufacture of shells, rockets and the like. I had seen many of the machines themselves, primarily at the Nassr establishment (where munitions were made) but also at Saad-16 and at factories and plants throughout Iraq. Now, by arresting members of the company's management, the authorities were following a policy similar to that of the Supergun. Not only to lock the stable door after the horse has bolted, but to throw the grooms in jail as well.

It began to look as if Kevin Robinson was wrong for once. We heard at the end of October that a definite decision to prosecute the suspected Walter Somers and Forgemasters personnel had been taken and that formal charges would be laid on 14 November. At that time Glenys and I would be, very thankfully, out of the country.

There was one small item of information I wanted to nail down before I left. There had been much scepticism about my claim that the Iraqis had used Ringway Airport in Manchester to fly out the 350-mm barrels made by Somers. Customs had apparently approached the Civil Aviation authorities, who had denied that any such Iraqi aircraft had visited the airport at the time. I decided to go to Manchester.

There is no accounting for luck or coincidence. The air-traffic controller I spoke to as he came off duty in the Ringway tower had been there when the Iraqi plane had landed.

'How can I prove it?' I asked.

'Well, that's easy. There's a mate of mine who's a bit of a plane spotter, and I often tip him off when there's anything unusual coming in. I told him about the Iraqi plane, and he came right over and photographed the thing on the tarmac.'

So evidence of the Iraqi Air Force jet's arrival at Manchester did exist. I knew it had been a Russian-built Tupolev, an aircraft bought and used in large numbers by Saddam Hussein's Air Force.

It was also an aircraft frequently seen passing overhead A.T.I.'s office in Baghdad. If photographs had been taken, then surely I would be able to locate them?

Shortly afterwards I was in possession of photographs from two quite separate sources. On one photograph the control tower of Manchester Airport could be clearly seen in the background. I knew this was the aircraft which had tranported the 350-mm tubes from Walter Somers. Nobody could be in any doubt now that an Iraqi jet had been in Manchester.

And so another official lie was nailed.

41

It was eight-thirty in the morning when the bedside hotel telephone woke me. I had not had a night of uninterrupted sleep for seven months but the warm, equatorial climate of Malaysia had given me one at last.

I reached drowsily for the receiver.

'Hello.'

'Are you awake?'

I recognised the voice at once. It was my son Bryn, calling from Bristol.

'Nearly. What's the problem?'

'Look, shall I call back in ten minutes?'

We had not arranged for Bryn to call us; in fact he didn't know where we were staying. I sat up in bed, bracing myself for another piece of bad news.

'No, no. I'm awake.'

'I just called Bangkok. They gave me your number.'

Muzzily, I worked out the time difference. Malaysia is seven hours fast on G.M.T. It must be half-past midnight back home.

'What's going on?'

'It's all right. I just had a phone call from Kevin Robinson. It's fantastic.'

'What?'

'The Crown Prosecution Service have withdrawn all charges against you.'

I shut my eyes. Bryn's news seeped rather slowly into my sleepy brain.

'Say that again.'

'They've dropped the charges, dad. You know Kevin was due in court to represent you at the remand hearing this morning? Well Annabel Bolt called him up just now. They must be working late or something. Anyway, all charges against you and Mitchell have been withdrawn.'

I must have said some words mechanically which expressed

what fantastic news this was. But it still wasn't quite sinking in. I said,

'Aren't they charging anyone else? They were going to arrest the people from Forgemasters and Somers today.'

'No, they're not. The entire Supergun case has gone down the drain. They've given up.'

For some reason I found myself thinking of Barry Riley and how relentlessly and determinedly he had pursued the case.

'We want these guys,' Barry had told me, more than once. 'They knew what they were doing, and we're going to get them for it.'

To Bryn, I said,

'Did the decision come from Customs, or what?'

'We don't think so. Kevin said they hadn't been told yet.'

'So who did make the decision?'

'Kevin doesn't know, but he says he can guess. *The Observer* had a story supposedly leaked to them on Sunday. It was to the effect that the Supergun case would be dropped for political reasons. But nobody took that too seriously, because the Crown has always maintained it had such a strong case.'

'Barry Riley's going to get one hell of a shock when he finds out.'

I lay there after Bryn rang off, trying to organise my feelings. I was stunned and I was ecstatic, simultaneously shocked and flooded with elation. After months of concentration on almost nothing but my defence, the news that I could now switch off was almost impossible to take in. I had been in prison. I'd been spied on and hounded. I'd travelled thousands of miles and spent hundreds of hours on the phone, looking for witnesses and documentary evidence. I'd lain awake at night sifting my memories for details and clues. Now I was free.

When something sudden like this happens, so joyful and such a relief, there is nevertheless an element of disappointment which other people find hard to understand. I had been like a river flowing towards a particular conjunction. Suddenly the flow had been thwarted, and then reversed. My life required rethinking around a new objective.

Or did it? The more I considered my position, the more I wanted the story I am now writing to be told. Bull, who was by this time universally either reviled or mocked, had been my friend. I felt I owed a debt to his memory. I wanted the world to understand what Project Babylon really meant. I wanted Bull and his death to be understood. Above all, I wanted the politicians and officials, who had ducked and dived their way through this affair, to be brought to book.

The dropping of my case, and indeed the decision not to proceed against any of the suspects in the Supergun case, was done without prior reference to the H.M.C. customs. That meant it was a political, not a judicial, decision. The prosecutor, Annabel Bolt, had made a long statement to the court, explaining why our case was being discontinued. It contained a good deal of dubious reasoning.

'With regard to the two defendants with whom you are concerned here,' she read (the other defendant referred to being Peter Mitchell of Walter Somers), 'the issue is not just whether they were involved in the exportation of parts of guns to Iraq, but whether they knew what was afoot and, knowing that, participated in the intention of evading export controls. It is a feature of this case that the Iraqis used a number of different manufacturers in the U.K. and elsewhere in Europe, manufacturing different parts of the weaponry.'

But it was hard to see how this paragraph, which was also included in a press release after the hearing, could refer to me. I had never made any secret of my involvement in Supergun, or of how the deal was arranged. This was why the Customs had always felt they had excellent prospects of sending me to jail.

Referring specifically to me, the statement went on,

'In those circumstances, (the Customs) consider that it would be inappropriate to proceed against Cowley alone.'

If the statement was implying that I was guilty but not worth pursuing, then it would tend to infringe natural justice, since it denied my right to public acquittal. It is also a situation rarely, if ever, seen in the British legal system. I was certain in myself that the decision not to prosecute – a right one in the sense that I didn't regard myself as guilty – had been taken for an utterly wrong reason. The reason was fear – fear of what might come out, fear of what I, and more particularly, of what Sir Hal Miller would say in open court. The whole business stank of political manoeuvring.

I thought how fortunes change, how good news, like bad, seems to come in waves. I was shortly to learn that the attempted murder charge against Billy Proudfoot had also been dropped. The prosecution had been informed of the defence's intention to 'rubbish' the forensic evidence. Billy could now seek compensation and I would arrange to collect the beer it had been agreed was owed.

I decided my own case could not be put to bed so easily. Until now I had concentrated on my defence. That phase was over. I intended to switch to attack.

42

When I reached home a few days later I decided to lose no time in contacting Barry Riley, but he pre-empted me. At nine in the morning, on my first day home, the phone rang and before I picked it up I knew who it would be. He was angry, though not towards me. It was the system which had let him down.

All that work. Late hours, endless travelling, the effort of coming to terms with an excessively technical brief: entirely wasted. He couldn't believe it. He'd been assured the whole way down the line of unqualified support. He'd been stabbed in the back.

I had a strange sense of the bond between us. We had, in many ways, collaborated on this business, although from opposite sides of the fence. If for me the outcome had been a little more tense, the degree of effort had been equal. I arranged to go down to Birmingham to see him four days later, to collect my bail money. We would talk further.

'I thought you might as well have this. It was going to be part of the case against you.'

Barry pushed several A4 pages across the desk. They were stapled together in the top left hand corner. The uppermost page carried the S.R.C. logo.

I picked up the document which I saw at once was headed 'Project 839' and dated February 1990 – correctly, this time. I began to turn the pages, slowly at first and then with increasing excitement. This was what I had been after: a full technical brief, prepared by Tony Slack and another S.R.C. gun designer, Paul Bottomley, under Bull's direction.

The brief confirmed much of what I had suspected about Project 839. It was to be an artillery offensive system whose ambition was breathtaking. If achieved, it would have been second to none in the world.

Bull had obviously told the Iraqis that, by using some of the ballistics test results already carried out in the one-third-scale Supergun model, many of the technical problems of a new 350-mm offensive gun (the S-350) could be quickly solved. The introduction to Slack's report stated that the Babylon test model had now been redesigned as an inclined military gun, capable of firing a 75-kilo projectile, containing 14 kilogrammes of high explosive, to a target 450 kilometres distant. This was the first stage in the development of the new elevating/traversing S-350 system. The report then proposed an entirely new weapon, a 600-mm L.R.S.B. 'launching system'.

This system has the drawback of limited lethality, given the small high explosive charge. In order to increase the payload delivered to the target, it will be necessary to prepare a new design, based on increasing the launcher calibre to 600-mm. The maximum tube length will be 60 metres. The system will have a slightly higher ballistic efficiency than the S-350 launcher.'

The report goes on to discuss the use of a carbon fibre missile, which would allow a H.E. payload of 116 kilogrammes.

It is difficult to say how long Bull would have taken to develop the S-600, although he was never a slouch. He already knew the design profile, and the type of installation. There would have been no less than 50 of these huge guns, each capable of firing a projectile, depending on the payload, up to a range of 750 kilometres. The projectiles would have been very long, two or three metres. But being – like the Supergun projectiles – slimmer than the diameter of the barrel, they would have been girdled by a sabot to fill the barrel-bore, which would fall away as the shot left the muzzle. This device, used by Bull on H.A.R.P. and intended for use with Babylon, would enable these offensive projectiles to be fin-stabilised and thus to be highly accurate over the range. Its use would also significantly reduce the problem of barrel-wear and enhance the gun's useful life.

A new S.R.C. projectile was already under development. From January 1990 an engineer named V.M. Bojic was recruited to this project, codenamed L.R.S.B. 11 GLR. The projectile was based on the design of the Martlet 3E, a design proven during the H.A.R.P. programme, but it was now to be made out of carbon-fibre composite, a material which Jim Fletcher, a S.R.C. chemical engineer, had been charged with developing. This projectile was in fact intended for the S-350, but clearly something like it would have been used in S-600 too.

The guns of Project 839 were intended to be strung along Iraq's border with Iran like an offensive Maginot Line. They would be protected between 20-metre embankments of earth or sand, to make low-level aircraft attack impossible. For firing they would be rolled out, elevated and traversed by means of a rail table onto the target. They could have created devastation in the Iranian oilfields and the population centres nearby.

The Iraqi Government intended eventually to produce the massive S-600 systems on their own soil. Saddam Hussein knew that an arms or technology embargo was a possibility in the future, and set out to acquire the necessary manufacturing plant. By using a series of middle-men, he proposed to purchase the Baytown Texas steel-plant, lock, stock and barrel. The plant, capable of producing the S-600 barrel-forgings, was available at a cost of fourteen million dollars. Funding, by now impossible from Iraq, was to be provided unwittingly from Texas's neighbouring state, Georgia.

I learned later that Bull had not gone immediately to Iraq with his ideas for these new, very long-range gun systems. Around Christmas 1988 he'd approached the U.S. Army offering them first refusal. He talked also to his old clients, the Chinese. Neither proved to be receptive. But when he discussed the idea with the Iraqis in the summer of 1989 the response was much more positive. They commissioned the modifications to the 350-mm Babylon test model and the construction of two prototype 350-mm elevating systems. The components were to be made almost entirely in Britain. They also asked for more detailed studies for the S-600 with a view to going into production with three prototypes.

Later still, I was able to produce a drawing of the S-600 design. It would have looked very like, although much bigger than, the old Paris Guns of the First World War, braced in a similar way to maintain the straightness of the barrel. The age-old problem of 'droop' in long-barrel guns was to be further countered by wrapping the low-pressure section of the barrel with Kevlar, an ultrastrong fibre composite widely used in body armour. Reading this made me smile. It was a typical S.R.C. innovation, a simple cure for a very old headache.

It is the Paris Guns that provide, I believe, the clue to Bull's thinking at this time. Bull's book, *The Paris Guns and Project H.A.R.P.*, published only in 1988, actually contained more pages on the Germans' First World War long-range artillery than on H.A.R.P., although it was H.A.R.P. that Bull knew the most

197

about. And if, for Bull, the 1,000-mm space gun was the realisation of his main obsession, Project 839 contained many elements in common with the book's other subject. These old 350-mm German guns, and the men who used them to bombard Paris (establishing in the process world gunnery records unsurpassed until Betsy in the 1960s) had a strong romantic appeal for Bull, as can be found in the language he used to describe the Paris guns' powerful public image:

> . . . a new super weapon, performed beyond the limits hitherto considered possible for a field weapon. A system developed and shrouded in secrecy, neither its numbers nor quality known. Capable of striking at enormous ranges, it required little imagination to foresee its potential to play a decisive role in shaping the events of war.

Here he might have been describing Project 839 itself. And, with his new departure in the summer of 1989, Bull, I think, saw himself as following in the steps of the men from Krupps who had built the guns powerful enough to bombard Paris from a distance of 127 kilometres.

43

A few days after I met Riley, three very worried men came to my house. All were directors of the lathes and tools firm, Matrix Churchill, and had been arrested only a few weeks earlier. Until recently their company – one of the largest in its field in Britain – had been enthusiastically encouraged by Government ministers to trade with Iraq. Now they found themselves in a similar position to the one I had only recently escaped from – on bail whilst awaiting trial on the charge that they had exported restricted goods. They were led by Paul Henderson, the managing director of the company.

What these men had to tell me was very interesting indeed. I already knew in general terms that the Iraqis were major share-holders in Matrix Churchill. Now I heard the full story.

'We were doing an awful lot of business with Iraq – it was keeping us afloat, quite honestly. But in spite of this, around 1987 things got very sticky, and it became apparent that our owners, the T.I. Group, wanted us off their hands. Well, of course, they couldn't find a buyer, so they considered putting us into receiver-ship. It was as simple as that. We, of course, wanted to do a management buy-out, it seemed the only viable option, but we couldn't get the finance. It was looking very bleak.'

Henderson explained that T.I. had a Deputy Chairman with very good contacts inside government. Since Matrix Churchill did such a lot of business with Iraq, the Foreign Office, through the British Ambassador in Baghdad, were asked to approach the Iraqis to see if they were interested in taking a share in the buy-out of the company. The Iraqis were interested and, in the end, provided most of the finance for the deal. Essentially, then, the British Government had sold the company to the Iraqis and then arrested Henderson and his two colleagues for trading with Iraq.

'And did you have licences for the machines you were selling to Iraq?'

They did, but it was all dual-purpose stuff, feasibly useful for both military or civilian purposes. But Matrix Churchill had teams of people out there, staying in Baghdad, Mosul, all over the place, setting the tools up, training the local workforce. Nobody at the U.K. end had raised a finger to stop them – until now, that is.'

Henderson recalled a meeting he attended between members of the Machine Tools Trade Association and Alan Clark, Minister of State in the Department of Trade, which took place on 20 January 1988, three months after Iraq had bought Matrix Churchill. The object of the gathering was specifically to discuss Iraqi trade.

The Minister had opened the meeting by congratulating members on their sterling efforts in obtaining such lucrative contracts in the Middle East. He went on to assure them that, since Britain's competitors were continuing to supply similar machines, there was no reason why the British Government should block the issue of export licences. However, Clark emphasised that manufacturers should submit their applications as quickly as possible, in case of 'bureaucratic interference' from other Departments.

I could see here evidence of differences of opinion between the D.T.I. and the Foreign Office, similar to those which Stephen Bryen had flagged up within the U.S. administration. Sir Geoffrey Howe, then the British Foreign Secretary, had recently been trying to have the rules of trade with Iraq tightened up. Clark warned the industrialists of this possibility, although the most important factor was the possibilty of a change in U.S. policy.

But I wanted to know more about the Iraqis' acquisition of the company.

'Who's the Deputy Chair of T.I.,' I wanted to know, 'the one who fixed up the original sale?'

'That was Sir John Cuckney. Appointed 1985. He has the most amazing contacts.'

'Mr Cowley, I must warn you that anything you say may be used against you.'

The scene was the offices of the Customs and Excise, in Birmingham and I was with an Italian judge and the two *caribinieri* police officers, who had travelled all the way from Milan to question me. They were investigating the Italian end of the Supergun affair. It was at this point that I almost lost my temper.

'There's no point in cautioning me,' I said. 'I'm here entirely of my own free will. You have no jurisdiction here, I don't have to talk to you and I won't if you harrass me.'

The investigating magistrate, Dr Carlo Mario Zampi, was very prickly, and kept appealing for support to the two police officers. They, more reasonable and perhaps more experienced, were talking rapidly in their own language, explaining that there was little they could do to me outside the frontiers of Italy. The judge then smiled at me and said,

'I wonder, Mr Cowley, if we could invite you to come and visit us as our guest, and – of course – at our expense, in Italy. We would like you to become a prosecution witness in our case against certain Italian nationals who we believe were involved in this business.'

I almost laughed. They had to be joking. But their faces were not smiling now. I said,

'I'll answer your questions if I can, orally. But I'll not sign anything and I won't be a court witness.'

There was another furious altercation between the three of them before we started a process of informal exchanges which went on for four hours. All the time the judge was writing, compiling, it appeared, a memorandum. It was when he suddenly placed the hand-written pages – all in Italian – in front of me and invited me to sign that I excused myself and left.

I passed Barry Riley in the adjaent office.

'They want me to sign something in Italian. So I'm leaving.'

He looked apologetic.

'I tried to explain that they can't do things like that. I obviously didn't get through.'

The subject of the Italian judge's investigation was Terni, who had made the Supergun breech. But there was much more to Italy's involvement in arms sales to Iraq. It had at this time been a year since the public heard of the astonishing unauthorised loans by an Italian bank, Banca Nazionale del Lavoro, specifically intended to help Iraq to acquire weapons and weapons-making technology.

B.N.L., three-quarters owned by the Italian Treasury, had a branch in Atlanta, Georgia. The branch maintained a staff of only nineteen, yet in 1987 or 1988 this insignificant banking outpost proceeded to finance Iraqi military procurement on a breathtaking scale. The 36-year-old branch manager, Chris Drogoul, was described by the bank's former Chairman, Nerio Nesi, as having struck him during their only meeting as 'a diabolic financial genius'. In February 1988, and for the next eighteen months, Drogoul used his genius to grant massive secret loans to Iraq, whilst allegedly evading the supervision of his superiors either in New York or Rome. Via B.N.L.'s electronic banking facilities, as many as six multi-million dollar transfers per day were leaving Atlanta and, in all, 2,500 export credits were dispatched to banks in areas where the Iraqis were making specific purchases such as the Matrix Churchill machining systems. Among the many other companies which received export credits were Mammesman Demag, Thiessen, Lummas Crest, Rotec and Potain so that, in the course of time, B.N.L.'s exposure to Iraq, created by Drogoul and his colleagues, amounted to about $3 billion. This meant that, with loans on Drogoul's authority alone limited to only $500,000 per client, he appears to have exceeded his threshold six thousand times over.

The surface commissions charged on these export credits amounted to a meagre 0.2 per cent, in a market where 15 per cent might have been the norm for a poor credit risk.

But it was not only through letters of credit that the Iraqi/B.N.L. connection worked. At the same time, $629 million in cash was gradually moved to the Rafidain Bank in the form of a straight line of credit from B.N.L. Atlanta. The enormous loan was guaranteed by the Rafidain Bank itself, a dubious arrangement since the reason it needed cash in the first place was that its coffers were practically empty. Nevertheless the cash served its purpose, which was to act as a fund for paying foreign suppliers on deals where dedicated letters of credit would be inappropriate and export credit guarantees were unavailable. It was by this means that Supergun was financed.

In the case of Walter Somers, cash deposits large enough to cover the entire contract for the 350-mm test model were made into a special bank account. Then, as the manufacturing passed a series of stages (reported to the bank by a Lloyd's inspector) staged payments were triggered. This had been essential ever since the Forgemaster's financial director, Philip Barrett, had made enquiries at his company's own bank (the Bank of Scotland) about the Rafidain's credit-worthiness, they had laughed at him. The Iraqi central bank's credit rating was regarded as so abysmal that reputable banks and manufacturers around the world would not deal with it unless cash was transferred in advance. In the case of the Supergun orders, this is precisely what happened, and the source of the cash was almost certainly the Banca Nazionale del Lavoro, Atlanta, Georgia.

Reflecting on the huge scale of the interbank transfers out of

Atlanta, it is hard to believe that nobody in the United States administration knew what was going on. The C.I.A., in a classified document dated 6 November 1989, discussed the Iraqi-Italy repercussions of the B.N.L.-Atlanta scandal. The C.I.A. were also aware that the B.N.L.-Atlanta rip-off was not some rogue operation but was also known to B.N.L.'s Rome Headquarters. In a document, Ref Rome 22019, marked Confidential – Entire Text, the Italian Ambassador discussed the subject with the U.S. Federal Reserve Board. The Italian President Cossiga was also being kept notified; his concern centred around the fact that B.N.L.'s major shareholders were the Italian taxpayers. The repeated emphasis on the wording 'damage control' reflected the desire to minimise any Italian political fallout. The American Government's awareness of the looting of the B.N.L. Atlanta Bank branch is also well documented in letters passing backwards and forwards between the U.S. Department of Justice and the Federal Reserve Bank.

In a letter dated 9 January 1990, the U.S. Department of Justice indicated they had located a Turkish national, Yavus Tezeller, who could provide information regarding, to quote, 'after sales services, unearned consulting fees, and other payments to Iraqis as well as kickbacks paid by United States and multinational companies to obtain Iraqi contracts'. The C.I.A., at their Headquarters in Langley, Virginia, maintains a large computer check entitled 'Follow The Money' on the flow of funds in and out America, and any sum larger than $200,000 automatically triggers a cue to investigation. With the activities of Drogoul and his colleagues the alarm must have been glowing red hot. So why did it take eighteen months for action to be taken? Certainly one of the reasons can be found in a classified document signed by George Bush, copied to the following addressees: The Vice President, The Secretary of State, The Director of Central Intelligence, The Director, United States Arm Control and Disarment Agency, The Secretary of Defence. And President Bush sets out, under the title, 'US Policy towards the Persian Gulf':

'Access to Persian Gulf oil and the security of key friendly states in the area are vital to the U.S. national security. The United States remains committed to defend its vital interests in the region, if necessary and appropriate through the use of U.S. military force against the Soviet Union.'

When I first read this document a chill ran down my back. It could all be summed up in just two words: 'power politics'.

44

When the British Government approached the Iraqis to see if they were interested in buying Matrix Churchill, the idea slotted neatly into Iraqis' objective of building a modern manufacturing base. In pursuit of this they had set up a network of legally-established holding companies owned by Iraq which went shopping for advanced machining systems or composite materials such as carbon fibres, and also for the companies which made them.

At the apex of the triangle was the Al-Arabi Trading Company, supposedly one of the few 'private enterprises' allowed in Iraq, although actually controlled by Kamil Hussein from the Ministry for Industries. In Baghdad a senior figure in the organisation was Dr Fadel Khadum, who moved to London in 1987 to take over the Technology Development Group, the company whose subsidiary bought Matrix Churchill and other companies such as Newcast Foundries, of Newcastle-under-Lyme. There was even a Matrix Churchill subsidiary established in Solon, Ohio, which, apart from contracting to build machine-tool and glass fibre plants in Iraq, was negotiating (ultimately without success) to buy a Texas steel plant for $14 million to manufacture large gun barrels in Iraq.

S.R.C. became involved in this procurement scheme a year later, when Bull's attention was caught by the existence in Northern Ireland of a defunct but extremely well-equipped company which had made a light aircraft chiefly out of carbon fibre materials. The company was the bankrupt Lear Fan Corporation, and the owners of its plant were now trying to sell. Bull saw this mothballed factory – at Newtownabbey, near Belfast – as an ideal source of the composite materials which he needed for the development of the Martlet missile, Supergun's space probe. He may also have been at least thinking about how to get materials useful in lightening the weight of a long-range military gun-barrel, such as he was later to develop in Project 839. But he knew, in any case, that Iraq would have many additional uses for advanced carbon fibre manufacturing, particularly in the Scud programme and for the Condor 2 missile, a joint on-going project with Argentina and Egypt.

In order to buy Lear Fan, Bull formed a joint company with T.D.G. called Canira, which itself spawned an offshoot, S.R.C. Composites (share capital £3.4 million). This was the company which, after prolonged negotiations, bought the Irish plant in May 1989 for £3 million. Eighty-five per cent of this was Iraqi money, almost certainly originating with B.N.L.

Bull was confident of success and he and his son Michel began to get organised. Pretty soon S.R.C. Composites had a small office and nine employees established at Newtownabbey. Next Bull started looking around for filament-winding equipment, difficult to obtain since this machinery is essential in the manufacture of carbon fibre to produce missile nose-cones. Purchase was restricted under the U.S. Missile Technology Control Regime, and similarly controlled by other countries. Various firms were canvassed by S.R.C. as to the availability and price of such a machine.

Then, on 11 July 1989 an agent, giving the evocative name of Philbey, approached the stand of a firm called Darchem Composite Structures at a trade exhibition in Birmingham. Philbey claimed to be designing graphite tubular composite drill guides for a petro-chemical application, and wanted to discuss placing an order. The Darchem people were surprised he needed such a high-technology component for a simple job, but Philbey convinced them that the loading would be such that this material was needed. In fact, these were not drill guides at all, but sabots to be used in the launching of the modified Martlet missile. Philbey then told Darchem that he was acting for a company called S.R.C.

Who was the mysterious Philbey? He had claimed to be a consultant, but in reality he must be an S.R.C. man. In my time there was only one figure who would have sought this role. John Heath was almost an Arthur Daley figure, a man who hated to stay in the same place for too long. He loved to consider himself a wheeler-dealer, a fixer who would boast about the deal he struck in Spain yesterday, and the one he's chasing in Iran tomorrow. The more I thought about 'Philbey', the more sure I was that this was Heath.

Martin Hughes, with Philbey and another S.R.C. man named Bradley, visited Darchem's factory at Huntingdon on 31 July 1989 to finalise the order. Preliminary discussions had already revealed that S.R.C. would be making the parts at their own factory in Northern Ireland, and they would be needing only tooling, prototype and pre-production batches from Darchem. The suggested value of the deal was now put at £150,000.

In the second week in September, however, somebody at Darchem had found an article in the magazine *Flight International* which linked S.R.C. Composites with Iraq. At the same time – after all the talk of Northern Ireland – there had been some alarm that this order was now for delivery to Brussels. Darchem immediately informed S.R.C. that in this case an export licence was required. S.R.C. replied in a letter dated 18 September requesting that the whole matter be now 'put on hold'. It was the last Darchem heard from Philbery or the Space Research Corporation.

The reason for the requested rerouting of the 'drill guides' was that the Lear Fan deal had fallen through. The factory could not be reactivated without a £2 million grant from the Northern Ireland Industrial Development Board, a British Government medium for industrial subsidies in the province. In a situation reminiscent of the Iraqis' attempt (through Colonel Kadoori) to purchase Flexible Manufacturing Technology Ltd from Vickers, the Board initially told Bull that they saw no problems. Meanwhile, however, they had begun to worry about the Iraqi connection and on 16 July they consulted the Foreign Office about the background of S.R.C. Composites. Officials investigated and two or three weeks later the F.O. killed the scheme by advising the N.I.I.D.B. to refuse a grant.

The fact that this advice came through the Foreign Office is interesting. The British Ambassador in Baghdad had been a key player in the Matrix Churchill sale, and through him the Foreign Office must have known a good deal about the status of Al Arabi Trading. In spite of the certainty that Matrix Churchill lathes were going to be used to make artillery shells, that deal had been smiled on. The Lear Fan purchase, however, was stopped. Why?

It's possible that, in the intervening two years, the Intelligence service had gained more information about the Al-Arabi missile programme, and about Dr Khadum in particular. In 1990, during the Gulf Crisis, Khadum's name turned up in the pages of Hansard, having been named in Parliament as an Iraqi intelligence officer active in Britain. It seems, however, that the real impetus behind the refusal came from the Americans. After the B.N.L. affair, the Americans had been investigating the activities of Matrix Churchill in Solon, Ohio, and they were alert to the activities of the Technical Development Group. The C.I.A. had also, apparently, heard that Bull was in the market for filament winding machinery, and had contacted British intelligence, asking for a meeting to discuss the Lear Fan sale. According to Bull's biographer, the C.I.A. waved a copy of Bull's business plan for S.R.C. composites, pointing out the sentence reading 'the Company has plans to acquire filament winding equipment in the near future' and asking the British to refuse the grant. M.I.6 said there was no need, at this stage, to take any action. They said they had good intelligence about what was going on within S.R.C., and could easily keep an eye on the situation. This is, of course, the classic posture of British intelligence: you keep an operation running and unsuspecting while you milk much useful information.

The Americans would have none of this. They told London to pull the plug and in the end that is exactly what happened. In a letter to Kevin McNamara explaining its decision to refuse the S.R.C. grant, the N.I.I.D.B. stressed that it was acting on Foreign Office advice, which was that 'the U.S. as a member of the Missile Technology Regime, is committed to do all that it can to prevent proliferation of missiles'.

The sentence more or less admits that America was tugging on the string.

45

I must come now to the murkiest part of this story. Wrapped up in it is the shooting of Bull in Brussels and, more than a year later, the killing of another man in the same city. But before we can begin to understand all this, we need to go back and reexamine the 1988 propellants contract which was signed between Azzawi and P.R.B.

Bernard de Witt and Serge Dumont were surprised by my information that the Belgian Air Force had flown the propellant out to Jordan, and they were very interested in the $25,000 that was paid in gold *baksheesh* to ease the path of each consignment. But this rather blatant palm-greasing was not the only corrupt part of the contract.

But before I get into that, it's necessary to understand something about how deals like this are done throughout the world. You don't expect to do business in the same way within West European or North American countries. These have their own effective controls to prevent the more obvious kinds of kickback. But in dealing with the government of any Third-World country, the businessman soon realises that he has entered an entirely different environment. Now the industrialised nations' rule book is thrown out of the window.

For a start the 'tender' stage takes on a completely new meaning. Usually tendering is about the customer seeking a deal at the *lowest* price, but when the customer is a government in Africa, South America or many parts of Asia and the Middle East, the process is turned on its head. Here, typically, the negotiators for the government agency in question are trying to harvest a large enough commission for themselves, and will frequently ask for the contract price to be jacked up accordingly. This results in the phenomenon of *over*cutting. I have sat in on contract negotiations in Kenya where the client has demanded of the supplier,

'You say you will charge our government one million dollars. We say, that's no good to us. *Two* million dollars would be better.'

In such negotiations, commissions payable by bank transfer (rather than the handing around of gold bars) are the preferred medium for the largest-scale corruption. I would add that, within Iraq, this is largely unknown, at least in my experience. Financial corruption by government officials is punishable by death, and I saw none of it in the course of my own dealings with the Iraqis.

Since there has been speculation about possible kickbacks from the Supergun tube contracts – those with Somers and Forgemasters – the special nature of certain payments made by these manufacturers require explanation. The contracts did indeed include percentage commissions, involving sums of the order of forty or fifty thousand pounds, which were paid into the bank accounts of two European shell companies, Perma Trading and Cometal. It's also true that these accounts were controlled by Bull, administered by Monique Jamine and used by the Iraqis. But the true purpose of the commissions was to provide cash-flow for Babylon in Europe. Iraqi bureaucracy and exchange controls, not to mention their shortage of liquidity, made it difficult to have ready cash available for the project's use. The commission payments, subtracted from the full contract price, provided a channel for this cash. The accounts into which they were paid had almost the status of petty cash accounts, and were extremely useful for odd payments or purchases for which it would have been difficult or tedious to transfer funds from Baghdad. Bull was fully accountable to the Iraqi Government for all payments made out of these accounts.

The money could be used for such contingencies as when one of our engineers, Big Ali, on (for him) a once-in-a-lifetime overseas trip to visit Forgemasters in Sheffield, went downtown on the customary shopping spree. His purchases, however, were later stolen and, with my approval, the impressed accounts were used to replace all the suits and shoes which Ali had lost.

Not all the payments were directly connected to Project Babylon. Dr Saadi's children's school fees in Germany were paid out of it, for example. But even this should not be seen as a form of underhand corruption. The perks of a job like Deputy Minister for Industry in Iraq were ill-defined but substantial. They included the provision of a Ministerial lift at the Baghdad offices, for his exclusive use. There would be many apparently spontaneous gifts from on high for him – a Mercedes car or a farm in the Tigris valley – but also more systematic benefits such as the education of his children at an exclusive school in his wife's native country (Saadi's wife was German). None of this treatment, in the context of Iraqi life, would be seen as unreasonable.

The commission payments built into P.R.B.'s formal contract to supply Babylon's propellants were a very different matter from all this, as I was eventually to discover. The order, covering shipments for both the 350-mm and the 1,000-mm systems, was signed on 17 November 1988 and the first delivery was due on 20 February 1989, in time for the test firing of the model at Tal Uwaynat. All told, 26 tonnes of 350-mm propellant and 210 tonnes of Supergun propellant were ordered – enough for at least 20 firings of the 350-mm systems and 17 firings of the 1,000-mm. That is about as much as I knew – or needed to know – about the deal while I was actually working for A.T.I.

It was only in mid-1990 that I discovered that the order was covered by the Office National du Ducroire, the Belgian equivalent of the U.K.'s Export Credit Guarantee Department: in other words, that the Belgian taxpayer was underwriting the deal, in case the Iraqis defaulted on the balance. Then I began to dig deeper. Eventually, I acquired documents which laid out the full structure of the contract, including the commissions. This document was provided by a source in England familiar with the financial shenanigans which accompanied the financial demise of P.R.B.

The first supplies of propellant ordered by Azzawi in 1988 were worth in contract terms a little over £3.25 million, of which 30 per cent was payable in advance. The contract was numbered E5397, and for form's sake, the purchaser was named as the Royal Jordanian Armed Forces. On the P.R.B. side the signatories were Jourdain and Ernoux, his deputy.

I had sat in Azzawi's office in the Special Projects Building while Jourdain and Ernoux had discussed the price per kilogram of propellant. Azzawi knew that the appropriate figure would be in the region of $3 to $6. Jourdain, however, was asking for an outrageous premium.

'It is because of the very special nature of this propellant that we cannot ask less than $12 per kilo,' stated Jourdain firmly, and he could not be moved. For once Azzawi's formidable bargaining skills were to no avail. Everyone around the table knew that as things stood, the Iraqis had no choice but to source the propellant through Belgium. Reluctantly, knowing that he was overpaying by $1.5 million on this contract alone, Azzawi signed. He had been sandbagged.

The advance payment was made by letter of credit drawn on the

Central Bank of Jordan but originating in Iraq and ultimately – there is no doubt – in Atlanta, Georgia.

The first documentary credits in P.R.B.'s favour were made on 22 February 1989 and, from then until the end of August, P.R.B. received about £1.5 million under this contract. There was a considerable balance left outstanding later in the year. By then events had occurred whose significance only became clear when I had tumbled to the fact that the hike in the *overall* propellants price had a very substantial tonic effect on a hidden aspect of the deal: the *commissions* paid by P.R.B. out of its Iraqi receipts.

Two commissions were to be paid on the propellants deal, amounting to about 17 per cent of the contract value. The first, to a company called Bilder Trading, a British-incorporated company which received a total of ten million Belgian francs (£175,000). The second company was Gerofin Investment Corporation, registered in Panama but with a box-number address in Lausanne. Gerofin's share of the commission was 11.77 per cent or about £385,000, and between 26 April and 20 July 1989 it had garnered more than £165,000 of this, in four stated payments.

˙ What were these companies? Everyday corruption through front companies over large-scale contracts is normally initiated by the buyer – government ministers or officials. But, as I've already said, such practices were unknown in Iraq. If Azzawi had participated in such payments, the punishment would have been hanging by the neck on a pole outside your home. I knew Azzawi and I knew him to be incapable of taking such a risk. Something else, something very unusual, was going on. Whoever controlled Bilder Trading and Gerofin must have thought they were going to gather some very tidy sums indeed. The on-going propellant needs for S.R.C.'s guns would potentially be worth at least $30 million – that translates into more than $5 million in commissions.

Then in September 1989 the fortunes of these shady companies took a sudden nosedive. P.R.B., it appeared, was in irreversible financial trouble and its owners Societé Générale de Belgique had determined to sell it. The buyer? There were two players in the game. One was a company which until recently had been an insignificant British fireworks manufacturer. The other was Gerald Bull himself.

46

Some of the constituent parts of Poudreries Réunies de Belgique had made gunpowder for Napoleon's army, and later for Robert E. Lee during the American Civil War. The company now had 1,400 employees at six Belgian factories making explosives, propellants, projectiles, ammunition cases and detonators. It also had firing range at Matagne near the French border and another similar facility in Canada. In the mid-1980s the company was doing well, with sales worth £175 million and a profit of £7.5 million.

Bull had known P.R.B. intimately since the 1970s. He had become friendly with the then Chief Executive of the company, Joseph Severin, who had not only persuaded Bull to start his first Brussels company (S.R.C. International) but had put up 38 per cent of the original equity. With Severin's encouragement, Bull developed the GC45 gun system and his Extended Range Full Bore shells, whose charges and fuses were supplied by Severin's company.

It was the Brussels base which had given Bull the European lifeline he needed after his American prison sentence. Once established here, he continued to work with P.R.B. on and off. He also maintained a useful informant inside the company. This was Tony Binek, a Polish-Canadian who had originally worked with Bull on H.A.R.P. and (unknown to P.R.B.) was also drawing a 'consultancy' fee from S.R.C.

In these circumstances it was inevitable that P.R.B. would be offered the contract for Supergun's propellant. However P.R.B. was now in serious financial difficulties. The previous year the company managed to generate a mere £45 million worth of business, and suffered losses of £25 million. It was against this background that Binek and Jourdain came out to Iraq to negotiate the details of the contract with Azzawi. Binek knew how desperate the company was for the order, and had long since informed Bull as much. Bull, of course, saw the implications. If P.R.B. went to the wall – or even fell into less friendly hands – where would Project Babylon obtain its propellant?

Yet there was a solution which immediately presented itself. I remembered a conversation with Bull towards the end of 1988, following a meeting he had had with Hervé de Carmoy, the Chief Executive of Société Générale. Carmoy had previously been Chief Executive of Midland Bank overseas operations and a main board member. Bull by now had acquired an early business plan drawn up by Astra Holdings, then considering a bid for P.R.B. Attached to it were projections of future business by P.R.B. itself. Bull made me read it, and a glowing future seemed in prospect. I wondered why S.G.B. would want to sell such a profitable enterprise.

'Exactly, it'll never happen. This is all fantasy.'

Bull flicked the P.R.B. plan dismissively with his fingers.

P.R.B.'s about to go belly-up. Astra will never buy it when they find out the true situation. S.G.B. will have to pay somebody to take it over. The Iraqis can have it for nothing, or at least a fraction of its value to them. It'd give them a very useful manufacturing capacity in ammunition, propellants, high explosives. And *we'd* have our own propellant capability for Babylon.'

Some time later Bull suggested to Dr Amir Saadi that S.R.C. could be the vehicle for an Iraqi-backed bid for P.R.B., and Dr Saadi must have been receptive to the idea. It would fit in with Iraq's technology procurement policy and, what was more, the funds were available through Atlanta, Georgia. If the Iraqis had been permitted to buy Matrix Churchill, then why not P.R.B.? True, the Lear Fan deal had been vetoed by the British Foreign Office, but attitudes in Belgium were very much more relaxed than in Britain.

The matter was broached and some negotiations in Brussels took place. The bankers through whom P.R.B. was to be sold, Banque de Générale, knowing Bull's background, were wary enough of him, but they nevertheless asked for a formal bid. Bull quickly put together a proposal, and sat back to await the reply. Bull was confident that the competition, if any, would not be serious. Companies with his type of expertise in this market were few and surely, he thought, Societé Générale de Belgique would jump at the offer.

However, bargaining with Astra had been proceeding for the best part of a year. This was a company from the U.K., and it was certainly a serious contender. Now, even as Bull put in his own proposal, P.R.B. and the British were coming close to an agreement.

Until recently, probably more children than adults have known the name of Astra. The company originally made much of its annual profits around 5 November, the nation's pyrotechnic celebration of the death, 400 years ago, of Guy Fawkes. But by the late 1980s Astra had changed. It was now a company with its eyes fixed firmly on the contemporary world – on the world of international military supplies.

In 1980 a group of ambitious men formerly employed by another fireworks company, Brocks, had bought Astra as a going concern, although with rather outdated plant. This takeover was backed by the 3i Group, and the intention behind the takeover was to turn Astra into a modern producer of explosives, fuses, military pyrotechnics, ammunition and propellants, a process which allegedly had the direct encouragement of the Ministry of Defence. As part of the Thatcher Government's privatisation programme, ammunition manufacture was due to be opened up to competition on a 'level playing field', following the sale of the state ammunition company, Royal Ordnance, to the private sector. Astra had even identified parts of Royal Ordnance that it would itself have liked to acquire.

Astra's expansion plans went well at first and by 1987 they had bought military-supplies plants in the U.K. and North America. But its Chairman Gerald James was furious when he discovered that Royal Ordnance had been sold off in one piece to British Aerospace, under a secret five-year agreement (known as E.P.R.E.P.) whereby 80 per cent of Ministry of Defence ammunition business would be exclusively reserved for B.Ae. Astra, James felt, had been led to believe that by making expensive diversifications it could tender for contracts previously enjoyed by Royal Ordnance. So much, he now thought, for level playing fields.

The solution, James and his Chief Executive Chris Gumbley thought, was to expand the company even further, to make it a truly international outfit. They already had North American plants, but they still lacked a presence in Europe and, when P.R.B. came up for sale, it looked ideal. Having secured backing in the City from the Prudential, Clerical and Medical and the 3i Group, Astra entered a lengthy bargaining process. They were worried by P.R.B.'s poor trading position over the previous two years and about its future prospects, despite being assured that, with lots of work in hand, the balance sheet for the current year was again healthy. Astra asked to see the outstanding contracts for this work, but P.R.B. refused, saying that if the deal fell through, Astra might have gained a commercial advantage by having seen them. Nor would P.R.B. supply Astra with a client list.

Eventually Astra's auditors, accounts Stoy Hayward, were allowed to look at the contracts, on the basis that they revealed no details to Astra. Stoy Hayward carried out their examination and reported to the client that profit forecasts from P.R.B. of around £2 million in 1989 looked secure. On 17 July, after months of talks, by which time Astra had beaten the asking price down from £40 million to £21 million, the deal was signed. Completion was on 11 September. On that day, and in one leap, Astra Holdings plc had apparently more than doubled in size. It had also unknowingly become the propellant contractor to Project Babylon.

Even before these events Astra had, in fact, already supplied materials to S.R.C. It had filled an order worth £300,000 for booster pellets, placed with Astra by a British company called B And J Industries. The ultimate client, however, was S.R.C. in Brussels, who required the pellets for the propellant of a new type of ammunition which Bull had designed to extend the range of the Soviet 130-mm M46 field guns. This weapon, deployed by armies throughout the Third World, was threatened with obsolescence in the face of more powerful 155-mm systems. Bull's shell, a version of his E.R.F.B. base-bleed shell originally developed for the 155-mm gun, was expected to give the M46 a new lease of life, and S.R.C. therefore hoped for profitable business around the world.

Bull's first client, however, was almost inevitably Saddam Hussein and in February 1989 an early consignment of Bull's new shells was actually sent to Iraq *via* Jordan in a Belgian Air Force Hercules transport, along with a cargo of Supergun propellant. Astra would probably have been unaware of this, since their end-user certificate and licence merely specified Belgium.

The situation at P.R.B. was, of course, completely different. Here the significance of the Babylon propellants order was taken entirely for granted and, once Astra were in possession of the company, they too would know the existence of Supergun. In the winter of 1990/91 I began to piece together the train of events which was set in motion by Astra's discovery. It was, I soon learned, no isolated event: it would end by destroying several companies, many thousands of jobs and more than one human life.

It would raise questions about the behaviour of senior P.R.B. employees, the possible role of the Société Générale de Belgique and the probity of the British Government.

47

In the first few days of September 1989, before the P.R.B. sale was finalised, Astra's Chief Executive Christ Gumbley was manning his company's stand at a Naval Equipment Trade Exhibition at Portsmouth. He was approached by a man who identified himself as Roger Harding, Deputy Director of Sales, Ministry of Defence.

Harding had a disturbing message for Gumbley. He'd heard that Astra Holdings were about to buy P.R.B. Well, he said, if they did go ahead, they should beware.

Gumbley must have been surprised, because he knew perfectly well that the M.O.D. – in particular Harding's senior colleague Sir Peter Levene – had been very anxious indeed that Astra should expand, supposedly to open up British armed forces' procurement to meaningful competition by buying companies like P.R.B. Exactly two years earlier, at the very same Portsmouth event, Levene had himself stood on the Astra stand and promised Astra 40 per cent of £500 million worth of ammunition sales if they got themselves in shape to take it on. However cynical they may have felt about this now, in view of the E.P.R.E.P. agreement guaranteeing B.Ae. 80 per cent of British defence sales, the warning seemed to Astra a strange contradiction of the public policy. Was there something the M.O.D. had learned and were not letting on about? If so, what was it, and how long had they known?

It was a question to which, when I eventually found out about the Harding warning in the summer of 1991, I too would have liked an answer. But at the time in 1989 the man from the Ministry had not been particularly forthcoming. He had spoken in vague generalities, explaining how, in his Ministry's view, the Belgian company might have a number of possibly untoward aspects to it.

Once Astra's James and Gumbley took control of P.R.B. they discovered what Harding may have been getting at. Their Belgian management, now becoming highly informative, revealed candidly that their factory at Kaulille was making a propellant charge for a gun of unprecedented size. They added that the client, ostensibly Jordan, was in fact Iraq. One of two men – Gilbert the Sales Director or Cardinael, the General Manager – was putting it about that Saddam Hussein was developing a weapon capable of firing projectiles tipped with nuclear and biological warheads.

But there was even more disturbing news to follow. P.R.B.'s Iraqi order was an absolutely vital one for the company; it was, in fact, the only extant business capable of sustaining P.R.B. into the future. Duronsoy, the former Chief Executive of P.R.B., told James and Gumbley that the rest of the business projections, seen and ratified by Stoy Hayward only six weeks earlier, were, in fact, seriously misleading. Without the Iraqi propellant P.R.B., far from being a live takeover target for Astra, was virtually a dead duck in the water.

Gerald James was justifiably embittered. He felt angry with P.R.B.'s owners, Société Générale de Belgique, who had misrepresented the financial viability of their subsidiary. But he felt hardly less disappointed with the British Government. They had, after all, suggested they had prior knowledge (at the very least a suspicion) of something wrong about P.R.B., but had allowed Astra to proceed regardless.

It seems to me that James had an uncomfortable dilemma. There was a real possibility that people in London, for whatever reason, had all along been playing with Project Babylon, like a cat toying with a broken-winged sparrow. If that was the case – although James could not then imagine why it should be – he knew that, unless he reported the propellants contract, he would expose himself to future prosecution for evading export controls. Yet by doing so he would inevitably cause the contracts to be lost and the entire future of Astra put at risk. What should he do?

If he felt tempted to try to conceal the Iraqi business and continue to make the propellant secretly, the matter would in any case have been swiftly taken out of James's hands. On 20 September he sent his most active non-executive director, a man named Stephan Kock, to Belgium specifically to visit the Kaulille plant. There, in the course of showing him round, the manager told Kock of 'an unusual propellants contract' and also spoke about orders being received from one Middle Eastern country whilst in fact being destined for another.

When Kock came to tell his version of the story to the House of Commons Trade and Industry Select Committee he claimed to have surmised that the propellant might possibly be for a very large gun, and to have telephoned the British intelligence services immediately to alert them. He says he later took expert advice and made a more detailed written report to military intelligence. Interestingly, as he confirmed before the Select Committee, he did not tell the Astra Chairman or Chief Executive about these reports. He did not even inform them of what he had found out.

In the meantime, however, James and Gumbley had bitten the bullet. In the last week of September, they set up a meeting with Harding to tell him about the Iraqi contract. Also present at this meeting, which was held at the Ministry of Defence's offices at Stuart House in London's Soho Square, was a man named Primrose and another who introduced himself as Holdness. Primrose was described as a director of M.O.D. export sales, and was in reality the intelligence representative in that department. The exact nature of Holdness's role was not spelled out, but James formed the certainty that he worked for the S.I.S., otherwise known as M.I.6.

The five men talked in detail about the propellant and its use in a very long range gun, with Primrose in particular asserting confidently that this was a large-grain, slow-burning propellant and must therefore be for such a system. Asking the officials' advice about how to proceed, Gumbley was told he could continue to make and deliver sample batches to the client. But he should on no account go ahead with substantive deliveries without seeking further advice.

A second meeting took place when James received a visit, from Holdness alone this time, at his London office in early October. Holdness proceeded to grill James at length, in particular wanting to know who in P.R.B. knew about the Iraqi propellants contract. Names like Jourdain, Binek, Glibert and Cardinael were among those mentioned. A further meeting between Holdness, Primrose, Gumbley and James took place later in October but, rather more significantly, Holdness made an unscheduled appearance at Astra's Grantham factory on 14 November.

The company was at this time considering the manufacture under licence of a vehicle-mounted machine gun, the Gikal 50. A major client for this weapon would be the special forces, the S.A.S. and S.B.S., and therefore, as he later told the Select Committee, Stephan Kock arranged the visit of an S.A.S. colonel to the Grantham plant, to test-fire the weapon. The soldier, to the surprise of James and Gumbley, arrived in the company of Holdness. Holdness wanted to talk not about the new weapon but about the Iraqi propellant contract. What would have been mentioned was the fact that by now Gumbley had decided, with his Manager John Sellens, to halt all deliveries of the propellant, although it was intended to continue production, at Kaulille.

However, design work on the charge for the 1000-mm System was three months behind schedule at A.T.I. I had received no help from Slack or Baynes, but there were still one or two people willing to be active on my behalf. In the winter of 1990/91, subsequent to the documents Barry Riley had passed to me, I began to receive additional progress reports and other papers from A.T.I. covering the last four months of 1989 and the early weeks of 1990. Among them was a memorandum from Dennis Lyster (a propellant scientist and S.R.C. Vice President) to Bull, dated 5 September 1989 and numbered DL.pf.112. Lyster's memo clearly laid out the position. By now Jim Chan had moved to Canada, and had been replaced by a new designer, Jan Kobes, a Dutchman who had worked for both S.R.C. and Muiden Chemie, whose major shareholder is the Dutch Government. Lyster indicates that Kobes had only just determined the web size of the charge, on the basis of which further tests were still to be carried out.

A second document brought the story forward a couple of months. This was a letter from Kobes dated 10 November, confirming the substance of a meeting which had just taken place between P.R.B. and A.T.I. At this meeting, writes Kobes, 'it was agreed that P.R.B. will start the production of the powder for this system'. If the original production and delivery schedule had been adhered to all 210 tonnes of 1000-mm propellant would have been delivered by 30 October and P.R.B. would have already banked the Iraqis' money. As it was, the giant press at Kaulille, in which the propellant extrusion was to be moulded, stood idle, still waiting for a final go-ahead.

Production never did get going. On 5 December, the workers returned from a tea break at the Kaulille factory to find that an explosion had occurred, destroying one of the press's supporting columns. The explosion had nothing to do with the propellant material itself, which would not have been in an unstable condition at the time. Whatever did cause the damage, it was ruinous. This equipment was one of only two presses of its type in the world. When James had the loss adjustors examine the event, he was told privately by one of the inspectors that they did not consider the explosion an accident. It was, in their opinion, sabotage.

When I heard about this, it got me thinking about my younger days at Henry Wigan, the subsidiary of International Nickel where I had worked in the 1960s. Wigan's was based at Hereford, where the S.A.S. also has its headquarters, and I can remember soldiers coming into the factory as part of their training programme. They came to learn about machinery – not, as you might think, how to make it work, but how to *stop* it working, how to disable it. A small charge was all that was needed. Even with a very big piece of kit like a hydraulic press, you merely had to fracture the frame and the entire machine was finished for ever. Such skills are undoubtedly routine in the training of special forces all over the world.

The fortunes of P.R.B. were now in irreversible decline and it was not long before those of James and Gumbley began to go in the same direction. By Christmas 1989 James had entered a long period of attrition as Chairman of the Board, during which he was subjected to criticism by Kock and by the institutional shareholders. There was a rift, also, with Gumbley. James had meanwhile begun the process of trying to claw back £12 million from S.G.B. in compensation for the misleading P.R.B. prospectus, on which Astra had paid £21 million for the business. Before James could get anywhere, he was suddenly forced to resign on 3 March 1990, as a result of a boardroom coup which had Kock's support.

Gumbley was not destined to last much longer. In the evening of 13 March 1990 a sergeant and a constable from the Ministry of Defence police visited his house with a search warrant. After searching his office and his house they took him off to the police station and interrogated him about his knowledge of the secret E.P.R.E.P. agreement between B.Ae. and the M.O.D. They wanted to know when Gumbley and James received details of the agreement and who had passed this information to them, and they also questioned Gumbley about a car which he had lent to a Ministry of Defence official. They finally let him go at two in the morning. Gumbley was by no means out of the woods. After a second interview a few weeks later he found himself under arrest, on a charge of corrupting a government official. He had become the first person arrested in Britain in 1990, on a charge associated with arms to Iraq.

Gumbley subsequently resigned from the company.

48

It was to be a year and more before I heard about the tribulations of Gerald James and Chris Gumbley, by which time they had begun to seem like small pieces in an increasingly enormous and bewildering jigsaw. And, as I beavered away at this manuscript, assembling as much documentary evidence and personal testimony as I could along the way, one very big piece of the jigsaw had fallen into place.

During Saddam Hussein's army's continued occupation of Kuwait, the Allied operation to oust it comprised of three distinct phases. From 3 August 1990 to 16 January 1991 – the withdrawal deadline set by the United Nations Security Council – the Western powers concentrated on the isolation of Saddam. They built against him a coalition of 26 nations, including the armed participation of 12 out of the 20 Arab League states. These armies, made up of various nationalities though overwhelmingly American, had been massing in the Saudi desert throughout the autumn and winter, but they were not unleashed immediately. As the deadline passed and Desert Shield turned into Desert Storm, General Schwarzkopf immediately initiated a six-week air bombardment, laying waste areas in and around Baghdad and in the south of Iraq with a terrible exhibition of overwhelming military technology. Then, on 24 February, the third phase, the battle to retake Kuwait, began. It was a completely unequal fight. Allied casualties were insignificant compared to Iraqi losses, estimates of which fluctuated wildly between 50,000 and 150,000. In only 100 hours the Iraqi army had fled back across its own borders and Kuwait, though now a ruined prize, was retaken, in what Saddam Hussein had promised would be 'the mother of all battles'.

I watched all this on television, like anyone, like the rest of the world, with a kind of horrified fascination: the smart bombs being dropped with deadly precision down the air shafts of buildings; the Patriot missiles downing Scuds over Tel Aviv; the tanks and troop transports churning relentlessly across the desert; the horrendous

222

oil-field fires; the smoke-darkened skies; the huge stain of crude oil spreading like black blood through the blue water of the Gulf.

I thought of the friends and acquaintances I had made in Iraq. I wondered how Azzawi had fared in the war, and thought of all the Farises and Alis who had worked in my team. I recalled the carpet seller in the Bagdad souk, wasting so many hours drinking tea with me under the misapprehension that I was the Swedish Ambassador. I remembered the roomful of Saad-16 workers I had once seen, sleeping away a long and hungry Ramadan afternoon in a tangle of snoring bodies; the Kurds and sheep-farming semi-nomads of the northern territories; the inventive owner of the antediluvian engineering shop in Mosul; the urbane, likeable Colonel Sharki. These people were caught up in events over which they had no control. They were nevertheless paying a heavy and disproportionate price for the cruelty and greed of their masters, and the cynical hypocrisy of Western Governments.

49

In the spring and early summer of 1991 there were three matters troubling me about the propellants contract and the Astra/P.R.B. debacle. The first was that the A.T.I. internal reports seemed to indicate Steve Adams, a long-time associate of Bull from the days of H.A.R.P. and the South African guns contract, had been in Yugoslavia, talking to the state manufacturer of propellants.

I worked with Steve Adams for five years and I cannot say I have ever trusted him. He had been a student of Bull's and, like so many of them, had remained part of the firm when S.R.C. became a commercial business. But Adams's loyalty was less than perfect. In 1978 he had gone to South Africa on S.R.C.'s behalf, where he had ended by accepting a lucrative service contract with Armscor, the state arms producer. Bull had almost wept when he heard of Adams's defection yet, four years later, he'd rehired the man when Adams needed a job. It was typical of Bull: he had done the same after I had fired John Heath in Baghdad. Adams had meanwhile worked his way into an influential position: he was one of the five vice-presidents of the company.

Over the past few years Adams had built up good contacts with the Yugoslavian Government. He had been instrumental in S.R.C.'s selling the Yugoslav Federal Army base-bleed E.R.F.B. ammunition for their 130-mm Soviet guns, and in a successful programme to re-fit some of those same guns with 155-mm barrels. During television news reports of the Yugoslavian civil war I have seen these guns in operation several times, pounding their targets in Vukovar, Dubrovnik and Sarajevo.

But ammunition was Steve Adams's great interest. It is a disposable commodity, so there is far more cash in it. The contract price for S.R.C.'s shells would be upward of $1,000 each which, given the volume of most ammunition orders, suggests the inclusion of very substantial commission payments.

In the report which he sent Bull from Yugoslavia, Adams confirmed that it would be possible to source the propellant from

Yugoslavia. But there was something about the way he phrased the report that suggested he was referring to the end-stage of a long negotiating process. Had S.R.C. started to transfer the propellants contract to Yugoslavia even before the explosion at the P.R.B. plant? Given the fact that P.R.B. was now a British firm, that would make sense.

Until the summer of 1989 there had existed another possibility. The Iraqi plant of Al-Qaqa, near Baghdad, was in part intended for propellant manufacture and the Iraqis had only ordered a small consignment of the 350-mm System's propellant from P.R.B. while, at the same time, sending a detachment of technicians into Belgium to learn how to make it with the object of setting up production facilities for the 350-mm charge at Al-Qaqa. Now, however, this Iraqi plant had been destroyed by the massive explosion (it had killed 1,000 Egyptian workers) which Farzad Bazoft had been trying to investigate.

So where were S.R.C. going to acquire propellant for the new *military* S-350 which was already being produced at Walter Somers and Forgemasters? Adams's activities in Belgrade seemed to provide the answer. Reading Adams's reports and memos, I felt a twinge of pity for the upright Azzawi, who had the task of negotiating the deals.

The second thing that was bugging me at this time was the number of individuals cropping up in the Astra/P.R.B. story who had been variously associated with the Middle East arms trade, the Midland Bank and the British intelligence services. The connections were brought sharply to my attention when, out of the blue, I was contacted by Gerald James, the ex-Chairman of Astra. The D.T.I. had begun an investigation of the Astra/P.R.B. affair, and James wanted to know if I could help him understand certain details about S.R.C. He was also sure he could provide me with much interesting background information. I arranged for him to come to my house.

One of the figures James told me about was the Belgian Hervé de Carmoy. He had previously worked in London, heading the Midland Bank's arms-sales division but, in July 1988, de Carmoy became Chief Executive of P.R.B.'s ultimate owner, Société Générale de Belgique. It was interesting to note that S.G.B.'s presence in London was at least geographically close to British intelligence: one of its offices was at a Whitehall address also used by M.I.6!

Another significant player in the Astra/P.R.B. takeover was Sir John Cuckney. He had been Deputy Chairman of T.I. when the group sold Matrix Churchill to the Iraqis, and a non-executive director of the Midland Bank with special interest in arms-related business. Between 1987 and 1992 he was Chairman of Astra's main shareholder, the 3i investment bank.

Cuckney has a reputation as an ex-spy. In his autobiography, the intelligence agent Peter Wright names him as a training officer with M.I.5 in the 1950s.

He undoubtedly has an impeccable Establishment profile and is regarded as a very 'safe pair of hands'. Prime Minister Edward Heath gave him the job of sorting out the strike-torn Liverpool Docks and then the Port of London Authority. He was subsequently appointed to restructure the Crown Agents, whose reputation had been damaged by fraud allegations and, in the 1980s, he ran International Military Sales Ltd, the Ministry of Defence arms sales department which made something of a specialism of deals in the Middle East. In the private sector Cuckney was Chairman of Westland Helicopters, where he famously outflanked Michael Heseltine in organising the merger with Sikorski, a deal strongly favoured by the Prime Minister, Margaret Thatcher. He has also continued in his semi-official troubleshooting role – most recently having been charged with tracking down Robert Maxwell's disappearing pension funds.

It was not only through Astra that Cuckney knew P.R.B., because it appears that International Military Sales – of which he was Chairman – had worked with the Belgian company in the past. It also appeared now, as Gerald James had told me, that Cuckney was taking a personal interest in Astra's purchase of P.R.B. At one point in the negotiations he became particularly anxious for the deal to go through quickly, and himself telephoned James twice in the course of a single day to ask him to hurry things along.

There was a third player with similar, if less senior, banking and intelligence connections and he was even closer to Astra. This was Stephan Kock. I was particularly interested in Kock because I could remember Bull mentioning him to me as long ago as 1988.

It was when I had come back to Brussels from Baghdad in the winter of 1988. I had discussed the Astra bid with Bull and been shown a number of papers which Bull had somehow got hold of. (Through Binek? I didn't know.) But among them was a list of those present at talks between Astra and P.R.B., held in November 1988.

'What's Kock doing at this meeting?' he wanted to know.

'Who's Kock?'

'He's a Yarpie – a Rhodesian. He works for the Midland Bank arms department, but he's also part of M.I.5 like Cuckney. And look, on this list they've misspelt his name. It begins with K, not a C.'

Bull was extremely suspicious when he realised that members of the intelligence world were closely involved in the Astra bid. Kock certainly appears to have been in military intelligence whilst serving as an officer in the army in Rhodesia prior to U.D.I., but naturally it is hard to prove any further intelligence links, since these are never revealed. However, Kock was proud of his former membership of the S.A.S. and was frequently to be seen wearing the S.A.S. Association tie. He was also happy for an internal Astra newsletter to describe him as follows:

Served in both the Air Force and the Army, including service in military intelligence and special forces. Following his military career he carried out special assignments for the Foreign Office.

This would fit in with his association with M.I.T.S., the Midland Bank arms trading department. Under its former Chairman Lord Armstrong, the wartime head of M.I.5, the Midland had been known to employ overseas representatives who were also spies. One such, a man named Dennis Skinner, had actually been assassinated in Moscow whilst working as the Midland's representative at the Narodny Bank. M.I.T.S. came after this, but it was originally set up with a staff of just such military and intelligence veterans as Kock was himself.

James, having been winkled out of the company he built up without a shred of compensation, is a man with a grievance. And on the subject of Stephan Adolf Kock he was fascinating.

Kock had come to Astra as non-executive director in October 1986, on the recommendation of a man named Richard Unwin, the proprietor of a company which Astra had taken over called Unwin International.

'He was first mentioned to me by the Midland Bank in Maidstone', James said. 'We were switching our account to the Midland and the manager there mentioned Kock as a person with a lot of influence. But it was through Unwin that he came onto the Board.'

'What do you know about Kock?'

'He's a very mysterious figure. It appears he has central European origins, apparently knows Arabic, and is ex-S.A.S. I know he was on the international board of Billiton, a subsidiary of Royal Dutch Shell.

He then handed me a cutting from the *Financial Times* dated 15 July 1991. Under a photograph of a rotund, grinning and weathered face was a profile of Kock and his connection with the Midland arms-dealing section. The article revealed:

> Mr Kock has been at the centre of some bizarre happenings in recent years. In one of these, on January 15 1990, he was involved in a shooting incident.
>
> Two men were trying to repair a broken down van in the dark on a lonely stretch of road at Barbreck in Argyll, northern Scotland. A car approached from a side road and stopped. Mr Kock, who had been driving the car, got out and beckoned to one of the men, Mr Argyll Macmillan. As Mr Macmillan approached the car, Mr Kock suddenly produced a semi-automatic pistol and shouted 'I'm a soldier, you know.' An argument developed between the two men. Mr MacMillan shouted to his companion, warning that the man was armed.
>
> At that point Mr Kock raised the gun and fired a single shot above their heads. Mr MacMillan, who lives in nearby Clachan, says, 'It's not the kind of thing that happens in the countryside in the middle of the night.'
>
> Police who made enquiries at the time describe the case as 'very delicate', because of Mr Kock's intelligence and special services connections, and because of the 'big names' who provided references . . . His solicitor at the court hearing following the shooting incident, said Mr Kock's defence work left him with an acute concern for his personal safety. He was fined £650.

Amongst Kock's friends in the Astra Group was Major General Donald Isles, Deputy Managing Director of an arms company called B.M.A.R.C. which Astra had acquired from the Swiss firm Oerlikon in May 1988. Isles had once been director general of army weapons and now became Managing Director of the Astra-owned B.M.A.R.C. and he was a strong supporter of any Kock initiatives within the company.

Having been originally against the purchase of P.R.B., Kock suddenly changed his tune in the summer of 1989, becoming very enthusiastic for it.

James told me about another interesting connection – not directly one of Kock's as far as anyone knew, although it was quite possible. This was the figure of Alan Curtis, the Chairman of Lotus. Curtis began to cultivate Gerald James assiduously in the spring of 1989, inviting him for frequent discussions at his suite at the Savoy Hotel, which doubled as Curtis's business headquarters.

Curtis spends much of his time entertaining senior politicians, civil servants and people in the defence business. He is also a friend of Mark Thatcher, as well as of Wafiq Said, a key figure in the huge Al Yamamah deal between a consortium of British defence contractors led by B.Ae. and the government of Saudi Arabia. James was rather baffled by Curtis's attentions, until he realised Astra might be on Wafiq Said's shopping list. For a while it looked as if the Saudis' company SIFCORP were interested in taking a stake in Astra and perhaps in financing the P.R.B. buy-out. In the event, nothing came of the idea, but the interest of SIFCORP woke up Astra institutional shareholders, 3i and the Prudential. From this point onward they were much more supportive of the P.R.B. deal.

After James left me, I started to wonder how Bull knew about Stephan Kock. Did he know the man? Or was it through his own intelligence contacts – George Wong perhaps, who was himself a banker?

I had a second thought. Kock's attitude within Astra had seemed so inconsistent. First he had opposed the P.R.B. takeover. Later he had become very active in promoting it – very active indeed for a non-executive director, one might think. Kock clearly had a number of different loyalties. He was a consultant with the Midland Bank. He knew de Carmoy, who had been his superior at the Midland Bank. He knew a lot of people in the Ministry of Defence and the special forces. The connections had one factor in common: the intelligence services.

When we'd met that day in 1991, James told me that the only director who then remained from his time at Astra was Stephan Kock. Moreover, although a new Chairman had been installed from outside, Kock had effectively taken command of Astra. They accepted £3 million from S.G.B. in compensation for the misleading business forecasts and then, though technically the company was still trading, Kock and the new Board effectively put it to sleep. New business was turned down on one pretext or another until the Astra Group was little more than an empty shell. The share value collapsed.

There was a third matter I could not at first reconcile at this time. It was something Monique Jamine had told me, but I couldn't discover its significance. Chris Gumbley had been in Brussels shortly after his run-in with the Ministry of Defence police, and he had come at the invitation of none other than Gerald Bull. Gumbley met Bull for about two hours at the S.R.C. office and then left. The arrangement was that he should return after the weekend for a second meeting, but there was no second meeting. The same afternoon Bull was murdered.

Whatever had happened at that meeting might obviously throw light on the reason Bull died. Gumbley himself is reluctant to talk about it. However, it became clear to me eventually that Bull felt sympathy for Gumbley's plight. He told Gumbley the M.O.D. police action against him was a ploy, a deliberately-engineered manoeuvre to discredit him and force him out of Astra. Bull hated dirty tricks – hadn't they been used against him by his enemies? He also had a strong dislike of S.G.B., whom he blamed for blocking his bid for P.R.B. and causing difficulties over the Supergun propellant.

Bull had apparently shown Gumbley a number of papers, internal P.R.B. memoranda and the like, which demonstrated some details of how P.R.B. sold itself to Astra, the misleading business projections and so on. But did they have any extra significance? I would have liked to know precisely what those papers were.

Gumbley was not willing to talk. Understandably, he was now a very frightened man. But quite possibly he was in possession of the key to Bull's murder.

50

One obvious theory of Bull's death is that he was killed by an intelligence agent acting on behalf of some government. William Lowther's biography of Bull, published in 1991, assumes this was the Israelis, citing an unnamed C.I.A. official who apparently told Lowther that 'it is the general understanding of Western intelligence agencies that Mossad gave the order to kill Bull'.

On this scenario, Supergun would not have been the direct cause of the murder. Project Babylon was not, in the Israelis' assessment, a particularly dangerous thing. It was more of a prestige toy and might even have been encouraged by Tel Aviv, since it soaked up Iraqi resources which otherwise might have been used more mischievously. However, since 1989, S.R.C. had become increasingly enmeshed in the whole of Iraq's weapons procurement programme. It was now supplying base-bleed ammunition for the 130-mm gun; it was developing three or four new gun systems – a 155-mm, a 210-mm self-propelled (the Al-Fao), and the new Project 839 guns; it was working on a unique anti-missile defence known as Project Bird, and advising on the programme to extend the range of the Scud missile. All of these S.R.C. contracts would have given Iraq's enemies cause for concern, and certainly their existence is the kind of routine information which it is Mossad's job to gather.

Of course Mossad would not have been the only ones. In fact, a good deal of their knowledge of Bull would have been made over more or less formally by the Americans. Michel Bull and Luis Palacio had visited the State Department in 1988 and told the Office of Munitions Control about the 155-mm gun, the Al-Fao and Project Babylon. The details of this meeting would have automatically been passed to Mossad *via* the C.I.A., quite likely coupled with other material, such as our proposal for a 1,000-mm gun system sent to the U.S. Army in 1987. That Israel had prior knowledge of Babylon was confirmed on a B.B.C. *Panorama* programme in June 1990. I remember seeing the Israeli Minister of

Defence Ariel Sharon stating firmly that, when Bull was killed, Israel had known about Babylon for more than a year.

In fact no intelligence service would have found it particularly hard to get details of Bull's activities. The gossipy arms-producing community in Brussels was a fertile source of this type of information, but there is another very simple reason – Bull didn't mind talking about them himself. On 19 March 1992, Robert Turp, a consultant in arms based in Jersey, wrote to *The Independent* to confirm that Bull had openly discussed Babylon with him, in a (successful) attempt to convince him of the viability of the system.

Bull told me of several similar discussions he had had with outsiders, even with diplomats and officials. I remember in particular one time in February 1989, when Bull arrived in Baghdad from London. During the flight he had sat next to a man describing himself as a military attaché at the British Embassy. He told Bull that he knew all about Babylon and the other Iraqi S.R.C. projects. He even knew the date I'd privately pencilled in for the firing of the horizontal system, to take palce at Tal Uwaynat the following month. It was a date I had kept dark, because I was still awaiting the arrival of some components from Somers and I was very disconcerted that Bull's travelling companion was privy to what I believed only three people knew – myself, Azzawi and Bull.

'But how could they keep tabs on decisions being changed on a daily basis?'

'Sigint,' said Bull. 'Signals intelligence. G.C.H.Q. monitoring telephone conversations, faxes, satellite traffic, you name it. They've got a major listening post on Cyprus which tunes in to everything coming out of the Middle East. Just don't worry about it.'

Bull's conjecture about British 'sigint' was confirmed in *The Independent* newspaper on 14 March 1992. A British civil servant, Robin Robison, revealed that his work in 1989 had involved sifting G.C.H.Q.'s electronic surveillance for the use of Joint Intelligence Committee at 10, Downing Street. Around October or November he had come across a transcript of a telephone conversation which he described as being between a London financier and a Brussels arms dealer. He added that they were clearly discussing the financing of a large gun project for Iraq, with the financier emphasising that there would be 'no problem' over any commission payments. Robison cannot remember any detail from a second conversation which he noticed, a month or so later, in which the same financier was speaking about Bull's gun to a man in north London.

It does seem probable that this information went through the 'Red Book'. Bull told Robert Turp, for instance, that M.I.6 'knew all about' Project Babylon.

Both these pieces of 'sigint' were passed to an assessment officer, whose job it was to decide whether they would go on to J.I.C. If they did, they would then appear in the so-called 'Red Book', an intelligence digest widely circulated to Cabinet ministers, British Embassies, M.I.5 and M.I.6 as well as to the Bank of England, the Export Credit Guarantee Department and other variously insecure recipients.

Robison was just one 'sigint' monitoring clerk, and he worked in the job for a limited period. He, like his colleagues, is gagged by the Official Secrets Act and it was only Robison's pacifist Quaker conscience which led him to speak out at all, three years later. The extent of additional and similar intelligence on Bull which came in and was passed upwards to the British Cabinet from 1988 onwards can never be known. How much found its way, through the dubiously secure 'Red Book' system, to foreign intelligence networks and governments is equally conjectural. That there *wasn't* any more 'sigint' about Bull and Sueprgun, however, would be incredible.

Lowther's theory that Mossad killed Bull was also, for a long time, my own presumption. I felt that the Israelis – whilst extremely reluctant to murder any European – would have had the ruthlessness and efficiency to do it if they felt it necessary. In addition, the way Bull died had certain hallmarks of the Mossad *modus operandi*. Of other countries with strategic objections to Bull's work, Iran would not be immune from suspicion, though it is questionable whether they could have carried out the hit without leaving more traces.

There is, however, another possibility, another explanation for this murder. It is to be found in the fact that, 16 months later, a second assassination took place on the streets of Brussels, and in this Mossad cannot be implicated. I am certain, however, that this, too, was linked to Supergun.

51

It was Bull, knowing so many influential people in the political and commercial flux of Brussels, who first introduced me to André Cools. This was in February or March 1988 and Bull and I were leaving the office together one evening. We thought we'd get dinner at the Hilton Hotel, which had one of the best restaurants in what is, in any case, an incredibly well-fed city. On the way, however, we dropped into the Neptune Bar on the Avenue Louis.

In the crowded bar, Bull spotted a man of about 60, wearing large distinctive square glasses and sitting with a much younger woman. Bull greeted him with obvious familiarity and introduced me.

'Chris, this is André, a good friend of mine.'

Cools invited us to join them and we sat down for half an hour or so. Bull and Cools got on very well together, gossiping and swapping opinions about the volatile political life of Belgium. I realised quickly I was in the company of a serious politician. Later, over dinner, Bull told me about Cools.

During the Belgian Socialist Government of the early 1970s, André Cools had been Deputy Prime Minister. He then became Chairman of his Party in opposition, heroically (some say single-handedly) saving the party from splitting along the sectarian fault-line which divides the Flemish from the French-speaking sections of the community. Later Cools retreated into regional government in his native Wallonia, the French-speaking area around Liège. But 'retreating' isn't really the word. Cools was always a figure to be reckoned with, a powerful opponent who inspired respect and fear in his enemies, as well as loyalty in his followers. One of Cools's enemies was S.G.B., which had plotted against his party when it had been in power. Cools knew as well, of course, that P.R.B., along with other S.G.B. firms, had been supplying arms to Iraq throughout the 1980s, in spite of the Belgian Government's professed neutrality in the war. In addition, S.G.B. had been blamed for an incident during an industrial dispute at a P.R.B. factory when a woman worker had died under suspicious circumstances. This scandal had provoked furious nationwide anger. For Cools's socialists, then, the giant conglomerate, with its unprecedented influence over Belgian life, was perennially suspect – the people's enemy number one.

I forgot all about Cools until July 1991. I was at that time still wondering how to find out more about the gross commissions received under P.R.B.'s Iraqi propellant contract by the two mysterious companies, Bilder Trading and Gerofin investments. I decided I needed someone in Belgium of influence and courage who was not afraid to shake the apple tree. Then I thought of Cools.

When we'd parted, Cools and I had exchanged business cards. I tend to keep packs of these cards, some of them dating back years. So I flipped through my packs until I found the card Cools had presented. Then I posted the documents by registered mail to his office in Liège, with a covering letter reminding him of my connection with Bull and our meeting in the Neptune Bar. I added that, if he knew, or could find out, anything more about the mysterious companies receiving these commissions I would be glad to hear it. Then I sat back to wait for the fruit to come tumbling down.

Meanwhile I had made another contact on continental Europe. Monique Saudan is a senior examining magistrate based in Zurich, and in 1991 she was given the job of looking into the involvement of Von Roll (and any possible government collusion) in the Supergun contracts. On 21 June I received a request from the Swiss Embassy in London for my cooperation in her enquiry and agreed to fly out a month later to see her.

I was sitting on the plane to Zurich, with a folded newspaper on my knee. We became airborne and I opened the paper, idly leafing through the pages as the hostesses moved efficiently up and down the aisles handing out breakfast. I may have been hungry, but any appetite deserted me in a moment, as my eye fell upon the stark headline: EX-DEPUTY PM COOLS OF BELGIUM MURDERED.

It is hard to describe the feeling of shock which came over me. I suddenly felt cold, and then hot. I could hardly take this in: I had just written to the man. I'd sent him material about Supergun, and now he'd been shot dead.

It was a while before I was able properly to read the details. It was apparently a cold-blooded killing in broad daylight. Cools had been leaving an apartment with his mistress Councillor Marie-Hélène Joiret. He had walked with her to their parked car, opened Ms Joiret's door for her and handed her in. He then walked around the bonnet of the car towards the other door when a man of about 35, in blue jeans and white trainers, stepped up to him. The man was armed with an automatic pistol. Without saying a word, and without hesitation, he shot Cools twice, once in the throat and again through his left ear. When Ms Joiret tumbled out of the car he shot her also, a bullet lodging near her kidney. He then ran off. By the time passers-by approached the bloody scene, Cools was already dead.

The fact that Cools was shot in the street provides a contrast with the mode of Bull's murder, but there are noteworthy similarities. Both assassins aimed for the head and neck, and both weapons, at 7.65-mm, were of the same calibre. A third important similarity is in the attitude of the Belgian police. They immediately announced that they held out little hope of catching the perpetrator of Cools's 'professional, cold-blooded and audacious' murder. What were the words Patrick Renoir had used to me over the Bull case? 'It was a professional killing. We will probably never find out who did it.'

And there was a fourth line of comparison, most telling of all. An hour before he died, Bull, as I now knew, had been with Chris Gumbley, showing him documents which revealed manoeuvres within S.G.B. and the British security services.

Now a second man had died, killed within a very short time of receiving documents, also connected with manoeuvrings inside P.R.B. As my plane droned on towards Switzerland I was more determined than ever to get to the bottom of the two companies whose details I had sent to Cools. There was one fact I knew about both of them – they had Swiss bank accounts, and I was in possession of the numbers. Maybe, I thought, I could use this visit to advance my knowledge from the numbers to the names.

My visit to Ms Saudan was useful for both of us. From her point of view, it was fruitful because I was able to confirm the participation of Von Roll of Berne in Project Babylon and give her an overall picture of the company's contribution.

Von Roll is a very large, diversified engineering group with plants all across Switzerland. One of their specialities is the manufacture of steel for arms and, in the mid-1980s, we had acquired forgings from them for GC45 155-mm gun barrels, which then went forward for finishing by Trebelan at Bilbao in northern Spain, the company that later made the Al-Fao gun for Iraq. When Babylon came along, Azzawi contracted Von Roll to make the breech for the 350-mm test model, with a number of other smaller components. The breech was hauled by road to Frankfurt and from there flown direct to Baghdad by Iraqi Airways, arriving in late February 1989.

With the contract for the 1,000-mm full-scale system, a larger job fell to the Swiss – the forging and finishing of ten massive recoil cylinders. No recoil cylinder so large had ever been made before. Its internal diameter (like the barrel of the gun itself) was a metre, and its weight, with the two support brackets, was 60 tonnes. A number of engineers had been involved in the tricky design, with the greatest contribution undoubtedly coming from Simon Hayes, a hydraulic specialist at S.R.C. One difficulty had been to prevent hydraulic leakage around the piston, the only solution being an immensely demanding specification, with extremely close machining tolerances and surface finishes of a very high order.

Provisional contracts were agreed with Von Roll while the design was still developing. This was a typical Bull practice. Agreement would be reached on overall dimensions, materials, mechanical properties and typical finished tolerances so that work could get started months before final designs were complete. Individuals within S.R.C. as well as the manufacturers often hated the uncertainty of this, yet it worked well, saving up to a year in the time between the first concept and a delivery.

For this reason the contract was continually renegotiated during development, and I was not sure of the eventual value of the recoil cylinders business to Von Roll. Each one probably cost Azzawi $300,000, and Von Roll also made the large support brackets on which the cylinders would have been fixed. So it was a job worth more than $3 million.

All this I told Ms Saudan. But now that I was in her country, I was also anxious to research the two company bank accounts. In Switzerland, banking secrets have the same prestige as state secrets everywhere else, so it seemed at first a hopeless problem. But by luck I was able to call in a favour from someone who had 'unofficial' access to this sort of confidential information.

Gerofin Investment Corporation (incorporated in Panama) had as its address PO Box 141, CH1005, Lausanne 5. The company banked at the Union Bank of Switzerland, account number 42131860N. Bilder Trading Company was registered in the U.K. and also had a Swiss bank, account number 657–809–404. I told my contact these details. They were fed into a computer; access codes were keyed in, passwords were entered, the restricted files accessed and, after a very short time, the answers had come back. Numbers had turned into names – the names of those individuals authorised to approve payments.

They were the same names for both companies, names I already knew well from the staff of S.R.C.: Jourdain, Glibert, Cardinael and Van Eetevelde.

52

The four P.R.B. men must have been alarmed when they realised their company was going to be sold to Astra. The British company would certainly end the (for them) lucrative Iraqi contracts and, if Gumbley also found out about Bilder Trading and Gerofin, it might even threaten their own freedom.

I wondered if Adams had known that P.R.B. executives were on the take. Adams was Binek's great friend, certainly. If he had known something, then his part in switching the contract to Yugoslavia was useful to the continued flow of revenue from the Iraqi contract into the Bilder and Gerofin accounts. It might even improve the commission possibilities, since Yugoslavia would manufacture the propellant for a much lower price than P.R.B. The Iraqis would not benefit from this lower price, naturally: the difference would be up for grabs.

I wondered too if elements higher up within S.G.B. had found out about the commissions. Gerald James believed the likes of Duronsoy and even Vicomte Davignon, the S.G.B. Chairman, were desperate to unload P.R.B. at almost any cost, and the knowledge that the company was a rotten apple might explain this. But was it a big enough motive to explain the murders of either Bull or Cools? I thought not. The scandal would need an international perspective to do that.

Another question which required explanation was the existence of *two* companies. What, after all, was the difference between Bilder and Gerofin? Of Gerofin the memorandum which laid out the structure of P.R.B.'s propellants was unenlightening. There was somewhat more information on Bilder Trading; they were described as 'P.R.B.'s former agents in Jordan'. It also said that, in addition to their 5.6 per cent on the propellants contract price, Bilder received ten million Belgian francs (£175,000) as a special payment 'in settlement of the old agreement'. What was this 'old agreement'? And what was involved in being P.R.B.'s agent in Jordan?

Suddenly, out of the blue, information came along which provided details of Bilder *and* the international perspective for which I had been looking. Just as I was completing the writing of this book, I was contacted by someone who could tell me just why this company was the 'Jordanian agency'. Much of the money in this account, I was told, was being remitted back to the Middle East; it was, in effect, a laundering service. And the recipients of the money were powerful Jordanian government officials who had authorised fake end-user certificates for the Iraqi propellant, and according to C.B.S. television investigation, one person who benefited from this was none other than King Hussein.

53

The British Parliamentary enquiry into Supergun, after almost two years of gestation, finally gave birth to its report on 13 March 1992, the day before the dissolution of Parliament. The report was rushed and, to my eyes, utterly inadequate.

Government ministers had always claimed that they had no prior knowledge of Bull's bid to provide Iraq with the biggest gun in history. Yet the longer the Select Committee's marathon ground on, the more dubious the claims seemed. My own scepticism – which I explained to the committee at length when I gave evidence – derives from the overwhelming likelihood that the combination of intelligence awareness and industry awareness must have resulted in Government awareness – of Bull and all that he was doing.

Industry's ignorance of S.R.C.'s real purpose was never too convincing. The pretence that Project Babylon was a petro-chemical scheme, that the tubes were pressure tanks, was a fiction which both sides implicitly agreed to maintain. Several times the veil slipped. Once I heard an executive say at a technical meeting that he didn't want to hear the word 'breech' mentioned again in his presence. Another time two of my engineers closely connected with the design of the project, announced to Forgemasters that they were aerodynamicists.

Once Babylons' revised version, Project 839 was under way in summer 1989, the petrochemical story was looking completely absurd. Take the eloquent testimony of another witness, David James, the Chairman of Eagle Trust plc, which bought Walter Somers in late 1989. James told the Select Committee how, on 11 January 1990, he had gone down to visit the steelworks at Halesowen and that, during his tour of the factory, he noticed three 350-mm tubes assembled together on trestles.

'There were several quite remarkable features which prompted my immediate response to Mr Mitchell when I asked him what the hell it was and he said to me 'Well, it is components for Iraq'. I said: 'I know that, but what is it for?' "We don't know", was his response.'

James was asked by a committee member what principally attracted his attention.

'The most conspicuous feature,' said James, 'was what one can only describe as a thumping great muzzle.'

Another M.P. asked,

'What led you to believe this was a "thumping great muzzle"?'

'If you went to the Tower of London or any museum of armaments you would see an identical piece of metal stuck on the end of another, which is a cannon to the naked eye . . . indistinguishable from any cannon in any period of warfare.'

The tubes for this gun were radically different from the flanged and parallel 'peashooter' sections shipped to Iraq by Somers for the Supergun test model a year earlier. The Somers people affected to believe that these three latest tubes were for the same project as the earlier ones. A photograph published in *The Daily Mirror* on 25 January 1991 make it perfectly obvious that James's instant judgement that the assembly was a gun barrel was fully justified. They belonged to the S-350, also known as the 350-E.T., elevating/traversing gun.

The manufacturers' obvious nervousness – not merely about Project 839 but from the time of their first connection with Iraq – manifested itself most clearly in the way they tried to alert the Government. They didn't do this very noisily, because (if at all possible) they didn't want to lose what were in sales terms very healthy orders. From the response they got they thought they'd been given the go-ahead, with that very British form of permission, the nod-and-wink.

In fact, I believe that is what did happen – unofficial permission was granted although, of course, on a completely 'deniable' basis. This, however, opens up a very sticky can of worms. It opens up the possibility of political complicity in the affair, even of several governments collaborating – first to manipulate events and second to conceal their manipulations.

In his evidence to the Select Committee, the former Industry Minister Alan Clark revealed that there had been an indeterminate number of meetings between British and Belgian officials, but only apparently at the lowly level of the diplomatic 'démarche'. Mr Clark did say that the Belgians had denied issuing any export licences for large gun propellants – something about which I know they lied, because I have the export licence numbers.

The Select Committee also established that British 'spooks' were informed by several sources about Bull's activities, but none, of course, gave evidence. In fact the non-appearance of several key witnesses in the story, especially with reference to Astra and P.R.B., tends to show what a half-cocked enterprise the Select Committee enquiry turned out to be, despite its two years of deliberations.

One of the most interesting of the figures who failed to appear was the mysterious Holdness, the M.I.6 man with the Special Forces connections who had three times grilled Gerald James about P.R.B. The M.O.D. men Harding and Primrose, who ought to be able to shed light on how early U.K. politicians really knew about Supergun, were also absent, on the dubious grounds that they were 'retired' from the service. Bill Weir did appear, but in closed sessions and his evidence is not publicly available. This is in spite of the fact that Weir could have given additional up-to-the-minute information on Projects Babylon and 839 since he had been part of the U.N. team which went to Iraq in 1990–1 to discover and destroy Saddam Hussein's war machine. Sir Hal Miller himself declined to appear, and could not be forced to do so. Several independent experts in the field of defence might also have helped the frequently deficient understanding of the M.P.s. Chris Foss, editor of *Jane's Defence Weekly* and a visitor to the Baghdad Military Fair in 1989, would have been extremely helpful, but he was not called. Nor was Robert Turp, who had discussed the technical aspects of Supergun with Bull, and who voluntarily offered his testimony.

Lastly, and I think importantly, there was no appearance by Bull's friend George Wong, a banker and close associate of intelligence agencies. Bull, as he himself told me, was in continuous touch with Wong throughout the 1980s, discussed everything with him and used his contacts.

There is no doubt Bull's activities *were* monitored by M.I.6 – sufficiently, for instance, to enable the Foreign Office to block his acquisition of the Lear Fan factory. Was it conceivable that Project Babylon and Project 839 failed to attract their attention? It was after all an 'open secret' which had been reported to the Office of Munitions Control in Washington. Major companies in half a dozen European countries had taken part in it. It had appeared in the signals intelligence gathered by G.C.H.Q. It was the talk of Brussels and Baghdad.

One who did present himself before the Committee was

Stephan Kock. In the following revealing exchange, he was asked by committee-member Stan Crowther if he considered himself particularly influential, even though only a non-executive director of the Astra Board.

'I think I made my contributions,' he replied.

'Did you know Mr Campbell Dunford?' Crowther went on.

'Yes, I did.'

'Did he become a consultant to Astra?'

'He never I think had a contract. I think he was used on a piecemeal basis to help on bridging loans.'

'Would he have liked to become a director?'

'He did want to become a director.'

'Do you remember a telephone conversation you had with him in about January 1990 on this matter?'

'I had several conversations with him. I cannot remember the exact dates.'

'Do you recall a conversation in which he referred to what he called "on-going internal problems in Astra" and you were able to reassure him there were not any?'

'I'm not sure what on-going internal problems he meant but I was not aware of any.'

'According to a tape recording of that conversation, which I understood Mr Dunford took not you, you were able to say to him this: "There is no on-going internal problem. I am in command. There is no question about that. I am in command because of all the people who have taken an interest in Astra." Who were all these various people whose interest in Astra led you to the feeling you were in command?'

Kock replied that all he meant by the phrase 'I am in command. There is no question about that' was that he had influence over the key shareholders, who could approve or block any new directors. At which point Keith Hampson M.P. broke in.

'How do you have such knowledge of them? Why as a non-executive director were you so deeply involved with all these powerful players [i.e. the Midland Bank, 3i Group etc.].'

'That,' said Kock, 'is a non-executive director's role.'

'Up to a point it is,' replied Hampson drily.

Then it was Stan Crowther again, putting a scenario to Kock which might explain his actions and his confidence about being 'in command.'

'If it was true, as Christopher Cowley told us, that at a very early stage the British intelligence services knew about Project

Babylon which became Supergun; knew from the beginning and no doubt monitored its progress all the way through, including the supply of tubes by a British company approved by their own Mr Bill Weir in the Ministry of Defence, it would make sense for the propellant company also to be taken over by a British firm so that if things started to go wrong, if it began to develop in a way contrary to British wishes, then the whole thing could be stopped dead . . . If it happened to be true, it fits in with the evidence we have received.'

'It does not make sense, and I do not believe it,' declared Kock. 'It's a flight of fancy.'

Well, was it? It is quite true that, as Crowther had said, the thesis fitted with the evidence heard by the Committee. But they were a very long way from being able to prove it, a long way from hearing the full truth.

If the embarassment over S.R.C. stopped with Supergun, the matter might not prove too damaging. But Supergun was only one of Bull's Iraqi dealings with a British connection. He had embarked also on a very broad transfer of long-range gun technology, as well as some assistance with Saddam's missile development programme. The most spectacular scheme of all was for the two new offensive gun systems, a 350-ET and S-600, to be ordered on a terrifying scale. In early 1990 the gigantic 600-mm guns were at the planning stage, but no less than 50 were to be ordered, guns easily capable of shelling over a range of 200 kilometres. Although very little has been made public about these systems, they obviously represented a far greater threat than the militarily innocuous Supergun. And if the Government's protestations of ignorance on Supergun lack credibility, what about these other guns?

The Select Committee did establish beyond much doubt that the British authorities, even as late as March 1990, were in the same frame of mind which had earlier allowed the Iraqis to buy Matrix Churchill, and indeed to buy sensitive technology on a very wide scale, not excluding material useful for nuclear and chemical warfare. In August 1992, when he was no longer a minister, Alan Clark was quite blatant about this, telling the *Sunday Telegraph* that it was true he had 'tipped off' machine-tool manufacturers about how they should frame their export applications. 'I did it for two reasons. First, I was Minister of Trade, so it was my job to maximise exports despite guidelines which I regarded as tiresome and intrusive. Second, Iran was the enemy – it still is – and it was clear to me that the interests of the West were well served by Iran and Iraq fighting each other, the longer the better.' If they had acted covertly to encourage Supergun, they were doing so in this spirit. At some point, something – the death of Bazoft, the nuclear triggers sting, the murder of Bull, a direct instruction from Washington, who knows? – suddenly shook them out of it.

It was late in the day. Only a few weeks before all perceptions of Iraq were irrevocably changed with the invasion of Kuwait. H.M. Customs were just in time to seize the last eight sections of 1,000-mm tube. If only we knew who gave Customs the order to act on 10 April 1990, and why they did so, we might solve the many unanswered questions surrounding this affair. But in their own evidence to the Committee, Customs (with Barry Riley amongst them) refused to say.

All I know is that the customs operation – codenamed Bertha – was handled directly from the Cabinet Office. Even the decision, on the eve of my trial, to drop all charges, came from this source. It was clearly felt that a public exposure of some of these events might prove too damaging. But damaging to whom? I still believe there are revelations yet to come about this.

There was very little discussion of what, to me, was the most outrageous aspect of the whole affair – the attitude of the authorities in Belgium to the murders on their soil. The files on the deaths of Bull and Cools appeared to be closed. Patrick Renoir was taken off the case and his superior officer redeployed to another section. Meanwhile the Belgian police refused to release the company records which covered Bull's Iraqi dealings and which they seized following his murder. Dealings between the Belgian Government and the British were not matters which the Select Committee Report felt it could concern itself with, although clearly it might have got much nearer to the truth had it done so.

54

My written record of this story ends as it began – with a dramatic phone call. Picking up the receiver in March 1992, I was totally unprepared to hear what I heard: that voice barking down the phone. It was a Canadian voice; it was in a state of great excitement; it was unmistakeable. I was listening to Gerald Bull once more.

The news of his killing had come to me exactly two years ago: now, through the earpiece of my telephone, I heard him say:

'We've got to have agreement. Christ knows *how* long I've been waiting.'

I was badly shaken and could hardly speak. I managed to get out,

'Dr Bull?'

Then I reflected. This was ridiculous. Bull is dead. What the hell was going on?

'Who *is* this?'

Then another voice came on, and this time it was from the land of the living, someone whom Bull and I had both known well.

'You recognise that voice, Chris, don't you?'

I said I was flabbergasted. I hadn't expected ever to hear it again.

'Yes, I thought you might be. It was a recording'.

By now I'd just about grasped as much, and confirmation caused an immediate echo in my memory, a scene from four years before. I had been in Bull's office and the voice I was listening to was again that of Bull, shouting into the phone.

'While *you're* making up your mind, missiles are dropping on Baghdad schools!'

Waiting to discuss some matter, I had been unable to avoid being a party to his end of the conversation, though I didn't know who was on the other end of the line. Bull talked for another minute or two, becoming increasingly exasperated, and finishing with a final flourish.

'I want collective agreement within a week'.

Then he'd slammed the phone into its cradle, sat back and waved his arms in the air.

'I don't know who's worse, London or Washington. They're all a bunch of liars. Over the years I've learned not to trust any of them.'

He dropped his elbows onto the desk and rubbed his face.

'All my important conversations I record, then they can't deny what they've agreed.

Now, back in 1992 and still shaken at having heard his voice again, I said.

'What was it, Bull on the telephone?'

'Yes. And you know what? He recorded everything, all his calls, for the last year of his life.'

At that point I had to sit down.

It is Spring 1992 and I am in the sitting room of a house in England. In the room with me is the person who played me the recording over the telephone line. A pile of audio cassettes stands on the coffee table, the tapes identical, none of them labelled or numbered.

A cassette tape deck is running and Bull's voice is booming out of the speaker. He is talking to George Wong. He is angry, saying those bastards at P.R.B. have deceived him again. They've sold out to Astra, a company quite incapable of running the business correctly. He thinks of himself as having been personally betrayed by P.R.B., a company he's been closely associated with for so long.

'*I* set up the Iraqi contract for them' he says. 'Astra will never do the contract, and Saadi will screw them.'

Bull says he's seeing Adams and Jan Kobes about Yugoslavia, where he was moving much of the propellant orders. Soon S.R.C. will have a fully-functioning Belgrade office.

'And when can *you* come over here?' he demands. 'We've got a lot to discuss. What the hell is going on in London? THey're changing their mind again, aren't they?'

Now there is a new conversation. Bull is talking to John Heath, discussing the need to relocate the A.T.I. office. Heath seems to want to move to Madrid, repeatedly mentioning his concern about office security. Really it would be best to separate the 1,000-mm project from the 'new systems', he says.

'Okay,' says Bull, 'I'll make a decision soon. What about the Bottomley proposal?'

I don't know what this is. Bottomley was the aerodynamicist who worked with Slack in the 1,000-mm system. It seems he has something to do with sabots, presumably for the Supergun projectile. Heath mentions an Austrian company, Pankl, and says,

'I'm going to Rome to meet Sagegnago.' Sagegnago had previously worked for S.R.C. in Brussels on gun design.

Clearly Heath was still running round the world, fixing deals.

Now Bull is talking to his old associate Luis Palacio. Palacio's just got back to Madrid from Baghdad and now reports on the mood in the Special Projects Office.

'Saadi's getting impatient about delays in the 1,000-mm system.'

'Why?' says Bull. 'Nothing's changed. Forgemasters are on schedule and we can start assembly soon.'

'Saadi's just trying to pressure us. But he's right about the slow progress on the guidance systems.'

'Well the new guy Bojic's making a big difference there.'

Bojic has by now joined Klaus Urbatzka in an attempt to speed the development of the guidance and control systems, apparently. Suddenly they are talking about Bazoft, and I realised this must be the autumn of 1989. It's irritating that Bull didn't date any of these tapes. What was the point of doing them unless he filed them properly? But that was Bull.

The explosion at Al-Qaqa would have been of great interest to Bull, because these facilities were supposed to be developing the capacity to make the propellant for Bull's guns. On the subject of Bazoft, Palacio argues pessimistically that the Iraqis are ready to hang Bazoft, despite what the West thinks.

Now Bull is on to Binek. There is someone else on the line but I can't identify him. Bull is behaving as if he's just heard further details of the Al-Qaqa explosion. He's in a fury.

'What a bloody useless lot the Iraqis are. They'll never get the propellant finished now. Are these the same people who came to Belgium for training?'

'Yes they are,' says Binek. 'But I'm not surprised about this. Those guys were more interested in going shopping than learning about explosive manufacture.'

I scribble a note on the pad on my knee. This is very interesting. It seems that the Al-Qaqa blast may have happened in the same section that was developing Bull's 350-mm propellants. With firing trials coming up in the New Year on the new inclined system, it would have been a blow to Bull's hopes for Project 839.

But now he takes up the topic of Farzad Bazoft and Daphne Parrish.

'We've had a lot of coverage over here about the arrests. I hope to Christ the Iraqis don't do anything stupid. They feel they're being bullied and this may affect their thinking. But still, I guess they'll lock them both away and do a deal later.'

Now Bull is talking to Tony Slack, about the S43 projectile – its design, payload and range. But he is more anxious about current Iraqi attitudes. What do Azzawi and Saadi think of recent progress? Slack is reassuring.

'They're really enthusiastic, especially about the S-600s. I told Azzawi they could be located on the Iran/Iraq border and cover the whole range of Iranian cities. They loved that.'

Bull must have been relieved. With Project 839 he was buying time for his precious Project Babylon, which must be nurtured at all costs.

Next, Adams calls. He is in Belgrade, bringing Bull up to date with the relocation of the 1,000-mm System propellants contract. Bull tells him to get Kobes down to Yugoslavia as soon as possible.

'It's vital we find another supplier urgently. I don't believe the story about the accident.'

If Bull is talking about the explosion which wrecked P.R.B.'s big press at Kaulille, it would place this conversation after 5 December 1989. Bull, of course, thinks it was sabotage. Adams doesn't comment, except to say he thinks it's in Jourdain's interest to move the whole of the contract anyway.

'And he'll have the support of the others in that.'

The *others*? It sounds as if the group running Gerofin and Bilder Trading are now ready to abandon P.R.B. Bull is contemptuous of them, still sore about the way he was rolled over in favour of Astra. He says,

'I don't care what Jourdain thinks. I don't trust him anyway. But will you contact Binek about Yugoslavia?'

In the next conversation Bull's talking with Binek himself, demanding clarification of something that's on his mind.

'Does Astra know you've been working for both P.R.B. and us?'

Binek thinks not; he reckons he would have heard if they *did* know.

'What about the front companies?' Bull wants to know. 'Is Astra aware of the P.R.B. front companies?'

250

Binek doesn't know the answer to this. Bull continues,

'Well if Astra finds out which Arab is behind Bilder, then the shit will certainly hit the fan. We'll never keep it quiet.'

Binek is reassuring.

'P.R.B.'s books will show that commissions have been paid to Bilder over a number of years. But it's unlikely anyone can trace the owners past Panama.'

'Well somebody has to approve all the end-user certificates issued by Jordan.'

I am writing furiously now. Bull *knew* about the Jordanian connections! The pad keeps slipping as I try to write too fast. The keeping of the Jordanian conduits secret was of course important to Bull – as it was to Iraq, for Jordan had long been a vital channel for military supplies to Saddam Hussein. I remembered the $275 million Anglo-Jordanian arms contract, which had been raised in May 1990 in the House of Commons by Allan Rogers M.P. This was the deal that had been signed in 1985 by Prime Minister Thatcher and from which, according to Rogers, as much as $150 million-worth of military supplies had found their way to Iraq. Yes, there might have been serious problems for a variety of arms manufacturers if, for whatever reason, that conduit became blocked.

Now I'm listening to another call: Bull talking to an American. Bull has mentioned Belcan, the P.R.B. subsidiary in Canada where Bruce Smith, our Vietnam-veteran gun captain from Tal Uway-nat, worked. He must be talking to Bruce himself.

They're discussing the latest set of firing trials which, as I infer, are the horizontal firings carried out early in 1990. I had read about these when first beginning to uncover Project 839 and noticed that Martin Hughes had been present – a sure sign that new designs (probably the breech and chamber) were being tried. Bull says now that he sees no point in holding any more of these trials: they were ready to go on to inclined firings. He wants the man he is speaking with to be present, as nobody else has the experience.

'I'll be there too. Will you be responsible for inspection and preparation of the site?'

'Okay.'

'You can go ahead and buy T.V. inspection equipment.'

'Okay.'

'Anything else?'

'Well, I still haven't been paid by Azzawi for last time.'

'I'll get Monique to pay and we'll invoice Azzawi. Can you also check out Al-Fao? It was damaged during the first firing tests – the traversing ring was distorted. See if it's safe to go again.'

'Right.'

Now Bull with Heath again, a conversation around the turn of the year, 1989/90. He's had a meeting with Slack and Bottomley, when Bottomley agreed to produce a revised project schedule for the 350E.T. system before the end of January.

Buffer cylinder assembly drawings for this project will be ready soon, and a company called Rexroth are mentioned as possible suppliers. Bull says,

'I'll get Pappas and Hughes out to Baghdad to look at the drawings, but the problem is Pappas is very busy with other Iraqi projects. On the S-600, Slack thinks we need extra engineering staff. Says the guys have enough to do and they can't design that as well. We need some more money, John. Get onto the Bonn Commercial Attaché [he meant the Iraqi one in Bonn] and arrange it, will you? Also the breech-block on the S-1000 needs redesigning; tell them we may need a new contract with Italy.'

I know Bull spent Christmas 1989 in America. In the next conversation he has obviously returned to Brussels, where a memo from Slack has been awaiting him. He now calls Kobes, who has clearly become increasingly central to Project Babylon since joining Space Research Corporation. Bull is telling him about the fresh test results Slack has reported. New gas velocities have been fed into the Martlet programme and these now confirm that orbital flight is available. Bull is excited. The S-1000 is inching nearer and nearer to completion.

'We have to let Saadi know,' he says. 'Also I've talked to Steuckers about some more tests at Kaulille. Since the so-called accident he's not so enthusiastic. Binek told me Glibert and Cardinael are both talking to Astra about the 350-mm and the 1,000-mm propellant contracts now.'

There's someone in the office with Bull during this conversation. He is now talking to this person, while Kobes listens in.

'Find out who I should talk to at Astra, will you?'

There is a pause, while he thinks. He wants to discover Astra's attitude to the Supergun, to know whether they'll be sympathetic. He says,

'Astra may not know about London. Let's find out exactly what Astra does know before we have a meeting.'

The other presence is probably Binek, because I hear him say,

'You're in a better position to set up a meeting, *via* Glibert, perhaps. If I arrange it they'll know I've been talking to you.'

'Okay. And it's urgent, but I have to go to Turkey and China, and I have to go to Iraq again.'

Binek says something which I can't catch.

'No, I have to go to China, it's something I can't avoid. We should set up a meeting before I get back from Iraq.'

More mumbling from across the room.

'Okay, just find out who the M.D. of Astra is, and I'll do the rest.'

Binek says he doesn't think P.R.B. will last much longer.

'And they'll take Astra with them,' says Bull.

'Can you believe the figure Astra paid for P.R.B. ?'

'Michel says it's right, but I don't believe it! The cupboard at P.R.B.'s bare.'

Now Bull asks Martine on reception to get Urbatzka in Geneva. After a pause, Klaus comes on the line.

Bull complains about the delays in the electronics. Klaus, deflecting the blame to his colleagues, starts to say that Slack and Bottomley are withholding information from him. Bull interrupts. He sounds tired.

'Klaus, Slack's given you everything you asked for. Now, what about the computer?'

This was the guidance computer, a very powerful mainframe tasked to control the projectile's flight path. Klaus says the French company Thompson have agreed to supply, but they've made Azzawi angry by asking twice the normal price.

'And it will take one year to deliver!' he adds.

Bull makes an obscene remark. He is jaded. There is none of his usual vitality or sparkle.

'Well maybe Hospes can get it for us from America.'

Guntrum Hospes was an old associate of Bull's from H.A.R.P. He had since helped to fix up training for Iraqi ballistic engineers in America. However, as I was eventually to learn the Iraqis were to obtain the necessary equipment from Swanson Analysis via an export licence applied for by S. Bull.

'I can't remember the name of the company, it's in California. It's the same company who are training the Iraqis, anyway.'

Now Bull is talking to Alec Pappas, back home in Waterloo having returned from a trip to somewhere or other. Bull has recovered a little of his good humour. He teases his old friend, who he knows works even harder than he himself does.

'You're always away on holiday, Alec!'

'Oh go shit in your hat!'

'Well listen, about Babylon. Have you incorporated the seals from Destec into the design?'

Destec are a high technology engineering firm in Lincoln, England, who later gave evidence at the Select Committee. They were approached in August 1989 by A.T.I. to manufacture seals to fit between the 350-mm pipes. Initially these seals had failed and Destec technicians went to Baghdad in November to fit a redesigned seal of their own. Bull was evidently now talking about the incorporation of these special seals into the 1,000-mm system.

Incidentally, from what Destec said to the Committee, they had been less than happy about Bull's style of doing business which they said

> caused so much commercial and practical panic that some of the
> urgency they required of us had the opposite effect.

As late as the end of March 1990, when Bull was already dead, a Destec director was in Baghdad, with the full approval of the D.T.I. to meet officials about future contracts. Destec was now dealing directly with the Ministry of Industries receiving, among other things, enquiries about the supply of seals for the one-metre pipe assemblies. 'The fact that they wanted us to machine the larger pipes', the Destec director who had been in Baghdad told the Select Committee, 'confirmed their satisfaction, it seemed.' In spite of the apparent friction between Destec and A.T.I., Bull and Pappas were also pleased with the British company's involvement.

'We need Destec to send engineers out to Baghdad to work on this at the Nassr establishment,' says Pappas.

'Well Azzawi might do the assembly somewhere else, we don't know.'

'Okay, we'll send Martin Hughes out there to check the latest design drawings. At the same time he can go to the test sites. The elevated tube assembly has arrived from Somers.'

Bull tells Pappas he had wanted to go to the test firings, but he can't.

'I've got to go on the 19th to Turkey with Fatso [i.e. Palacio]. Then I've got to get back to meet this Gumbley character.'

'Who's Gumbley?'

'He's at Astra, they bought P.R.B.'

Bull laughs.

'They told Astra that Space [S.R.C.] wanted to buy them at that price. They're fucking mad! Gumbley's trying to get their money back. He's also hoping to learn more about P.R.B.'s background.'

Bull and Pappas are now talking about the carbon-fibre sabot, a continuing problem ever since S.R.C. had failed to get the Lear Fan facilities. I hear Pappas say Heath was still looking for a supply and I wonder if he had continued to go around disguised as the "consultant" Philbey.

'Why not go back and speak to what's-his-name at Westland?' asks Bull.

'John Damon'.

'Yeah. Damon. Who is he?'

'Manufacturing Technology Manager. I know how important it is to get a supply of this and—'

'Well, will Westland supply us?'

'I don't know, maybe. Heath's also looking in Austria with Kranz.'

'I got to talk to Kranz about something else,' says Bull. 'I'll mention it to him.'

The sudden appearance in all this of Westland helicopters fascinates me. As I was listening to this tape, the Al-Yamamah bribery scandal was unfolding in the States, where it was being alleged that the Somerset helicopter firm, owned since 1985 by the American Sikorski company, had paid bribes on a massive scale to secure an order for 88 Black Hawk helicopters. The deal was part of Britain's huge rolling contract with Saudi Arabia – the largest arms deal ever put together – to exchange oil for armaments to be supplied by a consortium of companies led by British Aerospace. Wafic Said, friend of Alan Curtis and Mark Thatcher, is involved in Al-Yamamah as the B.Ae. agent in Saudi Arabia. The inter-connectedness of the international arms business is a phenomenon of our time.

Now Bull is talking in French to his son Stephen, who since the mid-1980s had been working with his brother Michel on the financial side of the company. Stephen is calling from Baghdad. He reports on the Al-Fao, which is progressing well.

'The new design should resolve the traverse ring problem.'

'Good. But what about outstanding payments?'

'I met Saadi and he said he's transferred cash to Bonn for us.'

'How much?'

'All the outstanding amounts up to the end of last month.'

'They owe us a hell of a lot of money.'

'Saadi also said you'd promised some calculations to increase the payload and range of—'

Here Bull broke in. Stephen was now talking about Scud missiles.

'Yeah, but a liquid propellant limits what I can do. They should develop a solid-fuel rocket.'

His voice sounds worried.

'But why do you keep promising them everything?'

'Because they *want* everything.'

'Yes, but we don't have the staff, dad. We're falling behind already and Saadi's using it as an excuse to delay payments. He wants to know when you're coming out to Baghdad by the way.'

Bull won't commit himself. He ends the call saying he'll see Stephen soon.

Now Bull is talking, again, to George Wong. The Bazoft execution is imminent and Wong is well-informed about secret British moves to save Bazoft's life.

'London's asked Kaunda to intervene.'

Kaunda is an old 'friend' of Saddam Hussein, but Bull sounds despondent, as if terribly exhausted.

'It's too late. They should never have driven him into a corner. It's a waste of time. And when the Iraqis hang Bazoft, a lot of people will quit Iraq. The situation was bound to change anyway, after August, but now . . .'

'Kaunda's worth a try.'

A lot of people know it's a mistake to hang Bazoft. But nobody will stand up to the Big Man out there.'

He rings off and the tape ends.

I look at the stack of further tapes. There's no time to listen to more today. I close my notebook.

From what I have heard on these tapes – only a selection from the total – I have found largely confirmation of what I know or have long suspected. Bull, to the end, was trying to exert influence in London through Wong and, possibly, other contacts. He was desperate to keep Babylon afloat, afraid that the propellant would not be there when he needs it, afraid that the supply of money would dry up, afraid that the Iraqis will finally, one day, ask too much or go too far.

But the tapes contain revelations, too. Bull knew about the Jordanian connection. He knew about Bilder and Gerofin – about the untrustworthy Jourdain and 'the others'. I had also learned a little more about Bull's contact with Gumbley.

There are many more tapes which I have not had access to. These are being kept for safety in different locations, and how many further revelations are lurking amongst them? What about Bull's supposed contacts with the Israelis? What about warnings of the type I myself had received? And what about Bull's conversations with Gumbley on the day of his death? It seems clear that Bull wants to tell Gumbley about 'London' – but what? In 1992 Gumbley indicated to the Select Committee that Bull told him the actions by the Ministry of Defence police against him and Anderson – another Astra employee who suffered harassment – were engineered to frighten or discredit him, and to get him off the board of Astra. Is that what he meant by 'knowing about London'. Or was Bull referring to his own contacts with Whitehall, and the unofficial agreement he believed he had received for Supergun?

The answers to these questions may be found in some of the tapes I haven't yet heard. In addition, new revelations have emerged, and continue to emerge, from other sources. Investigations by the U.S. Senate and media on both sides of the Atlantic into the so-called 'Saddamgate Affair' have pointed unexpectedly to Bull as a conduit for arms technology and sales to both Iran and Iraq, as well as to Yugoslavia. In August 1992 I learned from Bernard DeWitt that a man was in custody in Belgium having confessed to the killings of both Andre Cools and Gerald Bull. He is a Polish national and claims to be a professional hit-man. He will not say who his paymaster was. It is now clear that this could have been any one of a number of agencies. Some, though perhaps not all, have a connection with the Supergun story.

When, in early 1991, I first started looking for a publisher for this story, most recipients sent letters of rejection saying they believed that the Supergun saga had run its course. The concensus was then that the Gulf War had entirely superceded the question of military supplies to Iraq in the public's mind, and that my book would come too late.

In fact, the opposite has been the case. Supergun is a symbol, a very powerful and memorable one, of the attempts by Western governments to cover-up their long-term collusion with the tyranny of Iraq and the story of *that* scandal is still unfolding. At the same time, Project Babylon and Bull's associated Iraqi work make a continuing story in their own right, for the aftershocks of Supergun still reverberate and its legacy has, I believe, not yet been paid in full.

55

With all the arrogance of the victor, the U.N. Security Council has required Saddam Hussein to pay a heavy price for the invasion of Kuwait. The war machine he had assembled at such enormous cost has been dismantled and destroyed while his feverish attempts to delay the inevitable were contemptuously brushed aside.

I followed the process, from a distance, with the fascination of one who has walked the ground that was now being razed. Factories I once visited, if not previously destroyed by U.N. bombs, were now being obliterated. Explosive charges were detonated around their supporting columns. Walls crumbled, roofs fell and, as the dust cleared, vast areas of rubble appeared in one's view.

Even before the buildings were demolished, the weapons they'd manufactured or housed had been marked down. Scuds were neutralised; nuclear facilities eradicated; chemical silos emptied; ammunition dumps subject to controlled explosions. It was just a matter of time before the destruction got as far as Supergun.

In late summer 1991 it did. On the 23 August, photographers of the assembled 350-mm test model were printed in the press. It had been found by U.N. inspectors fixed in its inclined position at a quarry in the Jabal Hamrin mountains, on a heading of 210 degrees. This was consistent with the Project Babylon's purpose of test-firing projectiles into the Nafud desert of Saudi Arabia; for if, as has been repeatedly stated, the gun was aiming at Jerusalem, it would have required a different heading of around 240 degrees. The U.N.'s discovery thus disposed of another popular fantasy.

The U.N. also stated that the gun had been test-fired. Now they saw it put to the torch – the oxyacetylene torch.

The 1,000-mm tube sections, too, were soon located at a site to the south of Baghdad, as were the remnants of Project 839. Straight away Iraqi workers set about cutting the finely-machined forgings into ragged pieces. I watched the film of it on the B.B.C.'s *Six O'clock News*; a man's dream being converted before my eyes into so much scrap. The workman wielding his cutting torch could scarcely have been aware of the titanic effort that had gone into the creation of these objects: thousands of kilometres travelled, millions of words hammered out across conference tables, countless hours of computer time, gallons of perspiration. Much of that sweat had been my own.

A shaft of molten metal burned into the tube, sparks cascading around it, until a jagged lump fell away and dropped into the sand. How long would it rest in the desert? I imagined that once this work of destruction was done the men would simply move on to the next job, abandoning the bits to rust slowly in the dry air. Iraq hasn't the resources to remelt hundreds of tonnes of alloy steel: would anyone else bother to come in and reclaim it? If they didn't it would simply remain here, a monument in itself to a pair of egos whose very different purposes had combined to create a wasted and broken desert obelisk.

I might perhaps have felt some personal sadness, watching that destruction on television. But I didn't. I was glad.

Bull, as a man, a boss, a friend, was enormously attractive, and supremely gifted. No less than 600 mourners attended his funeral, which says a lot for his magnetism. But his character was nevertheless flawed, perhaps inevitably, for he wanted to be a creator in a destructive business. His obsessive drive counted no costs, neither financial nor human. His judgement became warped by it, until it led him down the road of personal destruction. And, as it destroyed him, it created much human wreckage around and about. It caused partial, collateral (and I'm glad to say temporary) damage in my own life – but then I had got out in time. Others were less fortunate.

I have said that Bull was my friend. But when I review his death and manner of his dying, I cannot feel pain. Bull's friendship was ultimately destructive. It was too powerful, too compelling, and there were few in his circle who had the strength to resist its force. In the end it pervaded and distorted their own independence, their judgements of value and morality, just as metal distorts and then melts in the presence of incandescent heat. To work for Bull gave me a marvellous feeling, but I would probably have been better off if I had not met him.

Bull never grasped the fact that he had struck a bargain with the devil. He was a man who valued rationality above all: he was proud to be regarded as a scientist. But his rationality did not extend to the world beyond technical calculations. Thus he never read the warning signs which another, less egotistical man would have seen blazing in his path. He was not, of course, the only one who failed to understand the changes in Western allegiances, as they occurred in the late 1980s. But he did not appreciate either the personal bind he was in as that gradual, fatal deepening of his identification with Saddam Hussein warped his own objectives. Bull's single-minded pursuit of Project Babylon led him to promise the Iraqis everything – just 'because they want everything'.

Bull, the prodigy, was the son of a failure, a father who had, in addition, rejected and abandoned his family. Bull himself grew up unable to countenance failure. He believed Babylon would vindicate him and bring him worldwide recognition and once he was committed to it there would be no turning back.

In the end Bull's lack of manoeuvrability made him fatally vulnerable. His importance to the powers which supported him was real for a time, but then he became expendable, a token in the game of international power politics. Truth and value are not, in this game, controlled by small men like Bull. They rest in the keeping of those who wield power, their forces backed up by huge industrial wealth.

He never realised it. He believed he was a mover and shaker. He believed he understood governments and their secret agencies and could influence the way they work. But, however dramatic the events surrounding the Supergun, Bull and his machinations were an unimportant sideshow. The huge international crisis which developed around Iraq, resulting in a terrible war and the loss of hundreds of thousands of lives, turned on the misguided policies of nations, and the short-sightedness of multinational commercial interests. Bull, in this, counted for little more than a candle blown out by a hurricane.

My own experiences have led me to the view that the international arms industry is an enormous and terrifying force for evil. That conclusion might seem trite. But I don't just mean that it is evil in the obvious sense of creating weapons of death. It generates evil in a more pervasive way, because wherever it goes, it creates political instability and personal corruption. A recurrent theme at S.R.C. was that we could justify what we were doing just because Belgian law allowed the easy transfer of weapons technology. In this regard one of the documents which percolated to me from the files of P.R.B. makes for illuminating reading. It is a memorandum written (in French) by Cardinael – one of the signatories, let us remember, of the Bilder Trading and Gerofin bank accounts – in which he discusses the future of P.R.B. within the Astra group. In one paragraph the P.R.B. manager discourses on the role of 'ethics' in their work, and how this may be threatened by the takeover.

> *Ethics*: In a field as 'sensitive' as ours, having a Belgian majority owner offers good protection. The functioning of the (Belgian) Ethics Committee and the 'obligatory back-up' (*couverture indispensable*) which it gives to the management in Defence must be guaranteed. The 'ethics' of Astra must be clarified.

This paragraph gives a pretty good idea of the meaning and function of the word 'ethics' in the international defence industry: if you can get government support, you are ethically O.K.

Very different from P.R.B. though it was, and unique in so many ways, S.R.C. was nevertheless a microcosm of this trade. Its own idealism – which at various times took political, commercial or scientific forms – could hardly survive in the swamp of corruption that was its habitat.

The rot sets in when Western governments support their own defence contractors as they compete for Third World orders. The most lucrative contracts emanate from despots like Saddam Hussein, Milton Obote, and General Pinochet, but there is plenty of money to be made from any insecure or paranoid regime.

Customers are treated by suppliers with invariable cynicism and (behind their backs) contempt. Their greed and vainglory are pandered to, as they are sold one obsolete system after another each with a 'state-of-the-art' tag on it. As far as the Third World is concerned, much of the arms trade is a gigantic fiddle.

The fiddle is operated by all parties. Sellers misrepresent the goods and grossly overcharge while customers and middlemen collude, taking their inflated percentages and salting them away in numbered bank accounts. The losers, as always, are the people. The hundreds of billions of dollars spent by Middle-Eastern nations in the last decade can scarcely be said to have benefitted the population at large. How many people in Afghanistan, the Horn of Africa, Yugoslavia, Nicaragua, Liberia, Nagorno-Karabak or Cambodia have been killed, wounded, made homeless and destitute as a result of the Northern world's desire to feed the monster of its own arms industry and to gratify its client states?

Democratic Western governments consistently refuse to take

responsibility. Checks on arms sales are half-hearted, systems of licensing are feeble and end-user certification is a joke. I had waited nearly two years for the Parliamentary Select Committee to report on exports to Iraq, assuming, naïvely, that this powerful body would root out and correct past mistakes. It did nothing of the kind. Ministers were allowed to hide behind civil servants, and civil servants behind veils of secrecy. The British system of government is supposed to operate the principle of ministerial responsibility. But members and witnesses alike seemed to have entirely forgotten about this, in a remarkable collective lapse of memory. Buck passing and political expediency were the order of the day, as politicians scrambled to blame civil servants and meanwhile endeavoured to say nothing which would embarrass any party whatsoever.

We need an independent legal procedure to investigate governmental malpractice. Parliament ought to be the context for this, but it has shown itself far too timorous. Perhaps it is because so many of its members hope, themselves, to gain office one day that they cannot ask or pursue uncomfortable questions. But if these questions are not posed we are all going to be losers.

The response in Switzerland to the Project Babylon scandal stands in marked contrast to our own. As I mentioned earlier an independent magistrate, Ms Monique Saudan, was appointed to investigate the actions of government officials and Swiss companies. In my own dealings with her I have been struck by the professionalism and strict neutrality of her approach, as compared with the inane and irrelevant comments which so often emanated from the Select Committee. Ms Saudan's enquiry (unlike our own) may have far-reaching effects. She may manage to convince the Swiss Government to introduce a constitutional change which specifically bans the sale of weapons and their technology outside the Swiss Federation.

On the day I finish these pages, *The Guardian* newspaper carries pictures of a 1,000-mm Supergun tube, seized two years ago by Customs at Teesport, being made ready for transportation to its final resting place at the Imperial War Museum. The news prompts a final thought about Bull's grand obsession.

Project Babylon has frequently and easily been dismissed as a piece of expensive vanity arranged between a fool and a maniac. Yet, what Bull had to say about big guns and space exploration, as I shall always maintain, has great merit. The American Government itself has now quietly accepted the principle of gun-launched orbiters, and are in the process of developing a number of space launch systems, the most spectacular at Laurence Livermore National Laboratory at a cost of $7 billion. The barrel of this – if it is ever built – will be truly monstrous: 3,500-mm in bore and 1,500 metres long. In its name alone the Americans are paying some kind of a tribute to Gerald Bull, the pioneer. They call it the Super High Altitude Research Programme – or S.H.A.R.P.

I can hear Bull's laugh of triumph, tinged with bitterness. He might well quote from his own book on H.A.R.P. 'Truth,' he wrote there, 'has become a purely subjective matter in the narrow contemporary context. In the long perspective of history, it may emerge objectively.'

One can only hope.

POSTSCRIPT

It is more than six months since I printed out the final hard copy of the foregoing chapters and switched off the word processor. I had spent the last two and a half years peeling back the layers of government secrecy. It was an onion whose outer skins were inedible, but as I worked on I found it increasingly nutritious.

But in life, as opposed to onion-peeling, there are no neat endings. I had not reached the onion's centre. I had not uncovered the heart of the mystery.

Nevertheless, since I typed that last full stop, the Supergun and the arming of Iraq have continued to mesmerise politicians and the public on both sides of the Atlantic. At the same time, vital additional facts have begun to come to light, stripping away further onion layers. In the United States, investigations by journalists like William Safire, together with the attempt by Representative Henry Gonzalez, through the U.S. House Banking Committee, to get to the bottom of the B.N.L. scandal, resulted in the christening of a new political scandal: 'Iraqgate'. In Britain, I have found myself in possession of new, almost hair-raising evidence about Gerald Bull's plans for Scud. And the attempt at the Old Bailey to try the three directors of Matrix Churchill has resulted in extraordinary revelations made in open court.

Twenty years on from the original Watergate affair, many scandals had been tagged with the '-gate' suffix, but few have had the potential of Iraqgate to hurt the man at the top. The Bush administration's published 'policy' towards trade with Iraq had seemed quite clear: in order to bring Saddam into 'the family of nations', non-military goods could be traded while the sale of sophisticated high-tech equipment, either with military or with dual applications, would be prohibited. Henry Gonzalez, however, has charged that President Bush and his close aides personally authorised a second, underlying policy about which the American people were not told. This promoted certain military transactions with Iraq and allowed others to happen by default.

Gonzalez alleges, for example, that members of the Bush administration knew about the funding of Saddam Hussein's weapons procurement programme through the Atlanta branch of B.N.L. and may even have helped to instigate it, in collusion with the government of Italy. He also insists that Bush and his aides have since tried to cover up their involvement.

It is now thought that up to $7 billion was advanced by the obscure Atlanta branch of B.N.L. to fund Iraqi deals. Much of it was in the form of 'agricultural credits', loans approved by the U.S. authorities overtly for food purchase. Gonzalez has shown how, covertly, many of these credits were diverted away from butter and into guns, and his investigations have caused scenes of near panic in Washington. Gonzalez was told by a senior official in the Agriculture Department that, prior to the House Banking Committee hearing on 27 October 1992, department aides had 'spent the entire weekend shredding documents'.

Apart from the use of agricultural loans, a fantastic array of banking techniques was employed to channel money from B.N.L. to the Central Bank of Iraq, to money-laundering shell companies or directly into the accounts of arms-trading corporations. But the real issue here is one of accountability. Drogoul, the manager of B.N.L. Atlanta, was eventually charged with several hundred counts of fraud and false accounting. He was accused of receiving some $2.5 million for his own use, including $750,000 spent on his home. But it is inconceivable to Congressman Gonzalez, as it is to me, that the Rome head office of B.N.L. and the U.S. banking and intelligence world were unaware of Drogoul's almost manic financial activity.

High-level Italian political involvement, and the stress this caused, may have been behind the suicide of a former Italian military attaché in Baghdad and the breakdown of the health of the Italian Ambassador to Iraq. Both these events followed the F.B.I.'s first raid on B.N.L. Atlanta in 1989. A thorough criminal investigation looked likely to uncover the role played by senior officials and politicians, a threat which apparently led the Italian government to make several approaches to Washington, seeking 'damage control' in the B.N.L. investigation. The most recent approach was on 25 July 1990, just prior to Saddam Hussein's invasion of Kuwait.

Of course, American officials who were party to the B.N.L. fraud would also have reasons to soft-pedal the investigation.

What is certain is that the investigation was seriously hindered by delay. Essential visits to Istanbul and Rome by Atlanta investigators were cancelled and, in the middle of his work, the Atlanta lead prosecutor was reassigned to another case – a bizarre decision if the B.N.L. investigation really was, in Gonzalez's words, 'the largest and arguably the most important case ever at the U.S. attorney's office in Atlanta'. After this the investigation was removed from Atlanta altogether and brought to the Federal Justice Department where, naturally, it would be under much tighter political control.

Gonzalez's associate Dennis Kane has told me that records of payments have turned up inside B.N.L. which were made directly from Atlanta, Georgia, into the account (held at B.C.C.I. in Luxembourg) of the Serodine Corporation – the S.R.C. Group's ultimate holding company. The reason for these payments has not been established.

Beyond B.N.L., Gonzalez's investigations have revealed important direct dealings between Washington and S.R.C. I had always been aware that in 1988 Luis Palacio and Bull's son Michel had visited the Office of Ammunition Control in Washington to talk about Supergun, accompanied by a lawyer, Chris Ohly. The U.S. registered office of S.R.C. in the same building in Maryland as the headquarters of Ohly's legal firm, Thomas, Fisk, and Beckhorn. It was from this building that, in 1989, requests were issued for licences to cover the export of computer technology to Iraq via Brussels. These were the systems, mentioned in Bull's telephone tapes, that were needed by Urbatzka and Bojic to develop the Martlet missile's guidance and tracking systems – based on two Iris super-380 computers. These machines, worth $161,000, were to be shipped from Silicon Graphics of Mountain View, California. The transfer of accompanying software – a ballistics calculation program developed by Swanson Analysis Systems of Houston, Pennsylvania – was also requested. The customer was named as Iraq's State Enterprise for Automotive Industries and, in spite of what the U.S. Government knew about Bull, Iraq and Supergun, in September 1989 the application was approved.

The cover-up followed. In February 1991, during the last days of the Gulf War, the State Department denied that it had approved 'any exports of equipment or technology by Bull or companies associated with Bull to Iraq'. But in October 1992, campaigning for re-election on A.B.C. television's *Good Morning America*, Bush found himself having to backtrack. He suggested any computers sold to Iraq were insignificant and the transfer accidental. 'If a

Tandy computer or an IBM PC ended up somewhere on a nuclear programme, too bad,' he said. 'But the policy was not to do that.' The trouble with this thesis is that the Iris is a machine capable of performing up to fifty million calculations per second: it is about as far removed from a Tandy as a Ferrari is from a skateboard.

It's interesting that two computers were needed. One, perhaps, for the Martlet missile, but what about the second? As I'd already discovered, Bull had in 1989 started to advise Dr Saadi on the development of the Scud missile. The second Iris must have been earmarked for this application.

It wasn't until 22 October 1992 that I realised just how far Bull had gone down this road. On that day I received, from one of my informants, a bundle of S.R.C.-headed papers with a technical brief for 'Project Bird'. The client was Iraq. I had previously thought the Bird designation was attached to an anti-missile 'shot-gun pellet' system on which Jim Chan had worked. The report I was now reading, however, effectively proposed an alternative to Supergun, but this time a missile system. Under the proposal, a technical team of about thirty-five was to be set up by S.R.C., probably led by Slack and Bottomley. They would provide Iraq with designs for an intermediate-range ballistic missile, capable of delivering a satellite into orbit.

The system would be based on the 'Saddam', the Iraqi-modified Scud. The first stage of the rocket was to be a cluster of these Saddams – four, five or six, depending on the performance required. The papers I acquired show computer calculations for the performance of each configuration and conclude that 'the present study confirms the feasibility of reasonably early orbital launches using the Saddam missile series. By this, a rough estimate would be within one year of commencing serious work on the project, and restricting early launches to relatively simple (but useful) pay-loads.'

A cynic might say that a nuclear device could be described as a simple payload – and may well have appeared to the Iraqis as a useful one, though it would not, of course, have gone into orbit. In any case, the type of rocket proposed here was undoubtedly cap-able of dropping a warhead onto a ground target, at a range of 2,500 kilometres from its launch site. If the rockets were rede-signed using carbon fibre composites – the sort of technology Bull had tried to acquire through the Lear fan plant – weight reduction could have doubled this range. London, as it happens, is approxi-mately 5,000 kilometres from Baghdad.

And it was in London, on 19 October 1992, that Paul Henderson, with both former Matrix Churchill colleagues who had visited me in 1990, finally came to trial. This was three years after the Matrix Churchill affair first hit the headlines. The defendants were charged with evading export controls in their dealings with Iraq, the country which the British Foreign Office had offered their company for sale in 1987. The case was heard under conditions rarely, if ever, seen at the Old Bailey. Visitors to the public gallery were asked to provide personal identification for the police at the door – in case, according to the police, they should need to be traced. But who might want to trace them? And why?

From the beginning the trial seemed like something of a nightmare for the prosecution. In evidence David Briars, an official of the Export Credit Guarantee department, agreed that as early as 1987 the British government allocated 20 per cent of its Iraqi exports cover to 'defence business'. Since a ban on weapons sales to both Iran and Iraq was still in force at that time, this was direct evidence of a secret and illegal push to provide Saddam Hussein with weaponry.

But it was another official, Eric Beston, who confirmed the truth of a much more remarkable allegation: that the defendant Paul Henderson was an M.I.6 source. Henderson himself then told the court how he had made business visits to top-secret Iraqi installations like the Nassr Enterprise, Saad-16 and Al-Qaqa where, the British believed, a nuclear weapons capability was being developed. He says he made reports on these to M.I.6. In order to maintain Henderson's access, export licences were to be granted on Matrix Churchill munition products, even though they were illegal – a policy which, according to Beston, was fully approved by ministers. Meanwhile it emerged that the company Export Sales Manager, Mark Gutteridge, was being run as a second intelligence source, this time by M.I.5.

Three days after these revelations, brown paper was pasted over the glass in the courtroom doors, the public gallery was roped off and the press were ordered by the judge to sit behind screens. This was to protect the identity of 'Officer B', an M.I.5 agent in the witness box. B then told the court how he debriefed Gutteridge in hotel rooms in England, receiving drawings of Iraqi machine tool orders, as well as political, military and economic intelligence. This information was then passed to M.I.6 and the Trade and Industry Department. When asked by counsel if he had told Gutteridge that Prime Minister Margaret Thatcher would see the reports, Officer B agreed that 'I may well have done that, sir.'

The case against the Matrix Churchill directors collapsed after Alan Clark gave evidence. The Crown was expecting him to say that, as Trade Minister, he had approved the machine tools' exports without knowing they were for arms manufacture. But lawyers were taken aback when Clark began speaking quite differently under oath. He said that he had regarded the regulations on arms exports to Iraq as 'tiresome and intrusive', even though, 'by their very nature the guidelines were elastic, the wording was a matter for interpretation'. Clark then admitted that he bent, stretched and economised with (as he put it) 'the *actualité*' in licensing military exports to Iraq. He regarded Iran as the enemy, he said, so that Western interests were 'well served by Iran and Iraq fighting each other'.

At last, here was clear evidence from the inside of political encouragement for exporters of war supplies to Baghdad. The strenuous attempt, through the issuing of public interest immunity certificates by four Ministers, to prevent this coming out simply shows how much the politicians wanted to keep this encouragement secret.

The trial also confirmed – in spades – what I had said to the Select Committee about intelligence awareness of Supergun. Among the information provided by Mark Gutteridge – which Officer B said he was passing directly to 10 Downing Street – was in fact that he had met John Heath in 1988 in Baghdad and received detailed specifications for the gun. When I heard of the contact between Gutteridge and Heath I recalled the interest Bernadette, the Belgian Embassy 'clerk' in Baghdad, had taken in our mathematician Graham Ingham. For spies, there is always more than one method of skinning a cat.

There is now overwhelming evidence that British and other intelligence services – with their governments behind them – did not merely monitor arms deals with Iraq but promoted them. Dwelling on this, I recall the scenario proposed at the Select Committee enquiry by Stan Crowther, M.P. His suggestion was that the British government may have secretly acted to keep the Iraqi Supergun deal in being, while at the same time (through the Astra/P.R.B. connection) maintaining a capacity to shut it down at will. They would have allowed Supergun to continue – as they allowed Matrix Churchill – in line with a general policy of maximising British industrial profits and protecting intelligence sources. Thrown into the recipe was a vague foreign policy objective of supporting Iraq and keeping the Middle East divided.

In front of the Committee, Stephan Kock dismissed Crowther's scenario (in relation to Supergun) as 'a flight of fancy'. When I myself said in evidence that I believed there were suspicious links between the intelligence services and companies involved with Supergun, I had been publicly scoffed at by officials and politicians. Now, in the light of the Matrix Churchill case, such links appear rather less fanciful and rather more suspicious.

It is even possible that the British were running a source inside S.R.C. The stakes and the risks involved would be high. The fate of Farzad Bazoft shows the consequence of discovery by the Mukhabarat within Iraq, and the exposure of such a policy at home, though individually less fatal, would be highly damaging politically. To make the game worth pursuing, then, an inside source would have to be very valuable. He would ideally have better access to more secret Iraqi installations even than Paul Henderson, would know Saddam's economic and military plans, would be extremely close to the top. There was only one S.R.C. man who fitted this description – Gerald Bull himself.

Bull's friendship with George Wong gives the thought some credibility. Wong's area of expertise is China, where the two men cooperated on military deals which Wong had originally set up. However, Bull's frequent telephone conversations with Wong, recorded by Bull himself and probably also by G.C.H.Q., show that Wong was privy to events in Iraq as well as China.

Sober reflection casts doubts on the idea that the Israelis really needed to kill Bull. A full dossier on S.R.C., placed in the hands of the press in Washington, London, Paris and Berlin, would surely have been enough to stop him. But suppose Bull was engaged in espionage, and the Iraqis found out. How would they react? Would they risk a trial? I think not. Bull was no Bazoft. He was a significant player and the consequences of his trial, however stage-managed, would have been unpredictable. There would remain an alternative means by which Saddam could exact revenge: on foreign soil, with bullets in the back of the head and the Israelis generally blamed.

Since it was set up in 1968, the Mukhabarat of Saddam Hussein has carried out many 'wet jobs' on foreign soil. In 1978 eleven Iraqi 'diplomats' were expelled from London for their involvement in assassinations. To such men, the killing of Bull would be just another routine operation. But the truth is, all intelligence services sometimes operate outside the law. If Bull had become an embarrassment to the Western agency to which he reported, or if he threatened to blow the gaffe, he might have been marked down for death by 'our side' too.

I have been told that, after Bull died, private contracts and very large sums of money were offered to senior S.R.C. staff to continue their work inside Iraq. It is quite likely that someone thought of trying to recruit me once more and, if they did, the moment for such an approach would have been about the time of the start of this narrative – March 1990. But by then I had already received my timely and anonymous warning. 'Never return to Iraq,' the sinister voice had said, and at the time I took that as a threat. But now I wonder. Perhaps he only meant it as a friendly tip.

After the collapse of the Matrix Churchill case it was widely seen as a triumph of justice that the 'public interest immunity' – under which Ministers sought to prevent the release of secret documents – had been overruled by Judge Smedley. Had he not done so, innocent men might have been convicted.

But innocent men *have* been convicted. I believe, for instance, that the case of Christopher Gumbley (convicted of corruption) should be reopened, as should that of Stuart Blackledge.

Blackledge was a former fuse-design specialist whom I knew because he had worked for S.R.C. on Bull's 15-mm shells. He was with Bull for four and a half years, having previously been with Royal Ordnance. In 1989 Blackledge left S.R.C. to go to a British company named Ordtech and was caught up in the series of arms-for-Iraq investigations which followed the discovery of the Supergun tubes. Ordtech had acted as a conduit for half a million U.S.-supplied artillery fuses to Iraq and, like Matrix Churchill, was an important link in the Iraqi arms procurement chain, Blackledge was offered a deal similar to the one Barry Riley had suggested to me: plead guilty and receive a suspended sentence after minimal publicity. Now, in handling the American fuses consignment, Blackledge had needed a temporary but secure storage facility. He had (quite openly) approached the Ministry of Defence, who had agreed to store the shipment at a Royal Ordnance depot. The M.O.D. had then billed Ordtech accordingly, with a revealing invoice. At Blackledge's trial, public interest immunity certificates were issued to prevent the production of this important document in court. Feeling he had no realistic defence, Blackledge then accepted the plea-bargain and so acquired a criminal record. Meanwhile, the government must have been pleased that it had escaped embarrassment.

Given the regime's human rights record, the way that Western governments cuddled up to Saddam Hussein had to be kept secret. But why did they do so at all? A half-baked idea about divide-and-rule in the Middle East had much to do with it. So did the possibility of maintaining the profits of the arms business and our industries in work. There was also the consideration that, with Iraq so deeply in hock to the West already, we couldn't afford to cast Saddam Hussein adrift.

But behind this there is the one consideration that, since 1973, has above all others influenced Western policy towards the Gulf region. This is oil. Oil imports from Iraq to the U.S. rose by a factor of six between 1987 and 1990 under deals which were seen as 'favourable' – i.e. cheap. By 1990 only Saudi Arabia sold more oil to America, but the Iraqi oil was especially attractive because it was coming in at bargain-basement prices, much of it being 'bartered' directly for military technology. For Henry Gonzalez, the fact that President Bush and his Secretary of State James Baker have extensive links with the oil business is a particularly relevant fact.

In Britain, too, the oil factor can be clearly seen. In 1987 the U.K. bought no oil from Saddam Hussein; by 1990 we were already importing 8.2 million barrels – a quarter of what we took from Saudi Arabia (much of which was itself bartered as part of the Al-Yamamah arms contact). Oil, it appears, was the mystery element in the arms-for-Iraq puzzle, the missing link which completes so many half-answers.

There is no further footnote to the story of the Supergun itself. On the afternoon of 30 November 1992, at the Lawrence Livermore National Laboratory in California, two test-firings were made of a new gun. This gun had a 350-mm bore dimension and was 47.2 metres long. The firings were horizontal, with the 'payload' being shot at around 4km per second into a wall of sandbags. This is the first trial in the new S.H.A.R.P. programme and the firings were reported as successful.